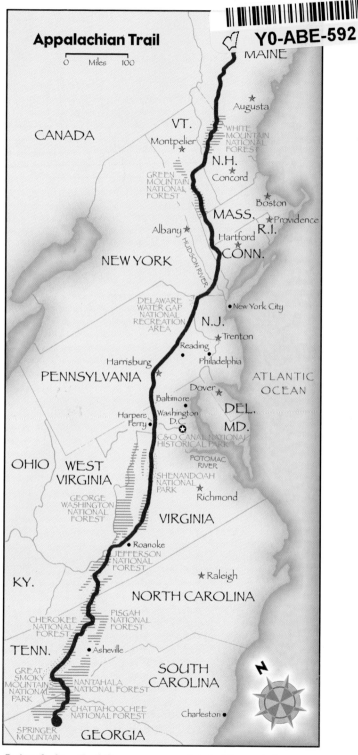

Appalachian Trail

© *Appalachian Trail Conservancy, reprinted with permission*

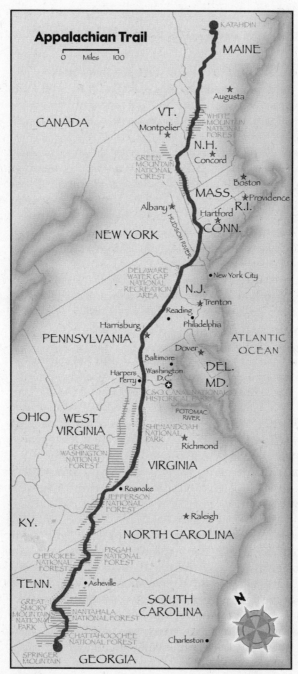

© *Appalachian Trail Conservancy, reprinted with permission*

What others are saying about *Hike Your Own Hike*

"*Hike Your Own Hike* is a helpful, fun book that combines everyday life with the outdoors. Walk the Appalachian Trail with Francis Tapon and learn practical insights that will get you ready for your own hike."
—Harv Erickson, Chairperson, Continental Divide Trail Alliance

"Don't buy this book if you just want a pure travelogue about the Appalachian Trail. *Hike Your Own Hike* is much more than that. It's about taking the lessons from the trail and applying it to your life. It won't just inspire and motivate you; it'll amuse and delight you. Francis Tapon transforms the wonders and wisdom of the woods into sound, useful principles."
— Peter Oorebeek, President, Advance Group

"The great outdoors is one of the best classrooms we'll ever have. It overflows with life lessons, as Francis Tapon so clearly and passionately explains in this wonderful book."
— Hal Urban, Author of *Life's Greatest Lessons*

"*Hike Your Own Hike* delivers helpful and sage advice for life on and off the trail. It is an extremely engaging and entertaining book!"
— Bruce Ward, Executive Director, Continental Divide Trail Alliance

"As his teacher, it is tremendous to see what Francis has learned about himself and about the world around him. The great thing about working with young people is that you get to see the future through their eyes...and you get to see yourself as you once were and can be again." — Joseph B. Lassiter III, Harvard Business School Professor of Management Practice

"Lisa Garrett, Francis Tapon's hiking partner, will inspire women throughout the world. She exposes her frailty and emotions, but never runs away from confronting them. It's fascinating to watch her draw deep into her incredible inner strength to overcome her fears. In some ways she's a superwoman because she is able to walk over 2,000 miles in less than four months, but she's also so human. Together, Lisa and Francis will motivate you to rise to a new level." — Susan McKee, National Sales Director, Pristine Water Treatment

HIKE YOUR OWN HIKE

7 Life Lessons from Backpacking Across America

By Francis Tapon

Unless noted, all photos in book are © Francis Tapon.

Cover photo: Mount Katahdin, Baxter State Park, Maine (photo by Sara Gray/Getty Images).

Printed using Soy Ink because it's much more eco-friendly than traditional ink. Printed on acid free, 100% recycled paper (70% post-consumer content) because we love trees. All this makes the book more expensive and so we'll sell fewer copies, but we figure this planet is worth it.

First Printing 2006
Printed in India by Thomson Press

Cataloging-in-Publication Data

Tapon, Francis
Hike your own hike: 7 life lessons from backbacking across America / Francis Tapon
p.cm
Includes blibliographical references (p.) and index.

ISBN: 0-97658-120-5

1. Self-actualization (Psychology) I. Title.
2. Hiking—Appalachian Trail.
3. Success—Psychological aspects.

158.1—dc22

Library of Congress Control Number: 2005904842

Visit SonicTrek.com

To Cartwheel

Table of Contents

Right before the Appalachian Trail, Lisa and I did one last 80 mile backpacking trip in our favorite stomping ground: California's Sierra Nevada. It's a magical place that always put a smile on our faces.

Introduction

I woke up wondering how a mosquito could have possibly bitten my rear end. I was covered in bites, so I suppose it's not incomprehensible that one ingenious insect found its way deep into my pants.

The night before Lisa Garrett, my hiking partner, had agreed that we should camp at the summit of the mountain where the winds were strong enough to drive away the mosquitoes. We carried an 18 ounce tarp instead of a 48 ounce tent, because we didn't expect that many bugs and we were eager to save as much weight as possible. We plopped down without setting up the tarp to admire the sky and to enjoy the brisk winds that kept those infernal insects at bay. We had been hiking almost nonstop since 4:30 a.m., and so when Lisa lay down at 9 p.m. she was asleep in seconds.

I managed to stay awake for two minutes—long enough to see a flash of lightning in the dark sky. I didn't say anything to Lisa. I took a deep breath and prayed it was just my imagination. Thunder rumbled in the distance. I gulped. A minute later I felt a drop of rain explode on my forehead.

"It's coming," I mumbled to Lisa, who was as alert as a corpse.

I shook Lisa hard, "Lisa, a storm is coming! You gotta get up. We have to set up the tarp. Now!"

She woke up in disbelief. When we had been hiking up the mountain there were a few clouds around, but nothing ominous. She couldn't believe that the weather had changed so quickly. As I stumbled out of the sleeping bag, I said dryly, "Welcome to Maine."

We pitched the tarp extremely low because with the fierce winds at the summit, the rain would surely come at a nearly horizontal angle. The tarp flapped violently in the blustery weather, but we managed to set it up. We had to crawl to squeeze under it. The tarp was so low that it halted nearly all the wind. Incredibly, within minutes, the mosquitoes descended upon us. Our wind-free environment had become an oasis for these God-forsaken creatures.

I always slept barefoot and with my feet slightly elevated to help decrease the swelling from walking all day. The next morning my exposed feet were swollen for a different reason: they were covered with bites. I couldn't resist scratching them until they bled.

The truly pathetic part was that the storm never hit us. During the night it passed just a few miles north of our campsite and we didn't even get a sprinkle. The token drop that hit my forehead was just a teaser. In other words, we could have slept without the tarp and without the mosquitoes.

While I miserably scratched my butt that morning I wondered, "OK, now how is this experience going to possibly help me find the way to get more out of life?" I shook my head questioning what I was thinking when I thought backpacking 2,168 miles would bring me some wisdom.

 The only difference between a rut and a grave is their dimensions. — Ellen Glasgow

Nine months before, I was stuck in a rut. I wasn't wild about my job. But I wasn't sure what to do next. The uncertainty of the future made me addicted to my daily routines—at least they were relatively comfortable. I clung tightly to the known instead of letting go and venturing into the unknown.

Part of my unwillingness to make any drastic changes was that my life really wasn't that bad. Many people struggled much more than I did. Yet deep down inside I realized that I wasn't getting the most out of life and that was bugging me. In short, I was settling for a pretty good life, but not an amazing one.

Lisa was also living on auto-pilot mode. She left behind her hometown in California's agricultural valley to pursue her dreams in Silicon Valley. However, after six years she was bored with managing commercial properties for the tech companies. Although her intelligence and strong work ethic helped her establish a successful career, she wanted to do something new, but she didn't know what. She also realized that her life was comfortable, but not magical.

It was during this period that we began backpacking. After car camping in the majestic forests of Big Sur, California, we agreed that it would be far more interesting to camp away from all the people. That meant backpacking, which neither of us had done. Our first backpacking trip was a four day adventure deep into Yosemite National Park, far from the crowds. We were hooked. We started backpacking almost every weekend. Eventually I started investigating some of the longer backpacking trips we could take. It wasn't long before I discovered something called the Appalachian Trail.

The Appalachian Trail (AT) is 2,168 miles long and crosses 14 states on the East Coast between Maine and Georgia. It typically takes six months to traverse the entire trail or "thru-hike" it. Few succeed: for example, when we walked it, only 17 percent of our fellow "thru-hikers" finished it. To put that into perspective, those who try to summit Mount Everest have twice the success rate (34 percent via the South Col route).[1] Embarking on a thru-hike usually entails quitting your job, moving out of your home, selling many of your belongings, and convincing your friends and family that you haven't gone completely nuts.

Lisa was initially skeptical about thru-hiking the AT. However, she concluded it might help her determine what she should do with her life. After encouraging Lisa to join me, we sold most of our belongings, and I convinced ten companies to sponsor our expedition. I romantically thought that thru-hiking the AT would help me gain profound wisdom. I yearned to uncover the fundamental Principles of getting the most out of life. I theorized that spending several months walking thousands of miles in the wilderness would help me discover these Principles. But while I was inspecting and scratching the dozens of mosquito bites all over my body, I started doubting this theory.

However, I would eventually get over the bites and many other challenges. Perhaps because of those trials, I ultimately learned

Lisa and I are goofing off on one of our training hikes in Yosemite. We had never done more than a four day backbacking trip before the AT. We both yearned for a break to recharge our spirits, get some wisdom, and have a few laughs.

what I had set out to discover, although not in the way I expected. Indeed, thru-hiking the AT was a life-changing adventure that taught me many values—especially the value of a bed, a shower, a toilet, and mosquito netting.

Wisdom in the wilderness

My idea of venturing into the wilderness to find wisdom is not original. Henry David Thoreau and John Muir both understood how communing with nature could reveal answers to the most profound questions of life. Religious figures such as Jesus, Moses, Muhammad, and the Buddha spent some of their most profound moments in the wilderness. Many who hike the AT hope that walking over 2,000 miles will reveal the answers to life's big questions. Indeed, thru-hiking is not just a long hike, it is a pilgrimage.

Pilgrimage (noun): An extended journey with a purpose.
— Webster's II Dictionary

Although your yogi may disagree, walking and sleeping in the wilderness is a form of meditation. Imagine waking up everyday before sunrise and walking up and down forested mountains until just past sunset, breaking only for meals and short rests. We walked 20 to 30 miles a day. Imagine doing that for almost four months. Many would conclude, "That's gotta suck!"

However, I quickly found myself in a groove and at peace. That state of mind allowed me to absorb lessons I might have otherwise overlooked. When I returned to civilization, I sought to summarize those insights. I distilled them into Seven Principles that not only apply to backpacking, but to life itself.

I can only meditate when I am walking. When I stop, I cease to think; my mind only works with my legs.
— Jean-Jacques Rousseau, French philosopher & writer, 1712—1778

Overview of the Seven Principles

Each chapter will discuss a Principle in detail, but first let's see how they all interrelate.

- The First Principle, Hike Your Own Hike, is the most important one. It's simply impossible to get the most out of life if you ignore this First Principle. Therefore, it forms the core.

- Principles Two through Six explain how to achieve the First Principle. They delve into the nuts and bolts of how to enjoy life.

- Finally, the Seventh Principle, The Hike Is Too Important to Take Seriously, puts everything into context. It gives us the perspective that no other Principle gives us. Indeed, those who truly follow it are usually masters at squeezing the most out of life.

The accompanying diagram depicts how the Seven Principles inter-relate. For example, it shows how the First Principle forms the core and is the foundation for all the Principles. The Seventh Principle wraps around all the other Principles, for it is one that should be sprinkled generously throughout life. Just because Principles Two through Six are not in the core or the outer edge doesn't mean that they are not essential. Each Principle is vital and should be followed if you want to optimize your life.

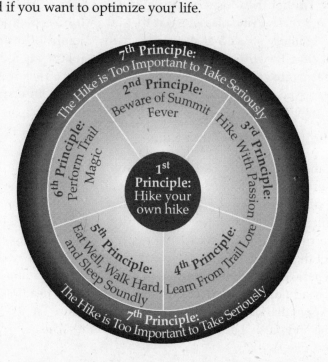

On the other hand, *this is not an all or nothing solution.* If you ignore one Principle, you will still get more out of life than someone who ignores five of them. If you're not prepared to make a radical change today, you can take one Principle at a time. It's better to follow one Principle than to ignore them all. The point is that each Principle you follow gets you closer to having a truly fulfilling life.

Some may argue that these timeless Principles are obvious. However, what's obvious is that most of us are not following them and are not maximizing their life. Therefore, when our lives get off track, it's healthy to remind ourselves what the Principles are so that we can realign our priorities. Furthermore, during my pilgrimage I didn't just focus on discovering the Principles, but I also focused on finding concrete, practical, and sometimes unusual ways to abide by them. Believe me, backpacking across America gave me plenty of time to think of such things.

Lastly, I'm not the Moses of thru-hikers. I'm not saying that God gave me these Principles or even that all thru-hikers agree with them. I simply arrived at them after many months of deep contemplation. For instance, someone else might follow my footsteps and be inspired to write a book called *The 7 Principles of Proper Trail Hygiene*. And alas, that book would probably easily outsell mine.

Katahdin—the adventure begins

In Maine's Baxter State Park lies the mountain called Katahdin, the northern terminus of the Appalachian Trail. For Native Americans, Katahdin means "The Greatest Mountain." Indeed, it is the tallest mountain in Maine and the longest vertical climb on the AT. Nearly all aspiring thru-hikers start in Georgia and make Katahdin the climax of their journey. Only five percent of the thru-hikers were doing what we were doing: starting at Katahdin and heading south. Most head north on the AT because it's easier than heading south (see Appendix 1). I started in Maine partly because I'm a nonconformist and partly because I'm just a foolish masochist.

It is only in adventure that some people succeed in knowing themselves—in finding themselves.
— André Gide, Journals, Oct 26, 1924

Katahdin represented a key Inflection Point in my life. Inflection Points are moments where one trend stops and a new trend begins. An Inflection Point represents a radical change from the way things have been going. Ask yourself:

- Do you feel like your life is stagnant?

- Do you feel like you're going nowhere?

- Are you content with life, but not thrilled?

- Do you really believe that you're getting the most out of life?

Whether you feel like your life is just fine, or whether it is rapidly spiraling downward, you need a positive Inflection Point in your life. That's what I hope this book becomes for you. It's that catalyst that gets you out of a rut and onto the ridge. It's that kick in the pants that sometimes we all need to get us off a moribund trend and onto a new trend line—one that soars to the sky like Mount Katahdin.

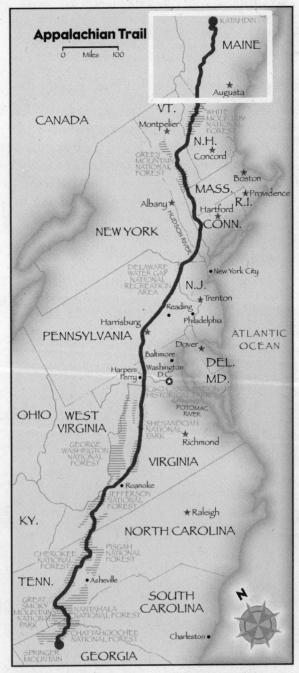

© *Appalachian Trail Conservancy, reprinted with permission*

Chapter 1:
Hike Your Own Hike

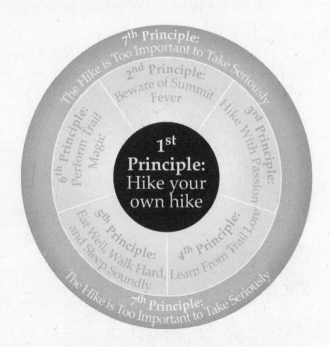

Standing on top of Mount Katahdin, the start of my Appalachian Trail adventure, I strained to see Springer Mountain, 2,168 miles away in Georgia. Of course I was kidding myself, but I tried anyway. I couldn't fathom walking across the entire Appalachian mountain range to get there. It sure would be easier to just take Greyhound.

It was June 26, there was not a cloud in the sky, scarcely a breeze, and the temperature was warm. There was so little wind on Katahdin's summit that there were several bugs flying about. This was almost unheard of, and a stark contrast with what most northbound thru-hikers experience when they reach the end of their journey. *Northbounders*, as we called them, or more simply, *Nobos*, leave Georgia in March or April and typically arrive in Maine in late September or early October. At that time of year the temperatures are below freezing on Katahdin and ominous clouds usually obscure the spectacular view. Even the lucky ones who have a clear day cannot linger long at the top because strong cold winds chill you to the bone.

On the other hand, *Southbounders*, or *Sobos*, don't end their journey in a tropical paradise either. Before they reach Georgia in November or December, Sobos usually get hammered with frosty weather too.

I shaved my head for the start of our thru-hike, while Lisa braided hers. On June 26th, we started our hike on Mt. Katahdin, the tallest mountain in Maine, and the northern terminus of the AT. The weather was warm and we were bursting with energy. We hiked 27 miles on the first day. Of course, it helped that mosquitoes were chasing us the whole way.

However, while I was standing on the tallest mountain in Maine, I wasn't worried about the weather conditions that I would face at the end of my pilgrimage. I assumed that I would simply walk hard, get to Georgia in October, and avoid the lousy weather. Little did I know that the AT had other plans.

Nevertheless, on that day the perfect conditions on Katahdin let me easily see over fifty miles in every direction. I suddenly realized that even if I could walk to the furthest point I could see, I would have only walked about two percent of the trail. I knew I needed some time to think, but this might be a bit much.

In any case, I touched the magical trailhead, the northern terminus of the Appalachian Trail, took a deep breath, and started methodically walking south.

 Wherever we go in the mountains we find more than we seek. — John Muir, US naturalist, 1838—1914

Discovering the First Principle

I met my first Nobo on my second day on the trail. He was a bearded, disheveled man resting by a lake. His resolute eyes hinted that he had walked from Georgia. His intense odor confirmed it.

He said that about six other Nobos had already completed their thru-hikes. They had all left snowy Georgia in January and slogged their way to Maine by the end of June.

He asked, "So how was Katahdin?"

"Tough," I replied, "But it helps if you leave most of your gear at the ranger station. After all, you have to return to the station on your way back down, so you might as well carry only what you need for the hard climb."

"No way," he said, shaking his head, "I've carried my pack and all my gear from Georgia, and you better believe I'm going to take it to the top of Katahdin."

What a stubborn, impractical man, I thought.

As if he had read my mind, he added, "Hey, you gotta hike your own hike."

He hoisted his backpack, smiled, and took off.

That statement puzzled me. In time, I would hear it over and over again. Clearly, this was a core belief of the AT pilgrims. What did it really mean and did it have any implications for life off the trail?

Hiking your own hike on the AT

Hike your own hike means that you should hike the trail in the manner that you enjoy, and not the way somebody tells you to hike it. Although you should ponder the advice of others, ultimately make your own decision and focus on having fun! For example:

- Some thru-hikers love to walk 30 miles a day and finish in three months, while others prefer to walk six miles a day and take 12 months.

- Some prefer carrying 70 pounds; others enjoy carrying less than 15.

- Some insist on eating at every possible restaurant along the way, while others contemplate the nutritional value of the bugs crawling in the mud.

Hike your own hike also means that you can backpack in any direction you want. Most hiked north, a small fraction went south, and others "flip flopped." A *Flip Flopper* might hike north from Georgia to Virginia, then flip up to Maine and walk back down south to Virginia. In the end, Flip Floppers covered the same 2,168 miles that the linear hikers did, but just in a different way.

In many cases, hiking your own hike may mean quitting the hike. Over 80 percent of the hikers who intend to hike the entire AT in one season quit. Some of them return the next season(s) to com-

Who hikes the entire AT in one season?

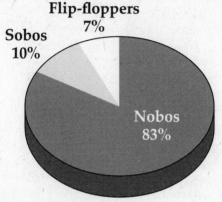

Flip-floppers
7%

Sobos
10%

Nobos
83%

Source: Appalachian Trail Conservancy

plete the sections they missed; thus, they become *Section Hikers*. However, many who quit never return because the hike wasn't fun for them. After all, digging a hole in the dirt and squatting can get old after a while.

 If at first you don't succeed, try, try again. Then quit. There's no point in being a damn fool about it.
— W. C. Fields

Whether you quit after 20 miles or you go the entire distance, the AT teaches you the same lesson: hike your own hike. All the hikers focused on having fun. Consider what Bramble and Bushwack, a married couple, wrote at the end of their 2001 AT hike:

 Some things you just can't escape, but this trip was a chance to do something few people get to do. We got away from many of the hassles and aggravations of 'normal' life and it was so nice. Life on the trail was much simpler, more spontaneous and a wonderful time for introspection. And our marriage survived! Not that we didn't have our moments (or hours), but it was nice to actually spend some real time together. The good times outweighed the bad 100 to 1. — Bramble and Bushwack[2]

Trail Names

Nearly every thru-hiker assumes a trail name that she either invents or another hiker gives her. Some adopt trail names like Swift or Strider; one couple chose the names Slow and Steady. Some name themselves after animals, such as Bear, Wolf, or Tortoise. Finally, some just have whimsical names such as Toll Booth Willy, Bloody Stumps, Doodle Bug, Krispy Kritter, and Happy Feet.

Trail names usually have a story behind it. For instance, in New Hampshire a thru-hiker named Blood gave Lisa her trail name. He anointed her "Cartwheel" because her pack was so light (less than 10 pounds) that he thought she should be doing cartwheels up the mountains!

Before I set off on my pilgrimage my friends named me "Mr. Magoo" due to my unusual amount of dumb luck!

Thru-hikers adopt trail names to symbolically shed their identity and adopt a new one for the trail. This represents the transformative power of a thru-hike.

Hiking your own hike off the AT

Although the AT's basic credo worked for thru-hikers, I wasn't sure if it applied to life off the trail. However, after enough back-packing and deep thinking, I soon realized that it did. In fact, the pilgrims applied the hike your own hike belief before and after their journey. For example, Aloha! Ann describes how the AT created an Inflection Point in her life. She finally summoned the courage to hike her own hike:

November 6, 2000: Cruise Missile Support Activity; Camp Smith, Hawaii
"What is this?" my boss demanded.
"Without looking at it, I would guess that it's my resignation," I replied.
"What do you mean you're quitting?"
"I mean that I'm not going to work here much longer."
"Who do you have a job with?"

"I don't have a job with anyone."

"Of course you do! No one quits without a job waiting."

"Oh… well, I guess you just met the first person that did."

"That's ridiculous. Where are you going?"

"For a walk."

"A walk?"

"Yeah… a walk."

April 1, 2001: Fredericksburg, VA (Four days prior to my "walk")

That was my conversation with my employer the day I turned in my resignation. Eleven years on the job, 21 years with the government and I was "going for a walk." It does sound crazy, doesn't it? What person in their right mind walks away from a good job, a decent retirement (when of age), and moves from a state that they truly love—to "go for a walk"? No one in his or her right mind for sure! But then again… what person remains in a job where they're unfulfilled, bored, frustrated, and truly dislikes being there? No one in his or her right mind for sure!

Upon finding out about my plans, friends, family and coworkers all asked that simple question—why? They're still asking it. Not why I quit my job or moved (well, many people ask why I moved from Hawaii but they're all from Virginia) but why am I going to attempt to walk across 14 states and 2168 miles. That's a hard question to answer. It's only hard because the answer is "because I want to and I can." Again, that's not looking very stable is it? But… it's the truth.

One day, a couple of years back I looked up only to find that I had been drawn into a Dilbert cartoon. I was sedately enmeshed in a job that I had limited to no interest in, working in a Dilbert-type cubicle, with coworkers that seemed to be unfulfilled and frustrated. However did this happen? Boredom ruled! It was obvious I needed a change, I needed a big change and I needed it soon!

— *Aloha! Ann*[3]

Aloha! Ann realized that she was not enjoying the hike she was on (her job), and that she could not afford to put off enjoying it any longer. She decided to create an Inflection Point in her life. The first step on her new hike was the AT.

Thru-hikers don't blindly do what people tell them they should do, they do what they know gives them pleasure. Those who just do what society expects them to do, thereby ignoring their inner voice, are missing the point of life. A pilgrim's purpose is to enjoy life now and not to put it off for retirement.

 We are here on Earth to fart around. Don't let anyone tell you any different! — Kurt Vonnegut

Many agree that the purpose of life is to enjoy it and will shout, "And it took you walking 2,168 miles to figure that out? C'mon, I figured that out this morning when I was doing the laundry!"

Yet for all those who agree, there are so few who fully enjoy it. Therefore, the challenge isn't understanding the concept, it's executing it.

Are you hiking your own hike?

The rest of this book will go into the *how* of hiking your own hike. But for now let's figure out (1) if you're enjoying life, (2) when to take action if you're not enjoying life, and (3) what it will take for you to enjoy life. Let's start with #1: Are you enjoying life? Some people know the answer immediately. For others, it's less clear and they should take a quick quiz. Just answer these questions with a simple YES or NO:

1. When you wake up the in morning, do you look forward to the new day?

2. Do you love your job?

3. Would most people who know you well describe you as a happy person?

4. Do you smile more often than you frown?

5. Can you look back on the last 12 months and say that you have no major regrets?

6. Do you feel like you have everything you need to be truly happy?

7. When you look at yourself in the mirror, do you feel good?

8. Would most people say that you're a giving and generous person?

9. Can you easily brush off the small irritations in life?

10. Do you go to bed eager to get up the next day?

Scoring: Give yourself 10 points for every YES. If your score is 70 or less, you need to make some changes to create an Inflection Point and start squeezing the most out of life. The rest of this book will show you how. If you scored 100, then go easy on the Prozac.

When should you take action?

Ideally, you should make every moment enjoyable. Don't sacrifice four years of your life to go to medical school if you don't enjoy school. Don't spend years in a lousy relationship. Don't hike the AT for six months if you can't handle eating the same unappealing dehydrated food everyday.

On the other hand, you can take this argument to an extreme; for example, someone might argue that she didn't enjoy medical school for the past two days, so she's dropping out. Another might say that his wife was being difficult last week, so he's filing for divorce. Clearly, these reactions are bit extreme, but it raises the issue: when you're down, when do you say, "Enough is enough"? I contemplated this going over Maine's Sugarloaf Mountain where, sadly, there were no sugarloaves.

Major Trails vs. Minor Trails

The first step you should take is to separate Major Trails from Minor Trails. A *Major Trail,* like the Appalachian Trail, is a long-term activity, such as a marriage, a job, or a home. It's a situation that usually lasts for years. A *Minor Trail,* like a section of the AT, is a short-term activity, such as a night out on the town, a football game, a trade show, a concert, a vacation, a picnic, a class, or a meeting with your mother-in-law.

Major Trails

Major Trails are more important than Minor Trails, so let's deal with them first. Here's the rule of thumb you should use on Major Trails: *if you're generally not enjoying a Major Trail for over four months, then create an Inflection Point by getting out of or changing that situation immediately so you can enjoy life again.*

Although it's not a perfect rule, it helps remind you that:

- You're going to have to put up with some bad times occasionally.

- You should not have to put up with them for long.

For instance, it's not a big deal if you have a bad day at work every couple weeks, but if you've been miserable at your job almost everyday for more than six months, you need change. Yes, you need the income because you have bills to pay, but don't succumb to Frog Psychology (see sidebar). *Instead, create an Inflection Point.* How? First, look around your company to see if there are any other jobs you would prefer to do. Talk with your boss or human resources to see what you can do to transition into the new position. Perhaps you will need more training, but many companies will provide it. They have already invested in you, so they would rather keep you happy because happy employees are more effective than disgruntled ones. Just ask Homer Simpson. If nothing

Frog Psychology

Scientists inadvertently learned something about frog psychology when they conducted two experiments.

In the first experiment, they threw a frog into a pot of boiling water, and it immediately jumped out.

In the second experiment they put the frog into a pot of cold water, and then slowly began to raise the temperature. As the temperature went up the frog showed discomfort but stayed in the pot. Eventually, the water hit a rolling boil. The frog never moved and died a horrible death.

Are you suffering from Frog Psychology?

Are you (or someone you love) in a situation that is progressively getting worse, and yet is doing nothing about it? Lousy Major Trails are sneaky because they usually don't get that way overnight; instead, the process can be a slow and steady decline. And like the frog, before you know it, you're dead.

Get out of that boiling water now!

works, then immediately start looking for a job elsewhere as discussed in Chapter 3.

One of the most challenging Major Trails is a declining relationship. Frog Psychology easily sets in when you've been with someone for a long time. After the initial honeymoon period, couples revert to their normal behavior patterns. In many cases, couples patterns are not compatible over the long haul. Nevertheless, couples have a tendency to become complacent with the moribund situation. Instead, they should either:

a) Create an Inflection Point and repair or radically improve the relationship.

b) Break up.

Those are your only two intelligent options. Most don't take either action because they, like the frog in the steadily warming pot, suffer from inertia. Isaac Newton described inertia: matter stays at rest or continues going in the direction it was traveling unless another force is applied. *Although Newton's principle on inertia focused on the physical realm, the same is true for the spiritual realm.* Your relationship will continue going the way it's going unless you exert a force against it. *Inflection Points happen because a force is applied; they don't happen on their own.* The effort to make a change may seem monumental—for who likes rocking the boat? However, you must realize that unless something changes, you will find it difficult to enjoy the relationship. And remember, unless you're Hugh Hefner, the dating scene only gets worse with age.

The reason you must limit miserable Major Trails to four months is that it allows for the normal ups and downs of life, but it compels you to reject extended down periods. By setting a limit of four months, you force yourself to put together a plan of getting out of it. Perhaps you want to make your own rule as short as two months or as long as six, but be strict about it. The most common excuse for not acting on a declining Major Trail is that we think we're experiencing unusual circumstances: "Oh, my husband has been having a few tough months at work," or "Her uncle died three years ago and she's still coping," or "He accidentally flushed his rubber ducky down the toilet."

However, bad news happens to all of us. Yes, some get it more than others, but there is always an excuse to be miserable if you're looking for one. If morose people are in a good situation, then they look back to their childhood to find something that didn't go quite right there and then get depressed about that. At some point you have to realize that you can't change the past and that you have only two choices:

a) Continue feeling sorry for yourself.

b) Get over it and move on.

Most people get over it, but some take more time than others. Chapter Seven discusses techniques on how to quickly get over misfortune and move on. For now, realize that you can either get over it today, or you can get over it in two months, or two years. Take your pick.

> *Any fool can criticize, condemn and complain—and most fools do. — Dale Carnegie*

As people age, there is a tendency to become complacent. Children, for instance, are always experimenting and look at the world with eyes of wonder and fascination. Adults, on the other hand, can get stuck in a tedious routine and accept it. You must commit to getting out of your rut and onto the ridge. If you don't want to make this pact with yourself, don't worry, even grumpy old men find something to be happy about a couple of times a year.

Minor Trails

A good rule of thumb for dealing with unpleasant Minor Trails is: *if you're not enjoying a particular Minor Trail, get out of it immediately if the repercussions are insignificant.* For example, if you're not enjoying a movie, then don't just keep watching it if it's not getting any better. Just discreetly leave. If you're watching it at home, it's easy to hit the off switch. Besides, maybe something more interesting is on TV, like Jerry Springer.

On the other hand, if the repercussions of escaping an unpleasant Minor Trail are significant, then tough it out; after all, Minor Trails pass quickly. The most common type of negative Minor Trail that is worth putting up with is one that's an investment for the future. Examples abound:

- Studying hard for a class you hate in order to get the good grades you need to get into a good graduate school or get a good job.

- Doing an undesirable project for work may be worth it to make your boss happy and get a promotion at a company you normally enjoy working for.

- Watching an uninteresting sports event with your boyfriend in order to keep your relationship healthy.

- Walking 20 miles on the AT even though you're tired, because you want to make it to the post office before it closes for the weekend.

- Doing the laundry so you have clean underwear tomorrow.

Whenever you feel yourself in a dreadful Minor Trail, ask yourself: "What would probably happen if I got myself out of this situation?" Then figure out if you can live with that outcome. In so doing you will identify if this Minor Trail is connected to a larger goal that you are pursuing. And if it isn't, then run away like a thru-hiker being pursued by a gang of mosquitoes.

Miserable Minor Trails on the AT

Most people find the AT thru-hike to be a miserable Major Trail. That's why over 80 percent don't finish it.

Those who do finish it will tell you that it was a *wonderful* Major Trail that was filled with a variety of *awful* Minor Trails!

Here are just a few trying Minor Trails that we experienced: being so dehydrated that we had to drink water with "floaties" in it; getting rained on for four days straight; walking 20 miles with blisters; living without a shower for five days during a humid heat wave; eating uncooked oatmeal; and sleeping on the grass near a venomous snake!

We couldn't get out of these Minor Trails without jeopardizing our hike. We had to press on. Had we taken a day off each time things got uncomfortable, a snowy winter would have halted our expedition. Yet despite all those arduous situations, hiking the AT was one of the most magnificent Major Trails I have ever experienced.

As Comer, a 64-year-old thru-hiker, put it: "It was the hardest thing we have ever tried but the most enjoyable and rewarding."

It's strange but sometimes the best Major Trails are littered with lousy Minor Trails. If you don't believe me, just watch *Behind the Music* on VH1.

Some sadistic trail designer made these trails. In Maine we often had to pull ourselves up the trail by grabbing the roots of trees. We could barely cover one mile per hour. This was particularly tough when swarms of bugs were constantly on our butts. Notice all the mosquito bites on Lisa's back.

Follow the Fun Compass

When in doubt, *let the Fun Compass guide you.* The Fun Compass tells you which direction is the most fun. We all carry a Fun Compass, but many of us ignore it. We settle for having a few enjoyable moments. Make a habit of frequently asking, "Am I having fun? Am I enjoying this activity?" If not, (1) look at the Fun Compass, (2) identify if it's a Major or Minor Trail, and (3) take the appropriate action. Don't linger in tedious situations. Get out of them as soon as possible. *Few people go overboard with enjoying life, most people put up with more hardship than they need to.*

What does it take to enjoy life?

If your hike is not fun, then you need to figure out what has to happen for you to enjoy your hike. There are many things that people think they need to be happy and to enjoy life. Go through this exercise:

- Write a list of things that have to happen or you need to acquire for you to enjoy life.

- If you're already enjoying life, then write down how much you could afford to lose before you would no longer enjoy life. In other words, how many things could someone take away from you until you are no longer happy?

You might have mentioned that you need a comfortable amount of money, a good education, personal freedom, equality, favorable social status, health, and other factors.[4] Even though you probably didn't mention all these, several might have made your list.

Take a step back

Now look at that list you just wrote and really ask yourself, are you paring it down to the minimum? When I was in El Salvador I met a woman who had a tiny dirty store in a humble pueblo called Suchitoto. This small Central American country has experienced nothing but misery for over thirty years. Yet this woman, who lived so modestly, was incredibly positive and happy. She was enjoying life despite having so little.

She knew what was going on around the world and how others lived. She had been to the United States. She was happy with her place, despite the erratic electricity and the poverty. She wisely realized that she did not need a $1,000 Aeron chair to feel good about life. Her wooden stool worked just great. Similarly, thru-hikers were perfectly content to eat their meals just sitting in the mud!

Happiness depends upon ourselves.
— Aristotle

In a broad study, two psychologists found that only 30 percent of those surveyed were "very happy." What was fascinating is that the percentage of those who said they were "very happy" or "fairly satisfied with life" was the same whether the person was black, white, Hispanic, Asian, male or female. Even more telling was that the percentages stayed the same over four decades of economic growth. In 1957 having a car was still somewhat of a luxury. Today in America, cars outnumber drivers. Compared to 1957, we now have microwave ovens, color TVs, TiVo, air conditioners, answering machines, cell phones, and spam both in a can and on our computers. So are we happier than we were in 1957? Not according to the survey. Still not convinced that you control your happiness? Consider that a year after winning the lottery, most winners are no happier than they were before.[5]

Simple Pleasures Deliver a Big Impact

Hiking your own hike, or following your Fun Compass, can have profound health benefits. Consider:

- ✓ A study showed that patients listening to Brahms in the operating room needed only half the sedative as those who listened to nothing.

- ✓ Looking at an aquarium lowered the blood pressure of patients suffering from hypertension.

- ✓ German research discovered that students who took daily saunas had less than half as many colds over six months as a group that did not take the saunas.

- ✓ Venturing outside can relieve depression.

- ✓ Research demonstrated that patients who were recuperating from a gallbladder operation got out of the hospital one day earlier, had fewer complications, and needed fewer pain relievers when they were given a room with a view of trees rather than a brick wall.

- ✓ You can steady somebody's heart rate by just touching them.

Therefore, improve your health by simply hiking your own hike and following your Fun Compass!

(Source: John Volmer, "The Balanced Life," Men's Health Handbook, *Rodale Press, 1994, p. 71.)*

Millions of Americans, who have one of the highest standards of living in the world, are not as happy as a poor woman in El Salvador. What's wrong?

How to compare yourself with others

When someone asks, "Are you happy?" we tend to look around at our peers and see how they are living. If we're better off than our peers, it's likely that we decide to be happy. *Therefore, one of the tricks of being happy is to change the group we compare ourselves to.*

Silicon Valley gossip columns enjoy pointing out that Oracle's software titan Larry Ellison, whose $14 billion net worth makes him one of the top 10 richest people in America, is not the happiest guy around, mainly because he always compares himself to Bill Gates. Meanwhile, back on the AT, some thru-hikers would feel smug because they got a spot in a shelter (which only has three walls and frequently has rodents nearby), whereas the latecomers had to set up their tent in the rain. For some reason most thru-hikers coveted the spots in the shelters, and preferred cramming next to snoring neighbors than setting up their tent. I suppose if we put Larry Ellison on the AT, he might feel better about himself if we somehow made sure that he always got to stay in one of the shelters (and Bill Gates had to sleep outside under a shoddy tarp).

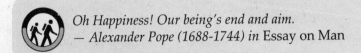

Oh Happiness! Our being's end and aim.
— *Alexander Pope (1688-1744) in* Essay on Man

Imagine I walk into a shelter and give you and your four friends an envelope. You open yours and it says that you get a free pizza at the next town. If you're like most thru-hikers, you'd do a somersault with your backpack on!

Clearly, you would be ecstatic: most thru-hikers value fresh food more than anything on the trail. Indeed, you might think that thru-hikers spend most of their time thinking deep thoughts during their long days of hiking in the wilderness. You might imagine that they are gathering the wisdom off every branch and every stream. On the contrary, most spend their time fantasizing about grilled cheese sandwiches, fries, shakes, and ice cream.

Therefore, if I were to ask you if you were happy about getting a free pizza, you would shout emphatically, "Yes! Woo-hoo!" But now imagine that your friends finish opening their envelopes and not only do they all get a free pizza, but they get to stay at the Ritz Carlton, have a foot and back massage, stay in the deluxe suite with a Jacuzzi, and have all their laundry done for them.

Now, all of a sudden, you don't feel so good anymore. You went from a state of exhilaration to one of melancholy. From a purely rational perspective, if you were happy before, you should still be happy now. After all, you still get your free pizza, and that's what got you so excited in the first place. I didn't take that away from you, so you should still be happy. However, when we're trying to decide how happy we are, we tend to look at how other people are doing to help us make that decision. This is natural and it's hard to fight this primal tendency.

Happiness, n. An agreeable sensation arising from contemplating the misery of others. — Ambrose Bierce

Use the urge to compare yourself with others in a positive way. *Instead of trying to stop comparing yourself to anyone, just change whom you compare yourself to.* If you want to instantly make yourself feel depressed, think about all the people who have much better lives than you. Conversely, if you want to make yourself instantly feel happy, compare your state to those less fortunate than you.

Moreover, don't just compare yourself with those less fortunate than you, take it a step further—compare yourself with people who are less fortunate than you *and who are happier than you*. It is at that moment that you will realize that you have no excuse. It's all in your head. What else can explain why so many thru-hikers, who effectively live like bums in absolute squalor, are happy and fulfilled?

One who is content with what one has is always happy.
— Chinese Proverb

The implication of this Chinese proverb is that the fewer desires you have, the easier it will be to satisfy them and be happy. Confucius reinforced this philosophy when he praised his favorite disciple, Yan Hui: "A bowlful of rice to eat, a gourdful of water to drink, and living in a mean dwelling; all this is a hardship others would find intolerable, but Hui does not allow this to affect his joy. How admirable Hui is!"[6] Clearly, this is proof that Confucius would have admired thru-hikers. Then again, it could also be used to prove that he would have respected participants in the TV show "Survivor."

Most folks are about as happy as they make up their minds to be. — Abraham Lincoln

Next time you feel like you're being short-changed on something, compare yourself to the following:

- **Wealth:** We've all met plenty of poor people who are happy. In case you haven't, just ask yourself if Gandhi or Mother Teresa were happy.

- **Education:** You don't need to have access to encyclopedic knowledge or a Ph.D. to be happy. There is a reason that we say, "Ignorance is bliss!" There are tribes in the world, such as the Aborigines, that have little access to the Internet, TV, newspapers, books, and other sources of knowledge. Are they despondent?

- **Personal freedom:** In every repressive regime there have been plenty of happy people. *The Diary of Anne Frank* demonstrates how a Jewish family in Nazi Germany enjoyed the simple moments of life even under the most confining of situations.

- **Equality:** South Africa's racist laws were extremely

40

unequal. Yet many of its citizens did not let that be an excuse for being miserable and depressed.

- **Health:** Stephen Hawking, the famous theoretical physicist, seems to enjoy every day of his life despite being confined to a wheelchair and living with ALS. Magic Johnson still maintains his ever present smile, even though he is HIV positive. Lance Armstrong kept a positive spirit in the face of cancer.

- **Social position:** Order takers at McDonalds aren't the pinnacle of the social ladder, but try to find an unhappy one among those who were selected to represent McDonalds in Utah's 2002 Olympic Games. McDonalds picked their most service oriented employees from all over the world and flew them in for that world event.

- **Life-events:** Some of us get big lucky breaks (e.g., winning the lottery), others get big unlucky breaks (e.g., getting paralyzed from a car accident). However, just like there are unhappy millionaires, there are happy paraplegics. A tragedy does not force you to be unhappy for the rest of your life.

I'm not suggesting that you learn to be happy living the monastic life. Nor am I saying that people who live in challenging conditions have no right to complain or to try to improve their situation. I'm simply suggesting that it is possible to enjoy life without all the things that we typically think of as basic requirements. Too many people think, "I'll be able to start enjoying life once I get _____." Don't put it off for tomorrow or next month. Even though there is some correlation between having the above things and enjoying life, they are not necessary to enjoy life. Just ask anyone who has thru-hiked the Appalachian Trail.

 Happiness doesn't depend on outward conditions. It depends on inner conditions. — Dale Carnegie

Common criticisms

A few might disagree with the *hike your own hike* philosophy. After all, declaring that we should follow our Fun Compass seems hedonistic. It seems to forget morals. What about helping others? Or bettering yourself? Or raising a family? Does that mean we shouldn't feel guilty for stealing a hotel's towels?

In short, it may seem like an irresponsible credo. To indulge the skeptics among us, let's think about it.

But what about morals?

Being moral and enjoying life are not mutually exclusive. Following your Fun Compass does not give you the right to be immoral or unethical. Just because you didn't get a raise, you don't have a right to go postal.

But what about self-sacrifice?

At Amherst College I majored in religion and studied a variety of faiths. The Bible and other religious texts frequently portray sin-

---

Morals on the Trail

Many people fear the AT. "Don't you carry a gun?" they ask. "Aren't you afraid some crazy person might attack you in the middle of nowhere?"

I tell them that I have those thoughts when I'm walking the streets of a major city, not when I'm in the woods!

A married couple that call themselves Bear and Honey run a hostel for hikers in Andover, Maine. Bear told me that for over 10 years he has left his wallet lying around the hostel, and even though hundreds of hikers have come through, no one has ever stolen any money from it. In fact, he gives his truck's keys to any hiker who needs to run an errand in town. He's never had a bad incident.

The AT's moral code is remarkable.

---

ners as pleasure-seekers. This leads some to conclude that a good moral life must be the opposite. But is that true?

Did God punish Moses for smiling when he saw the land of Caanan? Did Muhammad not enjoy reflecting in a cave on Mount Hira? Did the Buddha not take pleasure in his walks through the wilderness? Does God frown on Christians who enjoy singing? Did Confucius not extol his followers to pursue happiness in this life?

Religions aren't about making you miserable. They're about loving God, loving life, and being a good person.

Beer is proof that God loves us and wants us to be happy.
— Benjamin Franklin

Thru-hikers are akin to religious disciples: they suffer tremendously at times, but overall they enjoy the experience. Their purpose isn't to suffer, but to be happy and fulfilled. Sure it's tough backpacking the entire AT in one season. We would walk from sunrise to sunset up and over steep mountains with a pack on our backs. We would walk over 20 miles a day in the rain and the mud with an entourage of mosquitoes whining in our ears. We had to ignore our dehydrated throats and our ravenous stomachs. As one successful thru-hiker and retired Lutheran pastor named George Ziegenfuss told me, "There is no amount of money that you could pay me to work that hard." Yet George did it for free; in fact, a couple of years later, while in his late sixties, he attempted to hike the AT again! Incredibly, George has only one lung! Clearly, this was hard work, but he enjoyed it. This former pastor did it because he knew that accomplishing his goal would make him so happy that it would make it all worthwhile. If nothing else, at least it got him out of the house.

One of Buddhism's central beliefs is that much of life is about suffering, but Buddhists monks are taught to transcend the suffering. In conclusion, the most deeply religious people are the most likely to understand that the purpose of life is to enjoy it. It's no coincidence that the Dalai Lama himself wrote a book entitled *The Art of Happiness: A Handbook for Living* where the first sentence is: "I believe that the very purpose of our life is to seek happiness. That is clear."

But what about dreams?

Confucius advises us to have a few desires, but what about having big dreams? Isn't it important to dream ambitious dreams if we ever want to accomplish anything in life? If you don't want anything, doesn't that mean you won't achieve anything?

Dreaming and having big goals is extremely important. *The key is not making your happiness dependent on achieving those dreams.* For example, before starting the AT, most thru-hikers imagine finishing it. It's important to visualize it. But at the same time, don't tell yourself that you won't be happy unless you achieve it. No matter how much we dream and plan, things don't always turn out the way we expect. Have simple enough expectations that nearly anything will make you happy. Set up various scenarios in your mind and imagine being happy with all of them. Just have one ideal scenario that keeps you motivated; for instance, completing the hike without getting mauled by a bear.

> *I've been lucky enough to win an Oscar, write a bestseller... my other dream would be to have a painting in the Louvre. The only way that's going to happen is if I paint a dirty one on the wall of the gentlemen's lavatory.*
> —David Niven

Summary

Let's recap some of the important points of this chapter:

- Aim to make every waking moment enjoyable by following your Fun Compass.

- When life is not enjoyable, use the Major Trail vs. Minor Trail analysis to help you decide what to do.

- Identify when you're succumbing to Frog Psychology and quickly create an Inflection Point to overcome it.

- When you feel unhappy, stop comparing yourself to those more fortunate than you, and start comparing yourself to those less fortunate (and happier) than you.

- Realize that it takes far less than you think to enjoy life.

I'm reminded of my feelings when we crossed the state line of Maine into New Hampshire. We turned around to read the sign: "WELCOME TO MAINE: THE WAY LIFE SHOULD BE." Lisa and I looked at each other and burst out laughing.

Maine was some of the hardest hiking we had ever done in our lives. In preparation for the AT, we had hiked over 500 miles of trail in rugged California, whose peaks make Maine's mountains look like molehills. We thought we were prepared. We were cocky hikers believing that we could easily conquer Maine's diminutive peaks. We learned the hard lesson that a mountain's height is one thing, but the way the trail goes up it is another. Whereas California's trails are nicely graded for pack animals and have plenty of switchbacks, we encountered only two switchbacks in our first 400 miles of trail (the folks in New Hampshire don't understand the concept of "switchback" either).

Uh, I'm in Maine. I've been walking to Maine, and now I'm here. I had butterflies in my stomach all morning about 'the sign' and the Trail ending, etc. But after I got over it I started slipping on wet rocks and falling down and cursing and loving Maine and, well, I'm here.
— Mary Poppins, Nobo, August 22, 2001 Trail Journal

We were relieved to have finished the 284 miles in Maine in less than two weeks. Our pace was grueling, but we did it because we enjoyed pushing ourselves. We knew that Maine was the toughest state on the AT. Therefore, we knew that if we could get through Maine, there wasn't a state on the AT that we couldn't do.

It's a similar case here: once you truly grasp the concept of hiking your own hike, then all else follows easily. The key is not simply to say, "Yeah, yeah, yeah 'hike your own hike', OK so what's the next point?" First, you must truly want to change your perspective and habits. Second, you must let that notion permeate all levels of your life. *Commit to following your Fun Compass so you can hike your own hike.*

We've taken the first step on this epic journey by learning the most important Principle to getting the most out of life. However, if you disagree with this Principle, perhaps you might prefer the wisdom of Groucho Marx, who said, "The secret of life is honesty and fair dealing. If you can fake that, you've got it made."

Although Maine's mountains are short, the trail is steep. I accidentally got a few feet off the trail and had to take a big step to get back on it.

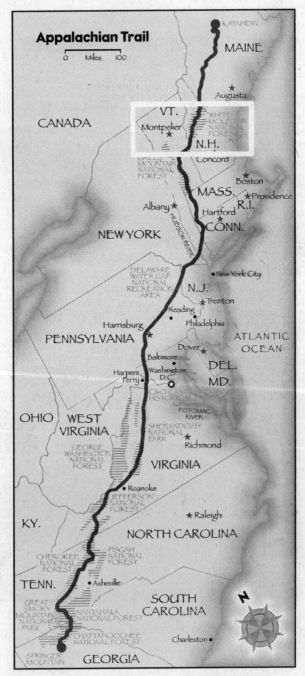

Appalachian Trail

0   Miles   100

KATAHDIN

MAINE

Augusta

CANADA

VT.

Montpelier

WHITE MOUNTAIN NATIONAL FOREST

N.H.

Concord

GREEN MOUNTAIN NATIONAL FOREST

Boston

MASS.

Providence

Albany

Hartford

R.I.

CONN.

NEW YORK

HUDSON RIVER

DELAWARE WATER GAP NATIONAL RECREATION AREA

New York City

N.J.

Trenton

Reading

Philadelphia

Harrisburg

ATLANTIC OCEAN

PENNSYLVANIA

Dover

Baltimore

DEL.

Harpers Ferry

Washington D.C.

MD.

C&O CANAL NATIONAL HISTORICAL PARK

OHIO

WEST VIRGINIA

POTOMAC RIVER

SHENANDOAH NATIONAL PARK

Richmond

GEORGE WASHINGTON NATIONAL FOREST

VIRGINIA

Roanoke

JEFFERSON NATIONAL FOREST

KY.

Raleigh

NORTH CAROLINA

CHEROKEE NATIONAL FOREST

PISGAH NATIONAL FOREST

TENN.

Asheville

SOUTH CAROLINA

GREAT SMOKY MOUNTAINS NATIONAL PARK

NANTAHALA NATIONAL FOREST

Charleston

CHATTAHOOCHEE NATIONAL FOREST

SPRINGER MOUNTAIN

GEORGIA

N

© *Appalachian Trail Conservancy, reprinted with permission*

Chapter 2:
Beware of Summit Fever

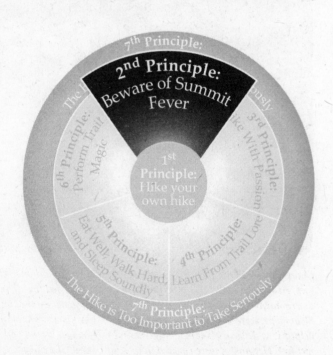

About 10 percent of would be thru-hikers quit because they run out of money. Lisa met two such hikers. Their experience would teach me the Second Principle on getting the most out of life. *This Principle is about managing your money.* Unfortunately, I never got to meet these two hikers because I was lost at the time.

It is hard to lose yourself on the AT, but somehow I managed to do just that. Lisa and I usually walked within eyesight of each other, but occasionally we would hike just a bit beyond the visual range. Although we appreciated each other's company, we also appreciated occasional solitude. This time we would get a bit more solitude than we had bargained for.

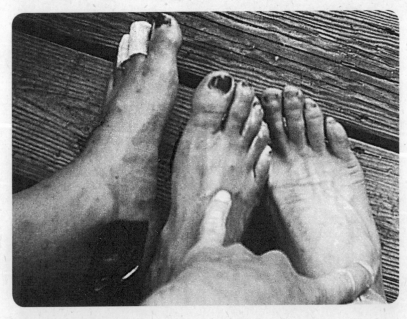

Maine destroyed our feet. Its 281 miles of brutal trail and nonstop rain tested our toes. At the end of the 100-mile Wilderness I had twisted my right ankle, creating a permanent bump on my right foot (see far right foot). By the time we entered New Hampshire we had been hammered with four days of incessant rain which helped Lisa develop blisters all over her toes. Bandages would barely stick to her wet feet. Her ankles were covered in mosquito bites. She covered her heel with duct tape to prevent a blister from getting worse. She also had a painful bump on the top of her right foot. At Pinham Notch we concluded that we deserved a day off.

We had left Maine behind and were hiking the rigorous White Mountains of New Hampshire. For me, it was the most spectacular section of the AT. In the Presidential Range the AT crosses well above the tree line, offering panoramic vistas everywhere. On the other hand, clouds frequently form in the Whites because three weather systems converge in that small area. Park rangers brag that the fiercest winds ever measured were on top of Mount Washington—an insane 231 miles per hour. Try setting up a tarp in that weather!

Our climb to Mount Washington, the tallest mountain in New England, was intense. The Outdoor Life Network put Mt. Washington on the list of the Top 25 Most Dangerous Places on Earth. We got a hint of its danger as we approached the summit via Mount Madison. It began to rain, but climbing 3,000 feet makes you work up a sweat. Backpackers wear layers to help regulate their body temperature, but in this case even my thin shirt was making me hot. On the other hand, being wet would make me too cold. Therefore, I took my shirt off and hiked up in shorts and with an umbrella. A group of school kids wearing heavy duty storm gear stared at me with their mouths open, incredulous that a nearly naked man was walking right into a rainstorm; the teacher joked, "Expecting sunshine up there?"

They had stopped at the tree line because the sounds of thunder meant lightning was near, and hiking on an exposed mountaintop is not the smartest thing to do. I smiled at the school kids and pressed on into the thunderstorm.

The rain made us particularly cautious as we walked over the wet boulders on our way to the summit. We heard the rumble of thunder to our left, and then about a minute later we heard another roar on our right. I had to tilt my umbrella at a sharp angle to block the horizontal rain. Even though Lisa was wearing waterproof tops and bottoms, the wind and rain started making her shiver.

"This can't be good," I mumbled under my breath.

I began to question if we were ready to summit this mountain. We were experienced hikers, but this could be pushing it. Throughout the climb up Mount Madison I had been scanning around to make sure that there was a quick way to get down the ridge in case the thunder moved over us. Knowing that hypothermia kills far more hikers than lightning, I focused on keeping Lisa warm rather than dodging lightning bolts.

Hiking with an Umbrella

I didn't bring a rain jacket on the AT because I find that there is no rain jacket that offers as much rain protection and *ventilation* as an umbrella. The ventilation is important because it postpones overheating.

For example, Lisa wore a rain jacket but by the time she would get to the top of a mountain, she would be soaked—in sweat, not rain. Either one would help take her down the path of hypothermia because of the cold winds at the summit.

An umbrella helps regulate your temperature because it lets the heat that your body generates while hiking evaporate quickly. Even "breathable" rain jackets trap a significant amount of heat. Near the top of a mountain, you can add a layer of clothing before your body starts to cool during the descent.

At nine ounces, a GoLite umbrella weighs about nearly half as much as a "breathable" rain jacket. Thru-hikers are fanatical about minimizing their pack weight, so this is yet another good reason to use an umbrella for rain protection. Moreover, since I wear glasses, I like how an umbrella does a much better job at protecting my lenses from getting wet than a simple hood.

Finally, when you're exposed to a scorching sun, umbrellas provide excellent protection and don't trap heat like a sunhat.

Lisa discovered that I was staying drier than she was, so after New Hampshire she sent her rain jacket home and used a GoLite umbrella for the 12 remaining states.

On the other hand, most hikers think I'm nuts. Although I encourage you try using an umbrella, what's more important is that you hike your own hike and use whatever rain protection makes you happiest.

As long as the sound of thunder was still in the distance and there was a quick way down, I figured it was safe to continue climbing—after all, one of the best ways to warm your body up is to hike uphill. I encouraged Lisa to hike vigorously, while I continued to make sure that an escape route was near and the thunder was not.

Fortunately, the thunder eventually grew more distant and the rain subsided. Lisa warmed up and stopped shivering. We hit the summit of Mount Madison in a swirl of mystical clouds. Park rangers warn that the weather in the Whites can change rapidly. They weren't kidding. By the time we reached the summit of nearby Mount Washington, we were basking in the sun enjoying the 50-mile visibility and the brisk winds. We breathed a sigh of relief and celebrated on the summit of the tallest mountain in New England.

By the time we got to the summit of Mt. Washington it was clear and windy. This is the tallest mountain in New England. The glory of climbing it is a bit diminished when you see that most people just drive (or a take a train) to the top. But who cares? We still felt like bad asses.

The next day I got lost. The Appalachian Trail is easy to follow—unless you're daydreaming. The day after walking over Mount Madison and Mount Washington, Lisa was hiking ahead of me at her normal swift pace and she got out of my visual range. I wasn't worried because this happened often—I found it hard to keep up with her brutal pace. So I merrily strolled across the ridges of the Presidential Range absorbing in the panoramic views and letting my thoughts wander.

Not until we are lost do we begin to understand ourselves. — Henry David Thoreau

Had I been paying attention I would have noticed the sign that showed that the AT took a sharp left. Instead I just continued going straight ahead, which was a completely different trail. I was in my own little world; it is easy to get "into a zone" on the AT. I walked over an hour and went down about 2,000 feet before it dawned on me that I hadn't seen a white blaze for a while. The AT is marked by these two by six inch white rectangles on trees or rocks to indicate where the trail went; we called these markers "white blazes." There are about 20,000 of these white blazes from Maine to Georgia, so only idiots get lost.

I finally ran into someone who confirmed that I was far off the AT and that I was, indeed, an idiot.

Fortunately, a road and a trailhead map was just another mile away. I certainly didn't want to walk up the steep mountain and attempt to catch up to Lisa. Who knows what she was trying to do. She was probably in that helicopter that kept circling over me.

We had about six hours of daylight left, so I felt we had plenty of time to run into each other somehow. However, we couldn't afford to get separated overnight. We hadn't equipped ourselves to get separated. We were 100 percent dependent on each other. For example, I carried our tarp, so Lisa had no shelter without me. Meanwhile, Lisa had our sleeping bag (which was effectively a blanket), so I had no way to sleep comfortably at night without her. I started having visions of mimicking John Muir and constructing a warm bed in the woods using dry leaves as insulation. Lisa was fine as long as it didn't rain. On the other hand, she needed food—all she had was a couple of X-Terra energy bars, because I carried all the food. Little did I know that while I was worrying about Lisa's lack of food that she was in the Mizpah Spring Hut relaxing with her shoes off, chatting with two Nobos, and enjoying some warm and delicious minestrone soup.

I have never been lost, but I will admit to being confused for several weeks. — Daniel Boone

About every ten miles along the AT there is a shelter. These shelters usually have only three walls and rarely have running water. In the Whites, however, these shelters become deluxe accommodations called "Huts." For $70 a night, you get the pleasure of sleeping in a bunk bed in a room with a few other snoring individuals. No self-respecting thru-hiker would pay that kind of money for those kinds of accommodations; they would rather sleep on the dirt for free. But thru-hikers are an important source of labor in the huts. The huts employ thru-hikers for a couple of hours in exchange for leftovers and letting them sleep on the dining room floor.

Normally thru-hikers will do the dishes, help cook, clean up, or do any other odd job. Since it was still the early afternoon, the huts didn't need any help, so Lisa and the other hikers just relaxed in Mizpah Spring Hut. Lisa was hoping that I would catch up. There she learned the financial lesson of the AT from two Nobos named Hot Sauce and Non-Existent.

Hot Sauce and Non-Existent had spent money as if hiking the AT took only a week or two. They went to restaurants at every opportunity, stayed in nice hotels (instead of hostels), and bought the most expensive and fashionable gear on the market. They weren't particularly rich, but they hiked the AT as if they were. As a result, they were now short on cash and did not expect to

Lisa descended to the Lakes of the Clouds Hut, the highest, most popular, and biggest hut in the Presidential Range of New Hampshire. We showed up at 8:45 p.m., just in time to eat leftovers and help with the cleanup. Lisa is holding up three fingers to indicate that we had hiked exactly three weeks and 333 miles to get here.

make it to Katahdin. In fact, they already had to compromise their thru-hike—they had skipped several states on the way up to New Hampshire. Their finances were stretched, but they didn't want to cut back their way of life on the trail, so they hitchhiked over half the distance. Now, with their funds near zero, and having grown accustomed to a certain way of life on the trail, they felt they had no other choice but to quit.

Before Lisa could tell me their tale she had to find me. We had no cellular phones because of the extra weight they bring, the challenge of recharging them, and the lack of coverage in the wilderness. But we were lucky—if there were ever a place to get separated on the AT, it was in the Whites. The huts have radios to communicate with each other. Lisa asked the ranger to notify the other nearby huts to look for me so I could call her. She gave a description of me so that the next two huts could identify me.

"Francis goes by the trail name Mr. Magoo," she explained. "He's wearing black spandex shorts, no shirt, sneakers, and has an umbrella."

"Sounds like a winner," the ranger quipped.

Several hours later and 30 minutes before sunset, we finally re-united at the Zealand Falls Hut. Thus, I avoided testing my John Muir survival skills.

 I don't panic when I get lost. I just change where I want to go. — Rita Rudner

Lisa eventually told me the story of Hot Sauce and Non-Existent. *Their tale taught me the second lesson of my pilgrimage: beware of summit fever.* In other words, don't upgrade your standard of living until you've got plenty of financial breathing room. It's important to explore how we can apply this lesson to our everyday life.

Don't summit before you're ready

Many mountaineers get *summit fever*—a burning desire to summit the mountain, no matter what the odds. When I was climbing Mount Madison, for example, I suffered from summit fever. I should have waited until the lightning storm passed before making my approach. Similarly, we can get summit fever in our financial lives too. We stretch ourselves financially and then we're caught in the open when a storm hits. The experience of Hot Sauce and Non-Existent taught me *the importance of living below your means.*

One of the most common questions people asked me was, "How can you afford to thru-hike?" They would say, "I'd love to go hiking for six months, but I can't afford that," or "What about your job?" or "You damn trust fund kids."

Most thru-hikers are not rich, nor are they poor. They have average incomes. Of course, we met people on the extremes, such as computer scientists, doctors, and lawyers on the one hand, and high school students, military officers, and Peace Corps volunteers on the other. However, the vast majority of the 300 or so who complete the AT thru-hike each year are regular people with average incomes. Observers find it amazing that those who have average incomes can take such an extraordinary "vacation." And yet thru-hikers return from the AT frequently aiming to do it again. They return changed. They look at all their "necessities" and realize that they are really not that necessary. The AT shows you the importance of adjusting your money management to maximize your options.

He who is attached to things will suffer much.
— The Tao Te Ching

One of the big lessons from the last chapter is how little we need to enjoy life. Let's learn how to practice this. This chapter is not about living like a monk, or worse, living like a thru-hiker (hey, at least monks have four walls and a roof over their head—some thru-hikers just have a flimsy tarp!). *This chapter is about learning to have the discipline to resist the temptation to raise your standard of living the moment that it becomes possible to do so.* It's about holding back on upgrading your way of life until you know that it's nearly impossible to fall back down. It's about freedom.

The value of freedom

Freedom is about having options so you can do what you love, pursue happiness, and get the most out of life. Yet how many of us are truly free today? How many of us can take a six month vacation? How many of us can afford to not worry about being laid off? How many of us can change careers and start at an entry level position in another industry? How many of us have the freedom to easily pack up our bags and move to a new city or country?

Most of can't do any of this. What kind of freedom is that? Who has put these shackles on us to inhibit our options and possibilities? Who is impeding our ability to squeeze the most out of life?

We are.

We are not truly free because we have chosen to believe that we need certain things to be happy. We let peer pressure persuade us that we will not enjoy life unless we have a certain standard of living. As a result, we kill ourselves chasing after these goals, hoping that they will make us happy. We waste our lives running after things that will supposedly make our life better while we wonder why we feel so empty even after we get them. In our rush to keep up with the Joneses, we don't stop and realize that the Joneses aren't that happy.

Are you climbing up too fast?

Here is a quick quiz to help you gauge how well you're following the Second Principle:

1. If all your income sources stopped today, how many months could you survive before you had to cut back your standard of living?

2. On a scale of 1-10, at what pace do you adopt new technology? (1 = "I get technology before NASA does!" and 10 = "I just bought a telephone!")

3. If you got a raise today, how much of it would you save vs. spend? (Rate it on a 1-10 scale where 1 = "spend it all" and 10 = "save it all")

4. On a 1-10 scale, how much do you worry about making ends meet? (1 = "It's hard to sleep at night" and 10 = "zzzzz")

5. On a 1-10 scale, how financially secure do you feel? (1 = "Bankruptcy courts know me well" and 10 = "I bathe in money")

Scoring: If you scored less than 36, pay careful attention to this chapter.

The trap of raising your standard of living

Do you remember the last time you raised your standard of living? Could you imagine going back to how you lived before? When you upgrade your standard of living, you become addicted to that standard of living. For instance, could you imagine living like you did when you were in your early 20s? You were probably crammed in a college dorm, or shacked up with three roommates in a small house, or dealing with your nagging parents. For those of us who have moved on to more comfortable situations, it's hard to imagine going back to that way of life. Most would rather endure weeks of Chinese water torture than return to our former standard of living.

Yet paradoxically many people fondly remember their early 20s as some of the happiest moments of their lives. Sure, you were cramped in a dorm, but you were enjoying life to the fullest. Sleeping in bunk beds in a New York City apartment was a minor annoyance compared to the joy you had during that period. Even putting up with your pestering parents was worth the good times you had. OK, never mind that last one.

The point is that even though we lived more humbly than we do now, we were just as happy, and perhaps more happy than today. This reminds us of the First Principle: happiness comes from within. However, few would be willing to return to that way of life and put up with those "meager living conditions" again. There is nothing wrong with feeling that way, it is a normal part of human nature—once we upgrade we never want to go back. Although we theoretically can go back, the pain and discomfort is monumental. *In essence, whenever we upgrade we pass a point of no return.* Therefore, it's vital to carefully think through each upgrade, lest we risk either diminished freedom or increased anguish. So the challenge is knowing when to upgrade. Luckily, the AT is a great teacher.

With limited funds to spend over four months on the AT, we faced decisions on when to give ourselves a treat. For example, sometimes we'd want to stay in a hostel to take a shower and do laundry. We also had to factor in our one big treat: going to Manhattan

The Chemist on the AT

Peter was a German chemist I met in Virginia along the AT. I asked him why he was hiking 1,000 miles.

He replied, "Because I want to remind myself how good I have it. I have a beautiful wife who is 25 years younger than me, a beach house in South Carolina, wonderful kids, a great job I enjoy that pays well. Coming out here to live a simple life will make me recall how good my life is."

Your life doesn't have to be as good as Peter's to appreciate such a perspective check. Most of us don't realize how good we have it. Putting yourself in an extremely humble environment can help you realize just how lucky you are.

to see some world class theatre and eat like monarchy. Since we would not have any income for at least four months, we had to budget carefully. The AT helped teach us to distinguish between One-Time Upgrades and Subscription Upgrades.

One-Time Upgrades vs. Subscription Upgrades

Upgrading costs money, and it comes in two flavors: One-Time Upgrades and Subscription Upgrades. A *One-Time Upgrade* is a purchase that you might do every few years. For example, a One-Time Upgrade might be a new DVD player, HDTV, backpack, laundry machine, car, kitchen appliance, business suit, or teddy bear. A *Subscription Upgrade*, on the other hand, is typically a small reoccurring incremental expense—perhaps only $3/day, or $50/month, or a couple hundred bucks a year. Examples include Internet access, cable TV, gourmet coffee, bridge tolls, monthly parking fees, car loans, gym fees, or an irritating timeshare.

Some upgrades are in a hybrid category. Buying a new house, for instance, is both a one-time expense (closing costs, commissions, down payment) and a subscription (mortgage payments and maintenance costs). Nevertheless, for simplicity's sake, we'll just focus on the two standard upgrades.

Both types of upgrades:

- Raise your standard of living.

- Cost money.

- Diminish your freedom.

Let's pick an extreme example to make the last point clear. Let's assume you live like a typical American: you have a decent place to live; you go out to restaurants occasionally; you go on a couple of vacations per year with your family; and you have a hobby that keeps you busy. In short, you have a decent amount of freedom. Then one day you decide to buy a Ferrari. The monthly car payments are so high that you can no longer afford to live in your house, so you must move into a small apartment. You stop eating out, you cancel your vacations, and you can no longer afford to pursue your hobby. You have become a *slave* to your car payments—now your purpose in life is to make money to pay for the car. Your freedom to change careers, to go to new places, and to enjoy life has vanished. In fact, your ability to enjoy the Ferrari may be restricted because filling up the tank costs so much and the repair costs are so high that you worry about driving it too hard. Besides, you don't want it to get scratched, because touching it up would be pricey. So you take the bus to work.

Perhaps it's an extreme example, but it illustrates the point: *every dollar you spend to raise your standard of living takes away a bit of your freedom.* If you raise your expenses dramatically, your options in life diminish dramatically. If you raise your standard of living slightly, your freedom diminishes slightly. Furthermore, the poorer you are, the more sensitive you are to nominal changes in your spending habits.

While most would agree that buying a Ferrari would diminish their freedom, it's hard to believe that an innocent $20 magazine subscription could possibly diminish one's freedom. On the other hand, most would agree that getting 400 magazine subscriptions would start to affect your ability to pay your rent. At what point does the process begin to erode your freedom? At 100 subscriptions? 20? The answer is the very first one. Of course, the impact is so subtle that it's nearly impossible to notice (unless your budget is hyper tight). Most people wouldn't even notice the impact of 10 magazine subscriptions, but at some point we would all start to feel it. Even Donald Trump.

The connection between money and freedom

Why do so many people envy the rich? Because we value freedom, and we understand that there is a correlation between money and freedom. If you have a billion dollars, you have the freedom to do almost anything: you can travel anywhere in first class; eat at any restaurant; sleep all day; live anywhere; and stay at hotels that put a Godiva chocolate on your pillow.

Of course, you can be pretty free without money, but money can help increase your options if you use it wisely. Some think that money enslaves you. It doesn't. What enslaves you is living beyond your means. I'm not saying that money is a panacea. As we saw in the last chapter you can enjoy life even when you are poor, and there are plenty of rich people who are depressed. Obviously, having lots of money isn't going to let you do back flips on a snowboard, nor will it help find true love.

 Happy is harder than money. Anybody who thinks money will make you happy hasn't got money.
— Multimillionaire David Geffen on "20/20" (ABC)

Having lots of money *may* increase your freedom, it's just not guaranteed. Whether it does or not is under your control. Whenever you receive money, you always have the same choice: *you can invest that money and increase your freedom, or you can spend it and decrease your freedom.*

One-Time Upgrade examples

To see how this works with One-Time Upgrades, let's say you get a $5,000 raise at work. That extra money represents freedom—you can either spend it or invest it. Here are some ways you can use that $5,000:

Increase your freedom	Decrease your freedom
Invest it in mutual fund	Buy a home theatre system
Invest it in your (or your children's) education	Buy jewelry
Help start up a business	Buy chrome wheels for your car

The One-Time Upgrades on the right immediately raise your standard of living, but lower your freedom. After buying the home theatre system, you quickly become accustomed to it and you can't imagine going back to a humble TV. By spending $5,000 instead of saving it, you diminish your future options. Just imagine, with an extra $5,000 you could retire to the inexpensive and ever-popular Sunni Triangle region of Iraq.

Saving your money is the purest way of increasing your freedom. Spending money on education or starting up a business also enhances your freedom, but not as much as investing it in assets. For instance, spending $100,000 to get an MBA will increase your options when you graduate: you will be able to work in jobs that you were not qualified before. However, had you kept the $100,000 in investments, you would have not only kept the option of going to business school, but also had the option to do a variety of other activities. Nevertheless, it's important not to clump spending money on education with buying a new car. Clearly, the former augments your freedom, while the latter reduces it. Moreover, this holds true whether you're making a $5,000 purchase, a $500 purchase, or even a $50 purchase. In every case you're biting a chunk of freedom, and its effect is far more pronounced the poorer you are.

Subscription Upgrade examples

Many people can understand how One-Time Upgrades can affect your freedom. However, it's hard to imagine how a little innocent

An Ancient Principle

The Second Principle isn't new. It's been with us for a while. Plutarch, a brilliant philosopher who lived in the first century, observed in *Of Man's Progress in Virtue*: "As those persons who despair of ever being rich make little account of small expenses, thinking that little added to a little will never make any great sum."

People had a funny way of writing back then, but basically he meant to say that people tend to ignore the little reoccurring expenses because they can't imagine that they make any difference at the end of the day. Plutarch recognized the fallacy of that logic 2,000 years ago, and so should we today.

$4 cup of coffee everyday can take away from your freedom. Yet it's a perfect example of a subscription, or reoccurring, expense. It's a good way to show how sneakily Subscription Upgrades can limit your options. So let's calculate the cost of a Subscription Upgrade. *There are two methods to analyze the true cost of a Subscription Upgrade: nominal costs or real costs.*

Nominal costs

This is the easy way, because it's simple math. Just multiply the transaction by the number of times you expect to do the transaction in a year. If you expect to do it for several years, you might want to multiply it by the number of years too. So in the coffee example, you would take $4 x 365 days = $1,460. This assumes you'll have a cup on weekends too, perhaps at a restaurant. This means that you spend almost $1,500 on coffee every year. If you keep that up for 20 years, you'll spend almost $30,000 on coffee! Just thinking about that might wake you up.[7]

The point of this calculation is to give you a rough idea of how a little expense can be significant if you do it repeatedly. Many Americans don't think twice about buying a cup of coffee everyday, yet they would rejoice if their Uncle Harry handed them a $1,500 check every Christmas. By avoiding the seductive coffee habit, we would effectively be getting a $1,500 bonus at the end of the year. Since the $4 transaction is small, we tend not to notice its impact over time. The nominal calculation gives you a rough estimate; however, this calculation *always underestimates* the true cost of a Subscription Upgrade.

Real costs

The real cost of a Subscription Upgrade would have to take into account what economists call the *opportunity cost*. In other words, we must answer the question: what else could you do with that $4 a day? What would happen if everyday for 20 years you put $4 into the stock market, for instance? Would you have $30,000 saved up as we calculated above?

No, you would have over three times that! Through the magic of compound interest, sometimes called the eighth wonder of the world, you would have an extra $93,231 in 20 years. All you would have to do is put $4 a day in the stock market, which has historically earned 10 percent annually. Some may scoff saying that $93,231 won't be worth much in 20 years, but assuming inflation stays around 3 percent, that's the same as someone handing you $51,630 today—or as a snotty MBA guy might say, the *present value* is just over $50,000. No matter how you slice it, it's not pocket change.

To put that into perspective, let's say your salary is $50,000/year today and you keep your same job for 20 years while your employer gives you raises indexed to inflation. In 20 years, your salary will be about $93,000. By avoiding that addictive gourmet coffee, you'll have the pleasure of getting a full year's pay in twenty years. It's not exactly a pension, but it sure beats working for a year!

Subscription Upgrades are particularly insidious because they can appear like One-Time Upgrades. Indeed, why make a fuss about a car payment that's an extra $50/month when most of us wouldn't think twice about buying a nice article of clothing for that price? However, Subscription Upgrades hit you over and over again, and you should be aware of them even if they cost $1/day.

Isn't it a wonder how expenses ramp up to meet our income? — Anonymous

Of course, for many people drinking that cup of soy-latte-espresso-Brazilian-mocha-without-cream-or-foam everyday is worth $1,500 a year, or even $93,000 over 20 years. They retort that if you live your whole life overanalyzing every expense you'll never spend a dime and you'll never have fun. Indeed, you could torture yourself with each little reoccurring financial transaction. For example, if you avoid going to the movies once a week for twenty years, you could have an extra $33,149 in 20 years. This could drive you insane. And you would have missed the *Star Wars Prequels*.

We'll address some of these concerns soon, but for now the key is to understand the connection between money and freedom, and the long-term impact of a reoccurring expense. Had Hot Sauce and Non-Existent understood how those frequent restaurant and hotel stops were adding up, they might have been able to complete their AT thru-hike.

Technology Adoption Cycle

Technology is one of the prime ways that people upgrade their standard of living; therefore, we must understand how society adopts technology. I'm speaking of technology in the broadest terms, not just computer technology. A toaster, for example, is technology. Technology goes through three phases:

1. **The Gee Whiz Phase:** This is when technology first comes on the scene. We all marvel at it. This happened when the first cars started overtaking horse-drawn carriages. Remember the first time you saw someone using a cell phone? Or the first time someone introduced to you an iPod? Or the Internet? It was cool.

2. **The Ho Hum Phase:** This is when a significant portion of the population has adopted the new technology and it's no longer novel. We are no longer

impressed if someone has a web site. Now when a cell phone rings, you're no longer intrigued or impressed—you're annoyed.

3. **The Must Have Phase:** This is when the technology has permeated so deeply into a society that it's a problem if you have *not* adopted the technology. We've come full circle: at the beginning we were amazed if you had the technology, now we're amazed if you *don't* have the technology! It was surprising if someone had a telephone in 1900, now it's surprising if you don't have a phone! Already it's strange if someone doesn't have an email address or a microwave oven, and soon you'll be a weirdo if you don't have a GPS implant and a fuel cell, hydrogen powered car.

It's important to understand that all technology follows this pattern. As new technologies come on the scene, expect that many will go through the cycle outlined above; those that don't usually flop at the starting gate.

It's also important to realize that once you adopt a technology, it's hard to go back. For instance, a couple of years after you bought your first cell phone you wondered how you ever got through life without it. Similarly, how many farmers would be willing to trade back their tractors for animals? And most of us shudder trying to imagine life without our remote control.

Therefore, before making a purchase, it's important to understand where the product is in the Technology Adoption Cycle. Unless you're exceedingly secure financially, you should always resist technologies that are in the Gee Whiz Phase. That's when the products are priced at a massive premium, and they don't really work that well anyway. The first automatic toasters were expensive and unreliable; so were the first cars, first cell phones, and first DVD players. Therefore, resist upgrading when a technology is still in the Gee Whiz Phase.

However, you should also resist upgrading when technology is in the Ho Hum Phase. Although the cost of upgrading will have dropped dramatically from the Gee Whiz Phase, it's far from being free! Satellite TV is definitely in the Ho Hum Phase, but it's not cheap—it's over $500/year. Those who have put off purchasing a cell phone have socked away hundreds, if not thousands, of dollars of income while their buddies haven't. Hence, don't succumb to the marketing hype of upgrading, even in the Ho Hum Phase.

Finally, the cost equation flips by the time we enter the Must Have Phase. It becomes more expensive *not* to upgrade than to upgrade. For example, if you live in the suburbs or in a rural area, then it is usually more expensive not to have a car than to have one. Not owning a watch can cost you more money in missed appointments. Given that a watch can cost less than $10, it should pay for itself in short order.

For a list of all the ways technology has failed to improve the quality of life, please press three.— Alice Kahn

Spider was a steady and strong hiker from Northern California. Although his gear was probably older than he was, he powered over the Bigelows in Maine and ultimately arrived in Georgia in November. He always had a smile on his face and was quick to laugh.

The Antique Stove

Some AT hikers prefer to hold off on upgrades. Spider, a 56-year-old AT thru-hiker from California, pulled out a rusted, creaky stove and an old lady in the shelter looked at it and said, "What year did they make that stove? That must have been before I was born!"

Despite the ancient gasoline powered stove, Spider was one of the most powerful and determined hikers I met on the AT. He completed it in less time than most kids half his age.

How will I know when it's safe to summit?

The Second Principle reminds us to beware of summit fever. Until now, we've focused on the cost of going to the summit. We've demonstrated that One-Time and Subscription Upgrades can limit our freedom and (as we will see in the next chapter) our ability to fully enjoy life. To effectively follow the Second Principle we need to know when it's safe to go up.

In some ways, it's impossible to know when it's safe to summit. Financial, physical, or emotional disaster can strike at any moment. Christopher Reeve, the famous actor who played Superman, was riding his horse when suddenly he fell off and was paralyzed for life. Major misfortunes can seriously derail us and are hard to predict. Nevertheless, there are two things we do know:

1. **Tough times will come.** All humans have had to overcome some financial, physical, or emotional challenge. Yet so many live their lives thinking that they will get lucky. We must expect downturns and challenges—being unprepared is foolish.

2. **There are ways to prevent most of these tough times.** Although random bad luck will hit all of us, most tough times occur because of our own actions. We can minimize the impact of these misfortunes, or avoid some altogether, thereby preserving our freedom and happiness. The key is to develop a few good financial habits.

Develop good spending and savings habits

Most thru-hikers have a good understanding of their expenses, know how to control them, are good at saving money, and know how to resist upgrading. Successful thru-hikers usually follow four steps to prepare for and complete their journey. Let's look at each step and how we can apply it on and off the AT.

Step 1: Know your expenses

First, you must know your annual expenses. Add up the amount you spend every year on all your major expenses, such as rent/mortgage, telephone, clothes, education, utilities, entertainment, transportation, fitness center, and booze. There are software programs (e.g., Quicken and MS Money) that help you figure out your annual expenses, and for the frugal, there are free financial web sites (e.g., Finance Yahoo! and MSN Money) as well. The super frugal can get by with just a pencil and paper! It doesn't matter what method you use, and you don't need an MBA or a CPA to figure this out. Just get a rough idea. Are you spending $10,000 a year? $30,000 a year? $50K? $100K? More than $200K?

Step 2: Save until it's safe to summit

Armed with that number, you can determine when it's safe to summit. The more cash you have stowed away, the better you will weather downturns. How much cash is enough? In the US, most recessions last under 12 months. *Therefore, saving a year's worth of expenses will provide a sufficient buffer to weather nearly any recession.* Once you have that level of protection, you can confidently adopt upgrades, as long as you maintain that one-year buffer. *You can summit without fear.* As a result, you will have the freedom to do what you love. Best of all, you'll finally get to buy that deluxe barbeque set that your wife has been resisting.

If you live below your means and you control your desire to upgrade, you probably won't notice recessions. Even if you are laid off, you won't have to change your way of life. If you're used to eating out twice a week, driving a Lexus, and schmoozing at the golf club, then you can still do that because you've saved a year's worth of expenses. Although this will chew into your savings, you won't have to tighten your belt (or at least far less than those who were overextended). On the other hand, those who constantly push the envelope of upgrades and live on credit will have to retrench their way of life significantly. The process of cutting back is depressing for anyone. That's why living beyond your means is so risky—you're bound to get disappointed.

Step 3: Resisting upgrades

Most of us don't have a year's worth of expenses saved. We feel pretty good if we have a month! *Getting a year's worth of expenses saved requires resisting every tempting upgrade until your life becomes highly inconvenient without it.* Before my thru-hike I learned to question every purchase. Ask yourself:

- You've gone this far without it, so is it really that important?

- Is there a truly compelling reason you need the upgrade today? Or can it wait a few more weeks, months, or even years?

- Has most of the world adopted the technology? Where is it on the Technology Adoption Cycle? Unless it's reached the Must Have Phase, do you really need it? Do not compare yourself with your peers if they are affluent and/or keep up with the Joneses types. These people tend to upgrade before the majority of the population, and before it's really necessary to upgrade.

The Amish off the AT

Nobody resists upgrading like the Amish. Although the AT doesn't cross through the heart of Amish country, it gets pretty close. Andy, a business school friend of mine, grew up in Lancaster, Pennsylvania. We stayed with Andy and his family for a weekend and learned about the Amish people. The Amish are a prime example of people who have withheld adopting new technology. Many outsiders get the impression that they don't adopt any new technology, but the reality is that they do adopt new technology—after much deliberation among the elders. They want to see the true value of the technology and its long-term impact on their society. Although thru-hikers may dress in quick-drying ripstop nylon clothes and eat high tech energy bars, thru-hikers are similar to the Amish. Neither of us have phones or electricity; moreover, we both hand wash all our clothes and let them air dry. Neither of us read newspapers, watch TV, or drive an SUV.

Incredibly, a thru-hiker's way of life is arguably simpler than the life of the so-called "Simple People." Let's compare the Amish with thru-hikers:

Amish	Thru-hikers
They have several articles of clothing.	We have one outfit that we wear all the time.
They have refrigeration and propane stoves.	We have neither (although we use Esbit tablets and a few stakes or rocks to prop up our pot).
They take horse drawn carriages to get around.	We walk over 20 miles a day.
They have a roof over their heads and four walls.	We have a tarp.
They sleep in a bed with a nice quilt.	We sleep on dried leaves or dirt, but we also have a nice quilt-like sleeping bag.
Everything they own and need to survive is in their house.	Everything we own and need to survive is on our back.
They have plumbing.	We drink from streams and dig holes.

In conclusion, thru-hikers have taken the simple Amish way of life to an extreme and found the pleasure of its simplicity. Some may feel it's austere, but thru-hikers can identify with the Amish. We admire and respect their way of life. Although I'm not suggesting that we all follow the Amish example, we could all learn something from this prudent and conservative society. Don't blindly rush to upgrade. Instead, deliberate on it and consider saving the extra cash to simplify your life.

Step 4: Always calculate nominal costs

Get into the habit of calculating the nominal costs of a Subscription Upgrade before committing to it. Figure out how much the subscription will cost you over a year, or even five to 20 years. When the next salesman tells you, "Hey, it's only $1 a day!" Remind yourself that it's $365 a year, and ask yourself if that extra $365 at the end of the year would be nice to have in the bank. Or you can suggest to the salesman that if it's *only* a $1 a day, then why not just give it away?

Cutting back

Although a few Americans live below their means, the majority does not. Americans have one of the lowest savings rate in the world, less than two percent.[8] Most live on extended credit. The same is true for many of societies in the world. Therefore, for most of us, trying to pull together one year of savings will require substantial changes. Thru-hikers used two ways to build up a financial buffer:

1. **Resist making upgrades until you reach your goal.**
   By avoiding upgrades from now on, you'll slowly build up savings. You'll effectively freeze your standard of living. For example, when everyone is upgrading to a plasma screen, you'll pocket the money you would have spent by hanging on to your current TV.

2. **Pull back.** Downgrading is difficult, and the Second Principle reminds us how to avoid that painful process. However, perhaps you are at a point in your life where you are psychologically ready to deal with a downturn. In fact, you may view it as

a healthy cleansing process. Choosing this method will allow you to build up that one-year buffer far more quickly than the method above.

Which method you choose depends on your current state. If you're the type of person who can't stand downsizing and would rather rack up some debt in order to preserve your way of life, then the first option is probably the only realistic choice. If you can stomach some downsizing, then pull back wherever you can. Finally, there's the *Returning to Base Camp* option (see sidebar), which may appeal to the all-or-nothing crowd.

Returning to Base Camp

Shock therapy sometimes works. Smokers and alcoholics who try to quit frequently go cold turkey overnight. Although it doesn't always work, it has some success. My Chilean grandfather, who smoked all his life, one day at the age of 57 gave up smoking forever. Just like that.

Similarly, those who hike the AT go cold turkey to get back to the basics. Thru-hikers, unlike most of the population, want to *downgrade* in a major way.

As pilgrims, we neatly summarized our lives: eat; walk; sleep. When we returned from the AT, we reexamined our lives. All those "must have" upgrades no longer seemed necessary.

If the thought of cutting back a little makes your stomach turn, then consider a more radical move by cutting back dramatically. I call it *Returning to Base Camp*—getting back to basics and learning to live a Spartan existence.

After living in the woods for several months or even several weeks, you'll be able to return to a far more modest way of life than the one you currently live—and you'll be happier. You'll be happy just to have warm running water and a comfortable bed.

The AT isn't the only way to return to absolute simplicity. Some people may volunteer at a monastery for several months, whether they are religious or not. Some may live with an inner city family. More adventurous people might live in a rural village of a third world country.

Returning to Base Camp is shock treatment, but it can be therapy for the soul.

However, the likeliest option for most people is a combination. In other words, there are certain aspects of your life you may want to preserve. For example, you may really value the $500/year you spend on tennis lessons, but you're willing to trade in your expensive car for a more economical one. Taking this hybrid approach will allow you to cut back while preserving the few things that give you the most pleasure and enjoyment. After all, as I quickly learned on the AT, you can't always pass up Ben and Jerry's ice cream.

The flip side

Sometimes people become so used to practicing the Second Principle that they forget the First Principle! They may have five years of living expenses saved up, and they continue turning down upgrades, even when they desire them. If you have plenty saved up, and spending it makes you happy, then enjoy it! Obviously, there's nothing wrong with turning down an upgrade if you really don't want it. However, make sure that you're being true to your desires. If traveling all around the world is your dream and you have two years of expenses socked away, go ahead and earn some frequent flier miles.

Money doesn't make you happy. I now have $50 million, but I was just as happy when I had $48 million.
— Arnold Schwarzenegger

Frugal millionaires

When most people imagine how millionaires live, we immediately picture Robin Leach parading through their lavish mansions, five car garages, and diamond encrusted pools "worth almost one million dollars!" Yet in the best selling book *The Millionaire Next Door: The Surprising Secrets of America's Wealthy* we learned that millionaires typically live *below their means*.[9]

John Bogle is the founder of the Vanguard Index 500 Fund, one of

America's two largest mutual funds with over $100 billion in assets. How does this high net worth man live? He owns a modest four-bedroom home in suburban Philadelphia. He drives Volvo station wagons, replacing them only when they get to be eight years old. And he wears a $14 watch, albeit for sentimental reasons.

Although I admire Mr. Bogle, there is no need for him to live so modestly if he doesn't want to. I don't know him personally, so it's possible that he has no deep desire to drive a fancy Mercedes or to live in a chateau. And he may splurge on other things that we don't know about. The point is that a few people deprive themselves of spending money on things that give them pleasure, even though they have more than enough money to justify buying it. There's nothing wrong with living *well below* your means, as long as you

---

Build Wealth like a Snowball

Cut back expenses and eventually you start experiencing a virtuous cycle, as money accumulates like a snowball. With a financial buffer you can:

- ✓ Raise your insurance deductibles thereby cutting your insurance expenses.

- ✓ Put 20 percent down on your next house to avoid pricey private mortgage insurance.

- ✓ Pay your credit card balances fully every month and avoid debilitating finance charges.

- ✓ Contribute the maximum to your employer's retirement plan to enjoy the tax break and maybe even a matching contribution.

- ✓ Invest in traditionally high return investments (e.g., stocks and bonds) now that you can stomach the downturns.

The more of these you can do, the richer you'll become. If you do it right, you'll have more freedom than ever.

(Source: Jonathan Clemens, "Getting Going—Dare to Live Dangerously: Why Ditching Some of Your Insurance Can Pay Off," The Wall Street Journal, *July 24, 2003 p. D1)*

truly don't wish for more. Just don't get mad if we all look at you funny for not being a materialistic pig like the rest of us.

Common criticisms

At this point you might have several questions and concerns about this Second Principle. Indeed, it may be hard to accept that one of the keys to squeezing the most out of life is to make sure you don't summit before you're ready. Let's consider the criticisms.

But isn't the purpose of life to enjoy it?

One of the immediate thoughts is, "Hey, in the last chapter we learned that we must follow the Fun Compass, and now you want me to resist buying a new car. What gives?"

I paid too much for it, but it's worth it.
— Samuel Goldyn

Let's face it: most of us don't have the self-discipline of a monk. Even though we may admire people who can live without cable, most of us scream, "I want my MTV!" Indeed, one of the greatest rewards of being alive is experiencing new things in life. That could include watching movies, eating tasty cuisine, going to the ballgame, driving a nice car, sitting on a new couch, traveling to exotic beaches, and climbing Mount Everest. To forgo these pleasures throughout your life is somewhat antithetical to the First Principle. In short, it may seem that to follow the Second Principle you need to go in the polar opposite direction of the Fun Compass.

There are two important ways to answer this criticism. First, the last chapter reminds us how little we need to enjoy life. You can learn to have fun and be happy by adjusting who you compare yourself to. Ultimately, you can learn that you don't need to spend money to follow the Fun Compass. Moreover, the next chapter will demonstrate how important it is to have the freedom to do what you love—otherwise, you will not be maximizing your enjoyment of life. You may have a few extra toys when you die, but your life will have been unfulfilling.

Second, I'm not suggesting that you shouldn't spend money extravagantly. I'm just saying that you shouldn't spend lavishly if you don't have lavish amounts of money! If you make $50,000 a year, spend only $20,000/year, and save $30,000, then there's nothing wrong with splurging on a few $200 dinners, a $5,000 vacation, and a $100/month fitness club. Similarly, if you make $300,000 a year, spend $30,000 a year and have $200,000 in liquid assets, then go ahead and buy a Ferrari, Rolex, and Gucci suit.

The Second Principle is neither anti-consumption nor anti-opulence. Although it's important to learn how little it takes to enjoy life, spending a few bucks can certainly help bring a smile to a face. Moreover, indulging can help recharge your batteries or give you inspiration. However, most Americans don't need much encouragement to spend money frivolously; we're pretty good at that. Instead, we need reminders to put more coins in the piggy bank.

But the downturns aren't so bad!

A common response to the Second Principle is that recessions and layoffs may be hard, but it's not the end of the world. They are painful, but not intolerable. Although this may be true for some people, downsizing is generally far more painful than maintaining the status quo. Hence, it's better to postpone an upgrade for a few months or even a couple of years, because you'll probably be able to upgrade later, and when you do, your upgrade will be cheaper and more up to date than ever since technology is always improving. Or, after waiting a few months, you may realize that you don't need to upgrade after all, because buying a boat isn't as interesting as you once thought.

Still, those who insist that the downturns aren't so bad should consider that when you upgrade at each opportunity, you are limiting your freedom to do what you love. If you want to squeeze the most out of life, you have to have a job you love. That's what the next chapter is all about. Therefore, even if downturns are not

Thru-Hiking the AT on $20

Many people ask how much it costs to thru-hike the AT. Answer: from $20 to $10,000.

It's amazing that we're all hiking the same trail, and yet some would eat out at restaurants at every chance they got, stay at nice hotels along the way, and rent cars to get away.

On the other extreme was a man named Cheapo who went from Georgia to New York on $20. He got nearly all his gear and food from "hiker boxes," which are boxes where hikers donate items they no longer need. When you go northbound on the AT, there are many hikers who discard perfectly good food and gear along the way. Having limited cash put another level of adventure into Cheapo's journey. He survived by living off the food and gear left behind in these hiker boxes.

The lesson is that there are always ways of cutting back. It just takes a little creativity while you systematically analyze all your expenditures.

For those who are still curious, the average thru-hiker spends less than $4,000 for the six-month journey, or $2 per mile. That includes everything. Not a bad deal for a six-month "vacation."

---

too bad, pushing the upgrade envelope cramps your freedom and, ultimately, diminishes your ability to get the most out of life.

But my new car is an investment!

Some consumers justify buying a Rolex watch "because it holds its value" or a posh Mercedes "because it's a good investment that will become an antique."

Give me a break.

Although these arguments are not totally crazy, let's not kid ourselves. Nearly every material item *depreciates* in value. The few that usually don't are precious metals and real estate. Otherwise, only the most rare and exotic material items appreciate.

Therefore, don't delude yourself when you buy a material good. Even if you think it might appreciate, just assume it won't. If it miraculously does go up, then consider it a bonus.

But you're a Luddite!

Some people may accuse me of being a Luddite (someone who hates technology). Although I understand the frustration that anti-technologists feel, I completely disagree with them. On the contrary, I love technology. I'm still hoping that Intel will develop a math co-processor and memory enhancement implant for my brain.

However, adopting technological advancements costs money, especially the earlier you adopt them. Of course at some point it will cost more money to *not* adopt a technology, especially if you're in the Must Have Phase of the Technology Adoption Cycle. For instance, not having a telephone today can cost you a lot in wasted time alone (e.g., having to walk to a store to find out something you could have learned over the phone). There's nothing wrong with upgrading, but you'll get more out of life if you put it off until you can really afford it. The Second Principle doesn't say that upgrading is inherently bad, it just reminds us to think hard before we upgrade.

But not all upgrades are technology upgrades!

True, that's why I mentioned that I'm using the term "technology" in the broadest sense. Some upgrade their wardrobes, carpets, and flower vases. The wisdom of resisting these upgrades holds true, even though they are not what we might consider technology.

But isn't a 12 month reserve a bit extreme?

It is tempting to upgrade as soon as you can. Although some financial advisors recommend a six month buffer, most recessions last longer and so you should have more stashed away. If you don't mind downsizing rapidly, then six months of savings is probably enough. Although some may feel comfortable summiting with less than three months of reserves, I don't recommend it.

But isn't this Principle paralyzing?

Some might believe that this Principle paralyzes them. For example, an aspiring artist may have the following thought process:

1. I love to paint.

2. However, every time I spend money, I decrease my freedom.

3. Painting costs money.

4. Therefore, in order to be free, I won't paint.

Clearly, this twisted logic will paralyze you forever. Whoever follows this logic mistakenly believes that freedom is the final goal. Freedom is important, but it is not the ultimate goal. The ultimate end is happiness, and freedom is simply a means to that end. A better logic would be:

1. I love to paint.

2. I will decrease my expenditures so I can increase my freedom.

3. With increased freedom, I can do what I love.

4. Doing what I love makes me happy.

But what if I live in the 'hood?

Fortunately, only 12 percent of the US population lives in poverty, so most of us don't live in the slums. Of course, some feel like we live in the slums compared to our wealthy peers. So if you need a reality check of the definition of a slum, go to a nearby inner city and drive around. If you really do live in a slum, then your reality check can be a trip to a nearby third world country like El Salvador. If you can't afford that, watch a documentary on the situation in Africa. Your "slum" will start looking pretty nice in comparison.

Nevertheless, living in poverty (or even feeling like you're living in poverty) is no fun. For those who live quite humbly, you might conclude that there is nowhere to cut back. The first step is to realize that there are probably still areas to cut back. I lived four months in Caracas, Venezuela, and in the poverty stricken shantytowns that I visited I saw families who would have a big screen TV with a satellite dish. Other times I'd see poor people wasting money on alcoholic beverages when they could drink water instead. Others spend a lot of money upgrading their cars with fancy gadgets, while others spend a large amount of cash on lottery tickets. All these little costs add up and make a big difference. Forgoing these luxuries can be the ticket to quickly getting out of a financial rut and onto the ridge.

Summary

In 1845 Henry David Thoreau moved to the remote location of Walden Pond, Massachusetts to conduct an experiment similar to the experiment that thru-hikers do every spring: he wanted to know how simply and humbly he could live and still be happy. Thoreau described how most people in his day thought that the more they acquire, the happier they would be. (Sound familiar?) He noted the irony that those very possessions ended up enslaving them. Having learned how happy he could be with nearly nothing, he returned to society with renewed vigor:

> *I went to the woods because I wished to live deliberately, to front only the essential facts of life, and see if I could learn what it had to teach, and not, when I come to die, discover that I had not lived... I left the woods for as good a reason as I went there. Perhaps it seemed to me that I had several more lives to live, and could not spare any more time for that one. — Henry David Thoreau*

Similarly, thru-hikers come away with lessons and want to return to society so they can apply them. The AT, through the story of Hot Sauce and Non-Existent, had taught me a valuable lesson. This couple was unable to complete their goal because they did not have a thorough understanding of the Second Principle. They went for the summit before they had a firm financial foundation.

We were on the Franconia Ridge Trail in New Hampshire's Presidential Range, my favorite section of the AT. We held up two fingers because we couldn't believe it took only two days to hike from the most distant mountains in the background. Only 1,800 miles to go.

If Chapter One was symbolic of the arduous journey through Maine, then Chapter Two is symbolic of the treacherous terrain in New Hampshire. AT hikers agree that Maine and New Hampshire are the two most challenging states along the AT. Like New Hampshire, this chapter might be a bit tough to deal with for some people. Let's sum up the key takeaways of this chapter:

- To fully enjoy life you need the freedom to do what makes you happy.

- Every dollar you spend diminishes your freedom; every dollar you invest increases your freedom.

- Beware of summit fever, so you're not exposed when a financial storm comes.

- When you raise your standard of living, you pass a point of no return, so do it judiciously.

- Evaluate if a purchase is a One-Time Upgrade or a Subscription Upgrade—and calculate the nominal cost of a Subscription Upgrade before buying into it (and recognize that the *real* cost is higher).

Lisa is hard to see, but if you strain your eyes you'll find her in the lower right hand corner. She's descending the spectacular ridge walk in New Hampshire. Except for the thunderstorm on our way up, we had clear weather throughout the Presidential Range.

- Identify where a product is in the Technology Adoption Cycle and try to avoid adopting until it reaches the Must Have Phase.

- Know your expenses and don't summit before you've built at least six months of reserves.

- Build a reserve by resisting upgrades and by downsizing wherever you can.

- If you're struggling to save, consider the shock therapy of Returning to Base Camp.

- Don't let the Second Principle make you forget the First Principle—don't be afraid to summit!

It's possible that you had opposite reactions to Chapter One and Two; you liked one and disliked the other. In a way, they are directed at two different types of people. The First Chapter is meant for the person who is overdoing the Second Principle; in other words, you are living so frugally and sacrificing so much that you are missing out on the pleasures of being alive. The Second Chapter, on the other hand, is directed at the person who is overdoing the First Principle; you are always spending more money than you have and living for the moment, but don't realize that doing so closes many options for the future. As we'll see in the next chapter, this can diminish your ability to squeeze the most out of life. Therefore, the person who takes pride in making lots of sacrifices might look down on people who follow their Fun Compass. Meanwhile, the person who takes pride in living for the moment might rebel against a Principle that tells him to hold back. *The truth is that following both Principles are necessary to get the most out of life. The trick is to strike a balance between them.* Don't go overboard on either one. The importance of the Second Principle may not be clear, but it will be in the next chapter.

 A monk becomes his own lamp and refuge by continually looking on his body, feelings, perceptions, moods, and ideas in such a manner that he conquers the cravings and depressions of ordinary men and is always strenuous, self-possessed, and collected in mind.
Whoever among my monks does this, either now or when I am dead, if he is anxious to learn, will reach the summit.
— The Buddha's last instructions while he was dying, from The Tripitaka

Far from Georgia, I clearly demonstrated that I still wasn't ready to summit Springer Mountain, the final mountain in my AT odyssey. Because I was simultaneously walking and reading my trail guide I didn't notice a thick protruding branch in the middle of the trail. I smashed my head against it so hard that I fell on my butt and cut a good chunk off my forehead. I didn't have summit fever, but my head was certainly throbbing.

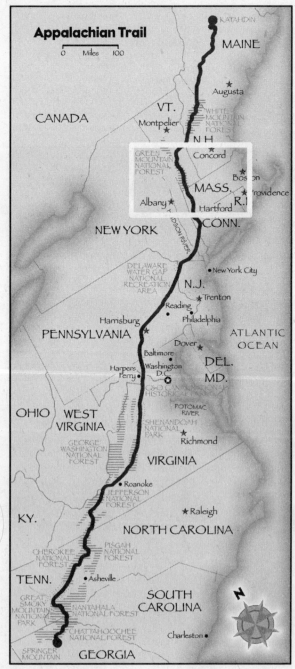

© *Appalachian Trail Conservancy, reprinted with permission*

Chapter 3:
Hike With Passion

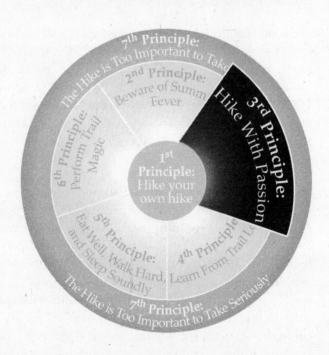

I was hitchhiking with a short muscular man whose arms were covered with tattoos. Soon after getting into his decrepit car, he suddenly turned to me and said, "I probably shouldn't be telling you this, but I have a passion for collecting meat cleavers."

Oh great.

I gulped and was about to say, "Um, right about here is just great, sir. Thanks, I'll walk the rest of the five miles."

But instead I held my tongue and nodded, waiting to see what would happen next.

Thru-hikers are hitchhiking connoisseurs. It's the only effective way to get into town when you're in the middle of nowhere. For example, the trail may cross a road that leads to the nearest town, but there are no taxis or buses in these remote areas. If you're out of food and the town is a few miles away, you must hitchhike.

Some people are amazed that thru-hikers will hitchhike even if the town is just one mile away. They say, "You're walking over 2,168 miles! What's another mile?" It's a lot. The reverse of that logic is: I'm walking 2,168 miles, and I don't want to walk one more stinking mile than I need to complete the trail! Most thru-hikers care about the miles they hike on the trail, not off the trail. Every mile that they hike off the trail is a mile they could have hiked on the trail.

Hiking the whole AT is not a walk in the park. For example, the total elevation gain for a thru-hiker is 471,151 feet. To put that in perspective: you would have to climb up Mount Everest 16 times *from sea level* to equal the elevation gain. A 5'6" person must take five million steps to complete the trail. Short people (around five feet) get to take an extra 500,000 steps, whereas tall ones (six feet) sneak by with taking 4,500,000 steps. Shaquille O'Neal could probably do it in about three steps. However, all these steps don't include trips into towns or taking side trails to view waterfalls. Now you're starting to think like a thru-hiker—that measly mile into town looks pretty big now.

Of course, the reason a mile doesn't seem like much is that most of us are accustomed to driving everywhere. The average American barely walks a mile a week! On the other hand, when I heard that a town was "only" one mile away, I would think:

- If it's flat, it'll take me 20 minutes to walk there—that's 40 minutes round trip.

- If the road into town is steep, then it will take me at least an hour, and perhaps more.

- What if it's raining or extremely hot and humid? That may make that extra mile even more arduous.

- If I'm hiking 20 miles today, then that two mile round trip represents 10 percent of my effort today—that's significant.

All of a sudden that seemingly harmless mile starts looking like quite a burden. As a result, thru-hikers would rather stick their thumbs out for 15 minutes, rest their tired legs, eat a snack, and wait hopefully for someone to take them into town. However, when my Hells Angels look-a-like driver started talking about his passion for collecting meat cleavers, I almost wished that I had walked those five miles.

Nevertheless, I gave him the benefit of the doubt because I've learned that tough-looking people are frequently good at heart. He turned out to be one of the nicest persons on the trail, and he drove out of his way to help me run errands, do a little sightseeing, and get back on the trail safely.

 Beware what you set your heart upon. For it surely shall be yours. — Ralph Waldo Emerson

This burly man's passion for meat cleavers made me think after I got back on the trail. No, I wasn't worried that he was on my tail with his prized meat cleaver clenched at his side.

His passion for meat cleavers made me start paying attention to how I hike. I enjoy hiking a trail passionately. That doesn't necessarily mean that I am walking fast or aggressively. It means that I try to absorb the smells of the pine needles, the sounds of the creeks, and the textures in the ground beneath my feet. This constant fascination with nature kept me entertained, whereas others might be bored and unhappy. Like the meat cleaver collector, I had discovered a passion of mine and was pursuing it vigorously. This helped me realize the Third Principle during my long pilgrimage.

The Third Principle for getting the most out of life is that you must *hike with passion*. If you can't hike a trail with passion, find another trail. In other words, don't waste your time pursuing dull endeavors; instead, pursue your passion. This is the third key ingredient to squeezing the most out of life. *After all, how can you claim that you got the most out of life if you did not spend most of it doing a job you loved?*

Nevertheless, the AT taught me that while many people want to pursue their passion, they simply don't know what their passion is. Indeed, many who hike the AT hope that the answer will come to them during the expedition. The AT adventure not only helps you discover your passion, it also instructs you on how you can pursue it immediately. It also helps you confront the worries and fears you may have about following it. First, let's think about why you should hike with passion.

Conscious hours are what really matter

Most people go about their lives working so that they can pay their bills and save a little bit of money. For most people a job is just a means to an end. As one song put it, "Everybody's working for the weekend."

Should we just work in any old job? Is a job just a job? After all, it's only 40 hours a week, right? Let's analyze this.

There are 168 hours in a week. Therefore, 40 hours is about a quarter of your time. You might be willing to sacrifice 25 percent of your life so that you can do other things you enjoy the other 75 percent of the time. Although it's not a great trade off, most people can live with that.

However, let's delve further. Most people are unconscious a third of their lives (we sleep about eight hours a day on average). It's funny to think that the average person spends 25 years of his life snoring!

Let's not count these sleeping hours as part of your life. While sleep is essential, it is not really quality time; after all, you're out cold! (Don't tell this to the shrinks whose job is interpreting dreams.) In a sense, you might as well be dead while you're sleeping. It's lost time. Therefore, if we discount those hours, the amount of *conscious* time that we have available every week is only 112 hours. Seen in that light, your 40-hour a week job is grabbing 35 percent of your conscious time—more than a third of your life!

Nobody can be successful unless he loves his work.
— David Sarnoff

But it gets worse. Let's start factoring in your commute time. The average American has a 30-minute one-way commute; that's one hour a day commuting back and forth, five hours a week. By the way, for many people those are usually five maddening hours! Now work is taking 40 percent of your conscious time.

What about the time it takes to get ready for work? Then there's also the time you spend thinking about work while you're not at work. Many of us claim that once we leave work, we stop thinking about it, but in reality sometimes it's hard not to think about your job when you're home. This is especially true if your job is as enjoyable as cleaning out septic tanks.

You might spend time discussing your frustrations with your spouse and/or friends. Let's tack on another five hours, making work a total of 50 hours per week. With only 112 conscious hours, that means you spend 45 percent of your conscious hours (*includ-*

ing weekends) devoted to work—that's almost half your life!

Others think about their jobs all time, whether they want to or not! They may be doctors on call, or Wall Street workers who think about the international markets when the domestic markets are closed, or radiation cleanup workers who wonder why they glow in the dark.

Furthermore, many professionals work 60-hour weeks. Similarly, some people have to work two or three jobs just to

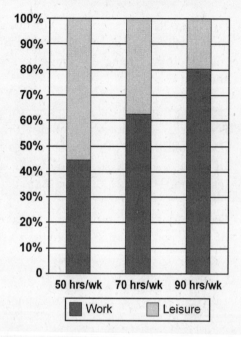

Work vs. Leisure Time Using Conscious Hours (includes weekends!)

make ends meet. They may work 80 hours a week! For these individuals, add another 20-40 hours of time to the base 50-hour work life—that's 70 to 90 hours of your 112 hours of conscious time. In summary, if you're a workaholic, you could be devoting up to 80 percent of your entire life to your job! That fact alone may compel you to call in sick.

This explains why when Friday night finally rolls around most couples spend it plopped in front of the TV staring slack jawed at *Buffy the Vampire Slayer*.

Make your passion your job

Suddenly it should become clear that a job should not be just about getting a paycheck. With so much of your precious life devoted to your job, it would be a total waste to be doing something you dis-

People who say they lack time to do what they want by age

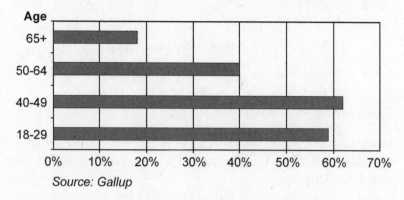

Source: Gallup

like. Imagine thinking on your deathbed that you spent 45 to 80 percent of your life doing something you didn't really care about. Talk about having a bad day.

You may have a high-paying job, a wonderful family, caring friends, and extravagant vacations, but if your job is unfulfilling, could you say you got the most out of life? Would you consider your life a success if you wasted over half of it doing something you cared little about?

Many people put off doing what they love for weekends or when they retire. One big problem with that thinking is that we have no idea when we're going to kick the bucket. Most people live their life believing they will live the average lifespan of 80 years, but are rudely surprised when their doctor tells them at 33 years old that they have cancer and have 12 months to live. Sadly, this is exactly what happened to Lisa's mother. Lisa was only six years old when her mother died of Leukemia. Unless you believe in reincarnation, you have only one shot to get this life right. Get it right today, right now.

 Choose a job you love, and you will never have to work a day in your life. — Confucius

There are three basic steps to hiking with passion:

1. Discovering your passion.

2. Finding a way to make it happen.

3. Summoning the will to make it happen.

Discovering your passion

Many people tell me, "But how can I pursue my passion when I'm not sure what it is?" I pondered that question as I walked through Vermont. Although many Nobos dread Vermont, Sobos welcome it. For Nobos it represents the beginning of the mountains of New England. After cruising through the relatively flat and easy Mid-Atlantic States, Nobos have to start working again in Vermont. However, Vermont is really just a warm up to the two toughies: New Hampshire and Maine. The Appalachian Trail Conservancy (the official governing body of the AT) rates every state south of New Hampshire a six or less in difficulty on a one to ten scale. New Hampshire and Maine both have sections that are rated from an eight to a ten. A score of ten means: "Use of hands required,

Maximum AT Trail Difficulty by State

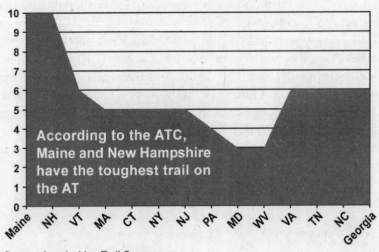

According to the ATC, Maine and New Hampshire have the toughest trail on the AT

Source: Appalachian Trail Conservancy

footing precarious—not recommended for those with fear of heights and not in good physical condition." In other words, you have to grab the roots of trees to pull yourself up—it's rock climbing without the rope.

That's why a popular AT guidebook says that there ought to be a sign near Hanover, New Hampshire that says: "Congratulations Northbounders! You've completed 80 percent of the miles! But unfortunately you've only done 50 percent of the work." This is yet another reason why we hiked southbound: we wanted to arrive in Hanover and say to ourselves, "Whew! We may have only done 20 percent of the miles, but we've done 50 percent of the work!" (See the Appendix 1—"Why Southbound?") We knew that when we got through New Hampshire and Maine, we could do the rest of the trail. Therefore, by the time we entered Vermont, I began to really relax and I had time to contemplate how one can discover one's passion.

Five questions

After backpacking about 240 miles through the green mountains of Vermont and the hot fields of Massachusetts, I came up with five questions you can ask yourself to help figure out what is your passion.

#1: The "Billion Dollar" Question

One of the best ways to determine your passion is to find out what you would do if you had tons of money.

> Write down what you would do with the majority of your waking hours if you had a billion dollars in the bank.

Obviously, with a billion dollars you wouldn't have to work, although some lunatics might. Don't worry about how you will spend the money. Yes, I'm sure that you'd donate 99 percent of your wealth to the poor and needy. Great. That's nice, but the goal here is to find out what you would do with most of your *time*. Clearly, there are many things you might do with your hours, but what would consume the *bulk* of your time? Would you travel? Teach? Write books? Help the sick? Build homes? Trade stocks? Collect meat cleavers?

Your answer is extremely telling. Look at what you would be doing; most likely, that is your passion! It's hard to believe that it's that easy to uncover your passion, but the Billion Dollar Question is extremely effective at revealing your hidden passion. Some people feel that their passion must be something that is deeply locked away in their subconscious and nothing short of hypnosis will reveal what it is.

It's not that complicated. In fact, once you realize what your passion is, you may not be surprised. This is normal. After all, you have probably been dimly aware of your passion for some time. It's just that we all have a tendency to deny our passions and not chase our dreams for a variety of reasons, and usually it's related to economics. The Billion Dollar Question removes that barrier and lets us think freely. Indeed, most people believe that they can't afford to chase after their passions because they think it's too hard to make money chasing their passion. After all, we have bills to pay like the mortgage, credit cards, car payments, children's education, groceries, and the NBA Sports Package on the satellite network.

These expenses are so overwhelming that it gives us no time to contemplate what life is all about. It reminds me of a funny exchange in Voltaire's hilarious 1759 publication, *Candide:*

*"Do you believe that the Pope is the Antichrist, my friend?" said the minister.
"I have never heard anyone say so," replied Candide; "but whether he is or he isn't, I want some food."* — Voltaire

Candide can't entertain philosophical questions because he's hungry. Similarly, we can't contemplate fundamental questions on life because we're too busy just trying to make money to put food on the table.

That's why the Second Principle is so important. *It's hard to hike with passion until you learn to beware of summit fever.* It's important not to raise your standard of living to a level that doesn't let you pursue your passion. Otherwise, you'll be so besieged with your day-to-day obligations that you won't have a chance to do what you really love doing. As we discussed in Chapter Two, you may need to make a few sacrifices to bring your standard of living in line with your earnings to give you the freedom to do what you love.

#2: The "What Catches Your Eye?" Question

If the Billion Dollar Question doesn't help you figure out what your passion is, then consider another exercise, called the "What Catches Your Eye?" Question. This exercise may help narrow down the list if you have many passions, or may help bring out the one passion that is deeply hidden in your mind.

> When you flip through magazines or newspapers, what catches your eye? What are the words or the themes that make your eye stop and want to read more about that subject? Write down all the words and subjects that come to mind.

The possibilities are limitless, but some examples are: movies; basketball; stocks & bonds; gardening; interior design; philanthropy; opera; sports cars; antiques; anthropology; pottery; tango; diabetes; Africa; hot springs; skunk wrestling.

Of course, you may have many interests, so just write down your top five, although it's best if you can narrow it down to your favorite one or two. If you're struggling for ideas consider looking at what pages you bookmarked on the Internet, or go to your bookshelf and pull out your favorite books to see if you can detect a pattern.

For example, in the 1990s my eye would naturally get attracted to the words "robotics" or "robots" or "artificial intelligence." (I know, I'm a geek.) I realized that the subject naturally fascinated me. Therefore, in 1995 I co-founded a robotic vision system company in Silicon Valley to pursue this passion of mine.

 Only passions, great passions, can elevate the soul to great things. — Denis Diderot, Pensées Philosophique, 1746

If you have several subjects that interest you, pick your favorite one. This is an area that you enjoy learning about, and may even be an expert in, and yet you're currently doing it for free! Imagine if someone were to pay you to research or be an expert in this subject! That's the beauty of hiking with passion! Above all, don't limit yourself to subjects that you think could pay money. Even if you can't imagine making money, don't worry about that now—we'll deal with that later. For now, just think without restraint and write down topics that grab your attention.

Perhaps you still can't focus on anything in particular because (a) you haven't found any one subject that stands out, (b) you've found many and can't decide, or (c) your neighbors are screeching their finger nails across their blackboard again.

If you have many interests, compare the answer of the What Catches Your Eye? Question with the Billion Dollar Question. Is there some common ground? Is something overlapping in both questions? If you're still stuck, then try the next question.

#3: The "Leisure Time" Question

Some people might not have gotten too many ideas from the last question because they don't read much! Then again, if you're *reading* this book, you're probably not part of the "My TV Is My Sole Source of Information" crowd. Brainstorm on this:

Analyze what you do with your free time. Write down everything you enjoy doing with your leisure time.

It rarely hurts to brainstorm some more, so use this question to increase your list of passions. This question helps identify what you enjoy doing. For example, some people enjoy remodeling; others see it as a chore. Some enjoy stargazing; others would rather be in a nightclub. Some people enjoy long backpacking trips; others think we're nuts.

If you do spend quite a bit of your leisure time watching TV, then analyze what you look at. Do you notice a pattern? Are you watching a lot of sitcoms? If so, write down that you might consider a career in comedy. Don't worry, that doesn't necessarily mean getting up on stage and cracking jokes. Somebody is writing all the scripts for those sitcoms. Maybe that could be you? Is there a local theatre company that could use you? What about trying to become the next Dave Barry? If you want to be a real comedian consider a career in politics.

Do you spend most of your time watching the news on TV? If so, what stories attract you? Write down that a career in media might interest you. Do you enjoy watching the political debates on TV? There are plenty of think tanks out there who need hard workers. Do you enjoy the local news? Consider becoming an activist for a cause that you're passionate about. Do you love following sports? The sporting industry is a multi-billion dollar industry with plenty of avenues to get involved.

It's fascinating to see what people do with their leisure time. It's those few hours where you're doing something because you enjoy it. Nobody is urging you to do it. You're doing it because it's fun. If you can transform that passion into a job or a career, then you're optimizing your life.

#4: The "You'll Succeed No Matter What" Question

Here's another effective exercise to uncover your hidden passion. Let's assume you drink a potion that gives you the power to succeed in absolutely anything. No matter what you decide to do, you're guaranteed to succeed. For example, let's say your dream is to become a famous pop star, but you can't sing. Thanks to this potion, you'll become famous anyway despite your voice, just like Jessica Simpson. If you can't act, you'll somehow become a superstar despite having zero talent, just like Keanu Reeves. And if being a writer is your dream even though you can barely write your name, then after drinking this potion you'll soon be writing self-help books based on the Appalachian Trail. (And yours will actually be good.)

If you were guaranteed that you would become successful in whatever you pursued, what would you do?

Would you become a poet? A stockbroker? A fashion designer? A media tycoon? A sports star? A great mother?

Nothing great in the world has been accomplished without passion. — Hegel, Philosophy of History, 1832

We frequently don't do what we love because we lack confidence. We fear the unknown. We tell ourselves, "I'm not good enough," or "I've just had a lot of bad luck." But now with the genie out of the bottle, you can have as much luck, skill, and talent you need to succeed. Analyze your answers and see how they compare to your answers in the previous questions. Are you starting to see a common thread? If not, try the last question.

#5: The "Who Would You Switch Places With?" Question

This question is somewhat tricky because you have to forget about the money issue.

If you could switch places with anyone, who would it be?

Although you might pick someone famous, it's perfectly acceptable to pick someone you know personally, like Bob at the corner store.

Two rules: first, you can't pick someone who is dead; second, don't take into account how much money the person makes—instead, look at the daily responsibilities of the job. The idea is to find the person you would like to switch places with today. Who do you look at and think, "Man, I would love to have her job!" In other words, whose job would you take and not even consider it a "job"? Be sure to think about everything that comes with the job too, not just the glamorous side.

For instance, you may fantasize about switching jobs with Julia Roberts so that you could live the lavish life, but would you be willing to put up with the stresses of fame and the process of making and promoting a movie if you didn't get paid $20 million per film? Would you do her job if you were only making $25,000 a year? Pick the person's job, not the person's pay. Look at what they do day-to-day, and figure out if you would enjoy doing that—even at a modest pay.

Once again the possibilities are unlimited. You might want to switch places with Larry King, Donna Karan, your Senator, the coach of the Nebraska Cornhuskers, the CEO of Ford, the local librarian, the editor of *Car and Driver*, the local building contractor, or Britney Spears.

> *I get to go to lots of overseas places, like Canada.*
> *— Britney Spears, when asked what she enjoyed about touring.*

Although I've named many famous people, you should consider people in your community. After you imagine their day-to-day life, the good and the bad, ask yourself if you would do their job even if it paid you 20 to 50 percent less than what you make now. When I worked at Microsoft, some employees wondered why billionaires like Bill Gates keep working. The answer is simple: they're pursuing their passion. They don't view their job as "work." These working billionaires would be doing their jobs even if they were paid a pittance. In fact, Bill Gates basically did just that when he started Microsoft. That's what hiking with passion is about.

Now that you've picked someone you'd like to switch places with, start scrutinizing her life. Log on to the Internet to learn as much as possible about her daily life, or if the person is local and not super famous, ask if you can have an informational interview. Find out how her life really is, not just the exterior image. Try to confirm that her job and life are what you imagine them to be. What are the downsides? Is the person away from her family all the time? Does the person work on weekends? Is the person in fact on America's Most Wanted List? If after all your investigations you still admire the person's way of life and wish you could follow it, then start learning how the person got where he or she is today (we'll discuss this more in Chapter Four).

For example, while I was walking through Massachusetts I thought I had discovered my dream job: Research and Product Development Executive at Ben and Jerry's. Why? You get paid to eat a lot of ice cream.

So later I investigated and discovered that it's not that glamorous. Arnold Carbone (who holds that position) said that when experimenting with coffee flavors he might create 15 batches per day. By the end of the day, his head feels like it's going to explode. Moreover, some ice cream concepts are just stupid. Somebody in B&J's research department had the bright idea of creating chocolate-covered-potato-chips-and-sour-cream-and-onion-flavored ice cream.[10] Yuck. That would even gross out a hungry thru-hiker.

So that's why today I'm a writer and not the Research and Product Development Executive at Ben and Jerry's.

Romantics—Read This

One of the challenges of identifying a suitable passion to pursue is figuring out if you'll get bored with it.

We face the danger of romanticizing an interest: "I love knitting, wouldn't it be great to do that all day…"

You may quickly discover that your passion is simply a hobby. Therefore, it's important to immerse yourself as much as possible in your potential passion to verify that you won't get sick of it in short order.

Discovering Your Passion on the AT

If you ask the average thru-hiker why they chose to quit their job, move out of their house, and leave their loved ones behind, many will tell you that they are on a mission to find out what they want to do next in life. In short, they want to discover their passion.

Although it is possible to conduct this deep thinking at home, there are obstacles to overcome such as the telephone, email, bills, friends and family, groceries, laundry, endless chores, and your landlord.

You escape these distractions on the AT. But the AT doesn't have a monopoly on peace of mind. There are other ways of finding solitude that don't involve slogging through the wilderness.

If you're having trouble getting away from it all, then consider a multi-week or multi-month trip to somewhere free of communications and distractions. It can be cheap and close—the key is isolation. That way you will have no excuse for not focusing on what you want to do next and how you would like to do it.

What if you can't seem to uncover your passion?

After going through these five questions, you may not come out with a satisfactory answer. You may go through the exercises and not find any compelling activity that you would do. Analyze why you cannot find anything that stands out. Are you sure you're letting your mind think freely? Or are you hampering your thoughts by thinking that you couldn't pursue your passion because it's not lucrative, or it'll make your spouse upset, or it's too risky? Make sure that you completely rid yourself of any insecurity during these exercises or else you won't get an honest answer.

What if you don't have a passion?

Take solace, many people are not born with a burning passion. Most humans have varied interests, but nothing that sticks out more than the others. This may explain why the average person makes at least three major career changes in his or her life.

Moreover, passions don't necessarily last forever. Beethoven was passionate about music throughout his life, but most of us mortals are lucky if our passion lasts for more than five years. You might have a passion today, but in six months or six years, you might have a new passion. And sometimes you might not feel a tug in any particular direction. This is natural and normal. Do not get anxious or desperate. Do not try to convince yourself that you are passionate about something you are not.

If you're in a lull and you're not sure what to do next, remember the First Principle: hike your own hike. Therefore, if you're struggling to follow the Third Principle, don't forget to continue to follow your Fun Compass as much as possible. That means minimizing your work hours, spending more time with your family and friends, and experimenting with new activities.

 We're lost, but we're making good time. — Yogi Berra

The process of elimination

You may not know what your passion is, but that doesn't mean you should continue doing what you're doing if it makes you miserable. Over 70 percent of thru-hikers go solo and so they have plenty of time to think. One thru-hiker told me that when he couldn't identify his passion he started writing down everything that he *didn't* like to do.

Therefore, write down the previous jobs that you have done that you did not enjoy. The process of elimination is a long way to get to an answer, but it still can be effective. Keep the list up to date. Ask people about their jobs and their passions. If you can't imagine enjoying a particular job, then add it to the blacklist.

 If it doesn't absorb you, if you don't love it, don't do it. — *D.H. Lawrence*

If you're not sure if you would like a certain job or activity, then try it! Don't quit your job and plunge headlong into it; instead, take small steps. For example, let's say you've been a lawyer for two years and you hate your job, yet you don't know what you want to do next because you don't know your passion. However, you know that you don't enjoy the restaurant business (because you were once a waiter), and you know you wouldn't enjoy working in the media business (because your best friend works in it and has turned you off of it). But you're intrigued with the investment industry because you've talked with some friends of yours and it sounds interesting. But you're not sure it's your passion.

Solution: join an investment club. You keep your job as a lawyer, but during nights and weekends you get together with an investment club and see what it's like to talk about stocks and bonds all day long. Perhaps you'll get excited and love it, or perhaps you'll lose your life's savings. But at least you'll have a better feel of the intricacies of the profession.

The same can be done with many activities that you think might be your passion, but you're not 100 percent sure. Dig deeper into them by talking with people in the industry and, if it still looks promising, start testing it yourself. If you love being around horses, volunteer at an equestrian ranch. You may adore feeding the horses and cleaning out the barn; on the other hand, it might get old pretty quick.

In conclusion, while you may not have a passion today, at the very least, don't do anything you don't enjoy! Keep experimenting every few months until something sticks.

The happiness of a man in this life does not consist in the absence but in the mastery of his passions.
— *Alfred Lord Tennyson (1809-1892)*

What if you have more than one passion?

It is natural to have multiple interests, and not feel like one pulls you more than any of the others. For example, you may be passionate about gardening, water-skiing, and studying 16th century France. Consider yourself lucky. Most people struggle to find one passion, and you've got several. What should you do? You have two options.

Combining passions

Try to combine as many of those interests into one job. In the above example, you could pursue a Ph.D. in French history and write your dissertation on the agricultural techniques of the Renaissance. This doesn't involve your passion for water-skiing, but you can do that on weekends.

Picking one

You could just focus on one passion. If no one passion stands out above the others, then pick the one that has the best chance to be lucrative. Let's say you're passionate about art, but you also love protecting people's rights. It's hard to make money as a painter, but defense attorneys don't do too badly. If you truly have no preference, then pick the one that pays better, and keep the other passion as a hobby.

What if your passion is kind of weird?

There's nothing wrong with pursuing your passion, even if it is a little odd. Some people might consider you eccentric, but take it as a compliment. Dr. David Weeks, author of *Eccentrics: The Scientific Investigation*, interviewed 1,100 eccentrics and admired their sense of humor, creative imagination, and strong will. Eccentrics are so curious that they are oblivious to the frustrations and stresses of daily life that most people perceive. Dr. Weeks found that not only do eccentrics live five to ten years longer than the norm, they are also, on average, healthier, happier, and more intelligent than the rest of the population.

Fireworks

George Plimpton wisely said, "I do feel that happiness is associated with being passionate about something." And his passion was fireworks.

Years ago he went to China to visit a fireworks factory and was envious of the person who had the job of naming each firework. Plimpton concluded that the simple pleasure of such a job would make his final years fulfilling.

His uncommon passion didn't embarrass him or discourage him from pursuing it. In his last few years he wrote a colorful book about his passion and became New York City's Honorary Commissioner on Fireworks.

"They don't try to keep up with the Joneses, they don't worry about conforming and they usually have a firm belief that they are right and the rest of the world is wrong," Weeks says.

Eccentricity, he stresses, is not mental illness. Eccentrics are aware of their uniqueness from an early age and are happily obsessed with their hobbies. They are often single, the oldest or only child, and poor spellers. They tend to be cheerful and idealistic, full of projects to improve or save the world. They may tinker with perpetual motion machines, discover how to assemble cars from rubbish, or, in the case of John Chapman (better known as Johnny Appleseed), traverse America planting zillions of apple trees. [11]

In conclusion, there's nothing wrong with pursuing an eccentric passion! Celebrate it!

When I was young I was called a rugged individualist. When I was in my fifties I was considered eccentric. Here I am doing and saying the same things I did then and I'm labeled senile. — George Burns

An Inspiring Career Change

My close friend Erich always had a profound interest in music and sound, but he was also good in biology. At Yale he kept music as a hobby by joining a singing group, but chose a major that was "responsible": Molecular Biophysics and Biochemistry.

However, after doing a couple of summer internships at a lab, he realized that he didn't enjoy it, and that he had been denying his true passion for music and sound. Most people would probably have just kept going on their career path, because who could turn down the lucrative six figure salaries in the hot genetics field? Most people might have just kept the sound interest as a hobby.

However, Erich had unusual courage. Although he graduated with his degree in MB&B, he immediately applied to Yale's prestigious Drama School to get a master's degree. His dream was to work for Skywalker Sound, George Lucas's prominent sound firm.

After graduating he accepted a six-figure job: $1,000.00/year. For almost two years Erich lived frugally in his parents' house doing whatever it took to break into the film and sound industry. To pursue his passion he built up his resume by doing film projects for free. As his debt grew, his determination never faltered.

In less than two years, his perseverance was rewarded. He became a sound designer at Skywalker Sound. In four years he did the sound work for over 40 movies including *Sixth Sense*, *Rainmaker*, *Cast Away*, *The Yards*, *The Young Black Stallion*, *The Recruit*, *Apocalypse Now (Redux)*, and *Final Fantasy*, among others. Today he works in Hollywood and earns a *real* six-figure salary.

Finding a way to make it happen

Let's assume that you've practiced the Second Principle: your expenses are under control; you have no debt; and you're free to hike with passion. What's next?

Although most of us don't have a billion dollars in the bank, that doesn't mean we can't pursue our passions. The standard reason most people don't hike with passion is that they believe they can't make any money that way. Although that may be true, more often we simply don't think creatively about making our dreams come true.

A life spent making mistakes is not only more honorable, but more useful than a life spent doing nothing.
— George Bernard Shaw

More importantly, we tend to forget all the people who make millions of dollars doing what they love. For example, let's say your passion is to watch football. You say, "I'd love to watch football all day long, but I can't make any money doing that." So instead, you stay in your unfulfilling job for the next 30 years and stick to watching football on Sundays.

A young kid from Brooklyn loved sports with a passion. He would study statistics and watch as many games as possible. He would go to the electronics store on Sunday so he would watch multiple games at the same time. He wondered if he could make a living doing this. He diligently pursued his passion. He didn't make much money in the beginning. In fact, the first several years were pretty rough. But in the end, he made it big. His name is Al Michaels. Michaels, one of the best sports announcers of all time, is perhaps most famous for covering Monday Night Football for ABC. He has three Emmy Awards for Outstanding Sports Personality and is a multi-millionaire. Do you think he loves his job?

What you do is more important than how much you make, and how you feel about it is more important than what you do. — Jerry Gillies

If you're stuck and can't figure out how to turn your passion into a reality, then consider these possibilities:

Sample passions	What you can do to pursue that passion
Eat out at fancy restaurants.	Become a food critic. Work for Gourmet Magazine. Become a chef.
Help the homeless.	Join a church that helps homeless. Work for a non-profit that helps find jobs and homes for the poor.
Work for charity.	Work for the Sierra Club. Work for United Way. Start your own charity.
Debate politics.	Run for local office. Work for the governor. Join a think tank.
Play golf.	Become a golf instructor. Work the grounds. Work to become a country club administrator.
Write books.	Start writing articles. Short stories. Just write the book!
Sit on boards of companies.	Join a very small company and join their board. Start your own company and create a board. Invest in a startup and join the board.
Cook all day.	Save to enter a cooking academy to become a sous-chef and work your way up.
Trade stocks.	Join an investment bank or brokerage.
Dance.	Join a dance group. Become a dance instructor.
Conduct scientific experiments.	Invent something and patent it. Join a university research team.
Listen to music.	Join MTV. Work for a radio station. Write for *Rolling Stone*. Open a music store. Volunteer for the symphony or the opera house.

The list could be endless, but the point is to brainstorm all the potential ways you could make money in pursuing your passion. Don't worry about how much money you'll make, but try to imagine if someone could somehow compensate you. Ask your friends for ideas. It's easy to forget, but people make money doing almost anything. Believe it or not, some people are even paid to sleep! Why? They're test subjects for psychology experiments!

You're never too old

Over 70 percent of the AT thru-hikers are male. Lisa and I wondered who would be the first female Nobo we would meet on the AT. That woman was definitely going to impress and inspire Lisa. Lisa was eager to meet her. She expected a 25-year-old, super fit Amazon woman to round the corner one day and tell her that she had walked from Georgia. This super woman would have Herculean leg muscles coupled with a fast and powerful stride. She would effortlessly carry her 50-pound pack up and down the mountains.

It took us less than three days of hiking to bump into the first female Nobo, but she was nothing like Lisa expected.

We were battling deer flies and mosquitoes in the swamps of the 100 Mile Wilderness in Maine. This is the most isolated part of the AT and is just south of Mount Katahdin, the starting point for Sobos. Until recently this 100-mile stretch of land had no re-supply points. At the beginning most thru-hikers average 10 miles a day, so many carried 10 days of food for this section. We met some hikers with 70 to 100 pound loads. When you consider that Katahdin is the single toughest climb on the AT, that the 100 Mile Wilderness immediately follows it, and that New England is the toughest section on the entire AT, you can understand why 90 percent of the thru-hikers start in Georgia. They prefer to avoid having a baptism by fire. Only the best prepared or the most foolish walk south.

Feeling like fools with the mosquitoes buzzing at our ears, we saw an old couple round the corner. Although we were hiking quite fast to keep the mosquitoes at bay, this elderly couple was plodding along, very slowly and methodically. The humidity was stifling, but they were fully clothed. Their beige pants and shirts were soaked in sweat. I got even hotter just looking at them with their hats on. We were under trees and in the shade, so I didn't understand why they had their sweat soaked hats on (except to keep the mosquitoes and the deer flies from biting their scalps). We couldn't believe that these old folks had picked such a brutal day to go for a walk in the woods.

"Hi, where are you coming from?" I asked quickly, hoping to be polite but short because I didn't want to linger in the company of the bugs.

"Georgia," they replied. "This is Jean, and I'm Comer," said the old man.

Lisa and I were stunned. "How old are you?" Lisa asked.

"We're both in our sixties," Jean replied.

Sadly, we were all so overwhelmed with bugs that none of us wanted to stay to chat. So we bid them farewell, but forever remember their lesson: you're never too old to hike with passion.

I want to see what's on the other side of the hill—then what's beyond that. — Emma "Grandma" Gatewood (1887—1973) who, at age 67, was the first person (male or female) to thru-hike the AT twice.

I eventually tracked down Comer and Jean while I was writing this book. I asked them to convey what they learned on the AT. In an email they wrote:

There is so much one can relate to but I think the trail reinforces that one can achieve a goal with their will power. To get up every morning from a warm sleeping bag when it's cold and wet, load up your pack and walk all day to meet all the challenges the trail offers and not give up when it is so easy to say let's go home. Not having ever backpacked before and not in the best of shape to climb the many mountains and go through as many weather changes took a lot of will power. — Comer and Jean, Nobos who were in their 60s when they thru-hiked

Pay particular attention to that first and last sentence they wrote to me. It brings up a key action we have to take to pursue our passion.

Summoning the will

The third and final step to hiking with passion is the hardest. You may know exactly what your passion is. You may know precisely what you need to do to pursue the dream and make it happen. However, you simply don't have the guts to do it.

Knowing is not enough, we must apply.
Willing is not enough, we must do. — *Goethe*

The list of excuses for not summoning the will is endless: I have a mortgage; I have a family to support; I would have to move to another city; I don't speak the language; I have no experience; I would have to sell my car and other possessions; I would have to give up my beloved cubicle.

What do you need to complete the AT?

There is no doubt that hiking with passion is hard. If it weren't, then everyone would be doing it. Similarly, thru-hiking the AT is hard. I met many successful pilgrims on the trail, and I tried to look for a common thread. Here are some characteristics I thought they would share:

- **Wealth:** I figured you might need the financial wherewithal to support the multi-month journey. *Wrong: one guy (Cheapo) hiked from Georgia to New York on $20.*

- **Good gear:** Those who travel with shoddy equipment are surely at a disadvantage. *Wrong: A man from Concord, California thru-hiked with the same old, decrepit gear he had 35 years ago.*

- **Superior nutrition:** Poor nutrition would certainly catch up to you during the hike and hamper your ability to finish it. *Wrong: A few thru-hikers survived mainly on Snickers and other junk food.*

- **Excellent cardiovascular conditioning:** Thru-hiking is the ultimate endurance sport, so surely cardiovascular fitness is paramount. *Wrong: In Virginia I met George Ziegenfuss who blew that theory—he was in his sixties and hiked the AT with only one lung.*

- **Disease-free:** Your body should be healthy and free of debilitating diseases. *Wrong: Sticks and Stones, two ex-military men, thru-hiked together to raise money for Leukodystrophy, which Sticks battled. Although Leukodystrophy is a progressive disorder that affects the brain, spinal cord and peripheral nerves, it did not stop Sticks from thru-hiking the AT.*

- **Youth:** I initially thought that being young and strong was a common denominator. *Wrong: I recalled the first female thru-hiker I met (Jean)—she was in her sixties. Others have completed it in their seventies. In 2004 Lee "The Easy One" Barry became the oldest person to ever thru-hike the AT: he was 81. The fastest thru-hiker our year was Linsey, a man who biked from California to Georgia, hiked up to Maine in about 72 days, and then biked back to California. He averaged about 30 miles a day on the AT and never took a day off. He was 63.*

- **Sight:** OK, at the very least, you should be able to see the trail! Right? *Wrong again: a blind man, Bill Irwin, hiked the whole trail with his trusty Seeing Eye dog named Orient. It took him nine months (50 percent longer than average) and he fell hundreds of times, but he made it.*

I was dumbfounded. I couldn't seem to find a common denominator among all the successful thru-hikers. Yes, the majority was young, strong, ate healthy food, carried lightweight gear, and could actually see the trail, but there were so many exceptions. It wasn't until I hit Georgia that I figured it out.

The only common thread that separated the successful thru-hikers from those who weren't successful was their *will*. Those who hike the whole AT in one season have an unbreakable will. They want

George and Murray Ziegenfuss, two former Lutheran Pastors invited us to stay with them in Bland, Virginia. Just a few of years before this photo, George thru-hiked the AT. He has only one lung. His breathing is labored even when he's resting. His incredible will and faith in God gave him the strength to walk from Georgia to Maine. Two years later we went again and got as far as New Jersey. In 2003, while hiking on the AT a hunter accidentally shot George in the back and collapsed his lung. He miraculously survived and is still hiking. (Photo by Justin "Stones" Matley)

to complete the trail so badly that nothing will stop them. Their rock solid courage triumphs over the fear and adversity that confronts them throughout their arduous journey.

Champions aren't made in gyms. Champions are made from something they have deep inside them. A desire, a dream, a vision. They have to have last-minute stamina, they have to be a little faster, they have to have the skill and the will. But the will must be stronger than the skill.
— *Muhammad Ali*

Mustering courage

It's tough to muster the courage to hike with passion, but ask yourself, "Why am I on this planet? To spend half my life doing a job I don't love?" Most people continue in dead end jobs that pay a decent wage. Others make lots of money, but still don't like what they are doing. Many of my Harvard classmates took 80 hour a week jobs that paid six figures, but a year or two later were completely disenchanted and quit.

Life is either a daring adventure or nothing.
— Helen Keller

It's hard to summon the will to pursue your passion when you have a well-paying job. I know what it's like to take a 100 percent pay cut. In 1997 I was in business school and I received an unsolicited email from Goldman Sachs, a leading investment bank. They had reviewed my resume (which I didn't even send them—they got it from the Harvard Business School directory), and they would really like me to work for their international division in Zurich, Switzerland. They liked that I was fluent in three languages. The *starting* compensation package would be $150,000/year. In less than five years, I could be earning about $500,000/year, and possibly more. It was tempting to say the least.

I politely told them that I was not interested, and I wanted to do what I had always dreamed of doing: starting my own company. I knew I would not be happy as an investment banker. I would constantly be thinking of all the other things I would rather be doing. Therefore, I graduated from business school and was the only one in my class whose starting salary was $0.00. I effectively took a $150,000 pay cut.

For one year I worked without a salary, while I focused on getting sales in the door. Eventually I closed some deals and I made about half of what I would have made in my first year at Goldman. I was doing what I loved, but it was certainly a hard decision. It takes a strong will and, in some cases, a tinge of insanity.

I worked myself up from nothing to a state of extreme poverty. — Groucho Marx

One of the secrets to mustering the courage is to visualize the end of each path. Project yourself into the future and imagine how you will feel in five or twenty years if you continue down the path you're going. Then imagine how much more happy and fulfilled your life would be if you created an Inflection Point today. Moreover, don't just focus on the destination, but also visualize the journey. *When you hike with passion, the path is more interesting than when you hike with apathy.* Viewing those alternate futures may motivate you to muster the courage to hike with passion.

 There is the risk you cannot afford to take, and there is the risk you cannot afford not to take. — Peter Drucker

But what about money?

Let's say you've come this far and agree that you should hike with passion, but you would really like to have certain things in life. You want a nice place to live, a luxury car, and you want an automatic garage door opener.

Although many dream of pursuing their passion, we don't do it because we fear that it will not produce any income. It's no surprise that most of us would agree with Groucho Marx: "Money will not make you happy, and happy will not make you money."

Of course, a few lucky people will discover that their passion in life is something that happens to also be fairly lucrative. If your passion is to save lives, nobody is going to worry about you making a living as a doctor. Similarly, if you love trading derivatives on Wall Street, your mom won't scold you for pursuing that passion.

Unfortunately, for many of us, our passions don't lead us on careers that can easily lead to big bucks. You might have a passion for writing, acting, or gardening. How are you ever going to make money doing that?

 I couldn't wait for success, so I went ahead without it. — Jonathan Winters

Think about the top of your ideal profession

No matter what profession you pick, think about the individuals who have made it to the pinnacle of that profession. Are they poor?

Let's examine a few professions that most people think are doomed to poverty, and let's see how those who pursued them to the top fared. These are professions that your parents would probably tell you not to pursue because "You'll never make any money that way!" Let's see what a few rebellious kids (or some with encouraging parents) did with their lives:

A profession and what people might think about trying to make a living pursuing it	Individuals who have hit the pinnacle of that profession and the rough lives they live
Music. Can you imagine telling your parents (or spouse) that you wanted to pursue a music career? It's filled with people living hand to mouth right? How can you ever make money doing that?	• Michael Jackson made (and spent) a few billion dollars. • Yo-Yo Ma brings home the bacon. • Even folk singers make decent money, like Tracy Chapman. • Pavarotti is a multimillionaire who gets to sing and eat all day long.
Sports. You love to play basketball, but can you make a living off it?	• Michael Jordan did. • Tiger Woods has been pursing his passion before he learned to walk, and he's worth tens of millions. • Phil Jackson coaches basketball teams and makes money to prove it. • John Madden goes "BOOM BOOM BOOM" all the way to the bank.
Painting. You wonder how well it would go over if you told your spouse that you wanted to become a painter? Talk about living in poverty, right?	• Picasso didn't care. He loved to paint and did it anyway. It more than paid his bills. • Monet made it through the tough times in Paris just by selling a few paintings.

Fashion industry. Here's another winner, "Mom, I want to make dresses." Yeah, right.	• Ralph Lauren didn't do too badly. • Donna Karan loved clothes and fashion ever since she could remember. She wasn't sure if she could make a living, but that was secondary. She wanted to do what she loved.
Cooking industry. How could you convince your loving spouse that you wanted to give up your $70,000 a year job to become a chef?	• Wolfgang Puck maybe didn't have a $70K job, but if he did, I'm sure he would have left it to pursue his passion. Now he can make $70,000 *a month*.
Writing. One way to produce a lot of chuckles in a crowd is to say you want to make a living as a writer.	• JK Rowling laughs all the way to bank. • Danielle Steele enjoys her 55 cars and wonders if she should buy another one.
Acting. Isn't "struggling actor" redundant? Guaranteed way to poverty.	• Jim Carrey makes $20 million per movie to make people laugh; is it obvious that this guy is pursuing his passion or what?
Psychology. You like to talk about people's problems and how to resolve them? No money there, right?	• Oprah Winfrey is the richest female in the entertainment industry, with a net worth of over a billion dollars. • Dr. Phil, her mentor, can't be doing too badly either. "Are you gettin' that?"

But these guys are the absolute best of their profession, and I can't expect to do that!

You're right. It would be irresponsible for me to suggest that you will do as well as the best have. You might, but you certainly can't bank on it. So now what?

If you look on the chart on the next page, we remind ourselves that in any profession there is a range of income. Entry-level people make far less than the outstanding performers and/or the more experienced people. The greater your excellence, the more you make.

Your excellence is a combination of experience, skill, and luck.

> *Wealth does not bring about excellence, but excellence brings about wealth and all other public and private blessings for men.* — *Socrates*

As you climb the Ladder of Excellence, your income rises accordingly. Those who are at the top of their profession today were not there several years ago. They were still struggling their way up.

Julia Roberts didn't make $20 million on her first film (the obscure 1986 film called *Blood Red*). She made maybe only $20,000 that year. On the other hand, she didn't jump from making $20,000 a year to $20 million either. It took four long years before she made her first hit, *Pretty Woman,* and she wasn't even making a million. It took her almost another ten years before she was offered eight figures. Julia journeyed up the income ladder, making more as her experience and her abilities grew. She wasn't an overnight success.

We tend to glorify those who are at the top of the profession, and forget the rest. We start believing that either we make it big or

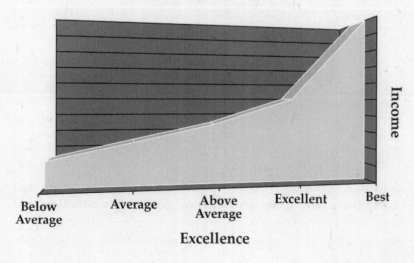

Ladder of Excellence

Income

Below Average   Average   Above Average   Excellent   Best

Excellence

we starve. It seems that if you want to pursue a football career, you either make $5 million a year, or you play flag football in the park. What about the people who play for the Canadian or Arena Football League? What about the backup players who make $100,000 a year? Just listen to this poor baseball player whine about his measly salary:

> *People think we make $3 million and $4 million a year.*
> *They don't realize that most of us only make $500,000.*
> *— Pete Incavigila, an impoverished Texas Rangers player*

Waking Up On The AT

When we would get up in the morning on the AT we would say that we felt like a pair of 70-year olds. We couldn't imagine what the real 70-year olds that we saw on the trail felt like!

Having hiked for 14 hours the previous day, our bodies begged us to stay in our sleeping bags. We could almost hear the creaking of our joints and tearing of our muscles as we propped ourselves up. Our feet were so swollen that we would sleep with our packs under our legs to keep them elevated.

The worst part was standing up. Utter pain would ripple through our bodies as we started walking. However, after five minutes of walking, we felt normal again. The blood was pumping through our bodies and we felt great to be back on the trail.

Thus, the AT had taught me another lesson about hiking with passion: it's those first steps that are the most difficult. Summoning the courage to do it is hard. But if you lack the courage, you can gain it by taking small steps. We wouldn't take big strides the moment after we got up. We took tiny steps and walked gingerly.

Therefore, look for small actions you can do today that will take you one step closer to pursuing your passion. After a few small actions, you'll say, "Hey, this isn't so bad," and you'll be walking with a confident and meaningful stride.

Career Bashing

I frequently give examples of someone who has a traditional corporate job but has a passion in a classic poverty related job (like writing).

Some may feel that I'm bashing "traditional careers." Not at all: I know people who love being a product manager, or a lawyer, or an accountant, or a factory worker. And if that's your passion, then absolutely go for it!

Those people rarely need encouragement and direction on pursuing their passion. Theirs is an easy road. Similarly, it's rare that someone is working in a "poverty career" and would rather be in a traditional career. It's not everyday that you find a sculptor who fantasizes about being a paralegal.

Therefore, I have focused on the most likely scenario. My goal is not to put down people who pursue "traditional careers," but rather to celebrate those who pursue their passion—whatever it may be.

So you want to be a photographer. You say it's either poverty or millions of dollars like Ansel Adams? Aren't there photographers who make $175,000 a year? Aren't there some who make $80,000? Maybe a photographer who works for National Geographic makes $50,000. And maybe a junior photographer for Vogue Magazine makes $25,000. There is always an income ladder.

Same goes for being the next Julia Child. Elinor Klivans spent four weeks in Paris and returned to Maine inspired. After searching for her passion using the classic tools a career counselor gave her, she concluded that she should write cookbooks. Her family chuckled. However, after eight years of pursuing her passion she's written four cookbooks, dozens of articles, toured the country to sign books and teach cooking classes, and has been a guest on network television morning shows, along with the Food Network cable channel. Her income is not the same as Julia Child's, but she's not living in poverty.[12]

In short, hiking with passion in a "tough" industry is not an all or nothing bet. It's hard to make a living making pottery, but if you're truly passionate about it, you will be persistent and you will eventually find a way to make decent money. If you're lucky and/or extremely good, you'll find a way to make lots of money. Don't worry about money; if you're hiking with passion, money will find you. It usually does for those who do what they love. And in the case that you don't end up making a fortune, you will still lie on your deathbed feeling better about your life than the man who sacrificed his life so he could have a few more digits in his bank account when he died.

 Without passion man is a mere latent force and possibility, like the flint which awaits the shock of the iron before it can give forth its spark. — Henri-Frederic Amiel

Isn't there another way to pursue one's passion?

Yes. I fully understand that quitting your secure job that pays good money to pursue your passion and take a 50 percent pay cut or more is highly uncomfortable. In some cases, it is simply impossible. You might have kids to support, and it would be irresponsible to live in a tent and have your kids worry about their next meal while you run off and pursue your acting career.

Is there a way to pursue your passion without giving up everything that you have? Yes. It is a compromise—but it's better than the status quo.

Let's assume that you're a controller at a solid company making $90,000 a year. Although you're good at working with numbers, it's not your passion; playing volleyball is. You think about volleyball all day long, you dream about it, you play it every chance you get, and talk about it in online chat rooms. You've researched it, and it's possible to make a living playing volleyball. The best volleyball players make over a million dollars a year. However, there's one slight problem: you're short and 43 years old.

Quitting your job and chasing your dream would be downright foolish. So do you give up and stay in a job that you hate?

No. You look at related fields. Ask yourself: "Why do I really want to be a volleyball player?" Is it because you enjoy watching volleyball? Or do you simply enjoy competitive sports? Analyze your true motivations and the reasons why you're attracted to your targeted profession. Following the example above, here are a few possibilities of related fields:

- You could start or join a company that sells volleyball related gear.

- You could become a part-time volleyball coach and eventually work your way up to the collegiate or Olympic level.

- You could set up and manage volleyball tournaments in your area or nationwide.

Go West Young Woman

Kathy Rogg, 54, was a partner at an East Coast law firm. An 18-day rafting adventure in the Grand Canyon caused an Inflection Point in her life. She moved to the southwest to practice law. Then one Colorado ski trip made the Inflection Point more dramatic.

For over 10 years Kathy has worked at the ski resort. She began at minimum wage as a snow making machine operator—talk about a salary cut from being a partner at a law firm! Now she runs snowboarding events and rafting trips in Utah.

When she started she did some legal work to make ends meet, but now that she's *Returned to Base Camp* (see Chapter 2), she doesn't need to do that anymore.

She encourages everyone to create an Inflection Point in their life.

(Source: Kelly Greene, "Travel Tales," The Wall Street Journal, June 24, 2002, p. R5.)

- You could work to become an announcer for volleyball tournaments on TV (announcing other sports to supplement your income).

- You could work for or start up a volleyball magazine or web site.

Without a doubt, if you were to pursue any of these options, you would take a massive pay cut from your $90K/year salary. Moreover, this would not be hiking with passion to the letter; these careers are related but not exactly your passion. Even though it is a compromise, it is not nearly as much of a compromise as continuing your job as an accountant. Of course, all these jobs pay less than your controller job, but how much is your happiness worth? Would you rather spend the rest of your days crunching numbers for a company that you don't care about? Or would you rather be knee deep in the sport that you love? Imagine, those work hours that steal 45 to 80 percent of your life will no longer seem like thievery. You'll enjoy going to work and talking about work all day long.

Will there be some tough moments? Yes, demanding Minor Trails occur in any job. It will be especially tough getting used to a decreased income. But would you have been able to take that extra income with you to the grave? *On your deathbed, looking back on your life, would you rather think of yourself as someone who spent the majority of his life doing an activity he didn't even enjoy?* Or would you prefer thinking that you were someone who earned $45,000 instead of $90,000, but who loved every minute of life and looked forward to going to work almost as much as coming home?

The double bonus

First bonus: Increased chance of success

You get two big bonuses when you hike with passion. The first is that you're more likely to hit the big time when you're doing what you love than when you are not.

This is true regardless of your wealth. We should pity those who have high salaries. They have more to lose than those who have low salaries, so they frequently don't want to take big risks. They're less likely to pursue their passion than those of more modest income because they're addicted to their income stream.

Dave Thomas, founder of Wendy's, didn't have a high school diploma, but was a millionaire by the age of 35 because he did what he loved and pursued it with all his passion. Wayne Huizenga sold trash-hauling services door-to-door before he started Waste Management, Blockbuster, AutoNation, Extended Stay America, and later bought three professional sports teams in Florida.

And it's never too late to start. Look at Ray Kroc: at the age of 52, with diabetes, he started McDonalds. He pursued his vision with a passion and energy unlike most 20 year olds could ever dream of doing.

If you're relentlessly hiking with passion, you will succeed. For some extremely talented or lucky ones it happens very quickly. For others it takes years. But it will come. And of course, remind yourself what you already know: money is not the best way to measure success.

A Harvard MD Pursues His Passion

Imagine you have two degrees from Harvard: a BA and an MD. Now imagine the guts it takes to decide that you will not be a doctor, but rather you're going to write fiction novels!

"To quit medicine to become a writer struck most people like quitting the Supreme Court to become a bail bondsman," said Michael Crichton.

This was especially impressive considering Crichton's Harvard writing professors gave him C grades. The odds of making more money writing fiction than being a doctor were slim. Nonetheless, he knew that as long as he pursued his passion, money would eventually come.

Ultimately he wrote *The Andromeda Strain*, *Congo*, *Disclosure*, *Jurassic Park*, *The Lost World*, *Rising Sun*, *Timeline*, the screenplay for the movie *Twister*, and created the "ER" TV series.

I always believed that if you set out to be successful, then you already are. — Katherine Dunham

Second bonus: Health improvements

Think about how you feel when you're doing something you enjoy versus something that bores you (or that you dislike). When you're doing what you love, your vitality soars. Compare that to the slouching, despondent, foot-dragging attitude you have when you must do something that you don't truly care about. Hence, hiking with passion brings the bonus of improved health and a *joie de vivre*.

What if you fail?

In a sense, you can't fail when you hike with passion. The hike itself is the reward. How does one judge failure anyway? Just because you don't make a lot of money doesn't mean you're a failure. As long as you faithfully hike with passion, you will enjoy life more than if you didn't and you will never be a failure. The only ones who fail are those who spend their lives coming up with excuses as to why they can't pursue their passion.

One of my favorite sayings is "Nobody ever lay on his deathbed thinking, 'I wish I had spent another day at the office.'" Although frequently quoted, those who are stuck in unfulfilling jobs don't repeat it enough. Write it down on your refrigerator, make it your screen saver on your computer, or think about it when you're in the shower. On the other hand, if you're hiking with passion, you might smile when you see that phrase and think, "Well, I'm glad I spent all those days at the 'office' because I was pursuing my passion and enjoying my life." Mark Twain quipped, "Work is a necessary evil to be avoided." The best way to avoid "work" is to make work your passion.

Serving one's own passions is the greatest slavery.
— Dr. Thomas Fuller

Summary

At just under 3,500 feet, Mount Greylock is the tallest mountain in Massachusetts. The best part of the mountain isn't the pretty view or the imposing war memorial that soars a hundred feet into the air. It's the Bascom Lodge at the summit that offers a lip smacking all you can eat breakfast.

No famished pilgrim would ever turn down half a dozen maple syrup drenched pancakes. It's rare to find such fine and abundant cuisine a few feet off the AT. Normally to get such a scrumptious meal you have to hitchhike into town with a meat cleaver collector.

Let's review what we've proven in this chapter:

- We spend 45 to 80 percent of our conscious time working.

- Life is too short to be wasted on a job you're not passionate about, so make that 45 to 80 percent count— do what you love.

- There is always a way to make money in any passion.

- There are always some individuals who make millions of dollars in every profession.

- There is always a progression of income as you climb up the Ladder of Excellence in any profession—it's not an all or nothing bet.

- There are always related career tracks in any profession that may be viable if you can't afford to pursue your passion in its purest form.

- Hiking with passion gives you a higher chance of succeeding in a competitive industry and improves your health dramatically.

Paralleling our AT odyssey, we are leaving the rigorous terrain of New England, and entering the more mild lands of the eastern mid-Atlantic. Although some may instinctively agree with the first three Principles, others may have difficulty accepting them.

However, we can already see how the Principles interconnect: to enjoy life (Principle #1) you must hike with passion (Principle #3), but to do that, you must beware of summit fever (Principle #2). As I mentioned at the beginning of the book, you don't have to follow all the Principles. However, the more you follow, the more you optimize your life.

Hiking with passion can be risky, especially if you're passionate about a field that is littered with failures and broken dreams. How do you increase the odds of success? That's what the Fourth Principle, and the next chapter, is all about.

> *It seemed the world was divided into good and bad people. The good ones slept better ... while the bad ones seemed to enjoy the waking hours much more.*
> — *Woody Allen, "Side Effects," 1981*

Umbrellas don't just block wind and rain. They also give you shade when the sun's beating down on you, like in this Massachusetts field. The downside is that some hikers might think you're a freak.

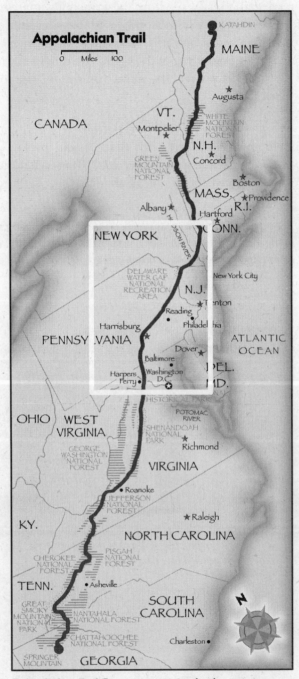

Appalachian Trail

0 Miles 100

KATAHDIN

MAINE

★ Augusta

CANADA

VT.

WHITE MOUNTAIN NATIONAL FOREST

Montpelier ★

N.H.
★ Concord

GREEN MOUNTAIN NATIONAL FOREST

MASS.

★ Boston

★ Providence R.I.

Albany ★

Hartford ★ CONN.

NEW YORK

New York City

DELAWARE WATER GAP NATIONAL RECREATION AREA

N.J.

★ Trenton

Reading •

Harrisburg ★

Philadelphia •

PENNSYLVANIA

ATLANTIC OCEAN

Baltimore •

Dover ★

DEL.

Harpers Ferry •

Washington D.C. ✪

MD.

HISTORICAL PARK

OHIO

WEST VIRGINIA

POTOMAC RIVER

SHENANDOAH NATIONAL PARK

GEORGE WASHINGTON NATIONAL FOREST

Richmond ★

VIRGINIA

• Roanoke

JEFFERSON NATIONAL FOREST

KY.

★ Raleigh

NORTH CAROLINA

CHEROKEE NATIONAL FOREST

PISGAH NATIONAL FOREST

TENN.

• Asheville

GREAT SMOKY MOUNTAINS NATIONAL PARK

NANTAHALA NATIONAL FOREST

SOUTH CAROLINA

N

CHATTAHOOCHEE NATIONAL FOREST

Charleston •

SPRINGER MOUNTAIN

GEORGIA

© *Appalachian Trail Conservancy, reprinted with permission*

Chapter 4:
Learn From Trail Lore

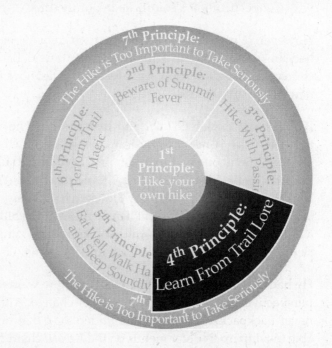

We descended Mount Greylock with plump, pancake filled stomachs. We easily crossed the Berkshires Plateau of Massachusetts and entered Connecticut. Out of the 14 states on the AT, we ranked Connecticut dead last on the enjoyment scale. It's really not poor Connecticut's fault. We just happened to walk into the small state during one of the summer's most brutal heat waves. The temperatures were around 100 degrees, and the humidity was over 90 percent. The conditions were incredibly debilitating as sweat poured down our backs. The only morons climbing mountains were thru-hikers—day and weekend hikers wisely stayed in their air-conditioned homes.

The higher you go up in altitude, the more you escape the heat. Unfortunately, the trail follows the low lying Housatonic River and the highest mountain in Connecticut (Bear Mountain, near Salisbury) is a miniscule 2,316 feet—so there's no escaping the inferno. Add some mosquitoes to the mix, and you'll understand why Connecticut left a sour taste in our mouths.

However, it was in Connecticut that we came across a man who had an unusual tale to tell, and his name was Party House. Of course, the first question we asked him was how he got a trail name like Party House.

Party House explained that one June morning he woke up and thought, "Gee, I need a physical challenge, something bold and exciting." Someone had told him of a 2,168-mile trail that crossed 14 states on the East Coast of the US and takes about six months of backpacking to complete. Party House, *who had never hiked a day in his life*, thought that such a challenge might fit the bill. Armed with a degree from a prestigious culinary school and zero hiking experience, he had no clue what it took to hike the whole trail.

He had been a chef for several years but now wanted to get some perspective and possibly make a career change. Although he had never backpacked in his life, he understood that he wouldn't be able to whip up five star menus on the Appalachian Trail. Mac and cheese is about as fancy as it gets out there.

His girlfriend drove him from Boston to the northern tip of the AT near Bangor, Maine. He walked into the only outfitter in town, declared that he wanted to hike the AT, and that he needed help purchasing the necessary equipment since he had absolutely nothing—not even a pair of hiking shoes. The salesman's eyes lit up, and in an hour or two he had helped him purchase hundreds of dollars worth of gear.

After loading up the shopping cart, the only item that was left to buy was a shelter. Most AT hikers start with a small, light, four to five pound tent, and then some switch to a one pound tarp during the journey as they realize that tents are overrated and too heavy for a thru-hike. Party House was dimly aware that he should minimize the weight he carried. So he asked the salesman to give him the "smallest and lightest tent" they had.

The salesman replied, "I'm sorry, but we're a small outfitter and we don't have a wide selection. The best thing I can get you is a nine pound, three person tent."

Party House, a gourmet chef, who hadn't even done a day hike in his life, set off to thru-hike the AT.

Without any other easy alternative and not fully realizing how quickly nine pounds can feel like 50, Party House said, "I'll take it."

It didn't take long for another thru-hiker to see Party House's massive dome tent. The thru-hiker, dumbfounded by the one-person palace declared, "With the powers vested in me as a fellow thru-hiker, I hereby name you 'Party House.'"

The name stuck. And the lesson of Party House stuck in my mind too: *learn from trail lore.*

The Lightest Pack on the Trail

Thru-hikers can be so obsessed with shaving every ounce of weight that they will clip the handles of their toothbrushes and trim the edges of their maps. In Connecticut, for example, we ran into Beat, a thru-hiker who took going light to a new level. Beat had some time off before he was going to go to Africa for the Peace Corps. Hiking the AT would be a great adventure before venturing into the bush. Beat got his trail name because he was always tired, or beat.

So after hiking over 500 miles, Beat ditched his 60-pound pack and bought a fanny pack and a compact, lightweight hammock, which he wrapped around his waist. Inside his diminutive fanny pack were rain pants, iodine tablets (for water purification), a few energy bars, and bagels. With the water bottle strapped to his side and a camera around his neck, he was carrying a paltry six pounds.

Most thru-hikers thought he was insane, yet Beat managed to hike several hundred miles of the trail in this way. The nights were so hot and humid in the Mid-Atlantic States that he really didn't need a sleeping bag. So Beat just slept in his rain pants when he was cold.

Of course, the first cold spell in the highlands of Virginia made him quickly realize that his days of featherweight backpacking were over—autumn was coming.

If the young only knew; if the old only could.
— French Proverb

It amazed me how many people were attempting to thru-hike the AT and had done little to no research on what they were about to do. Every spring thousands of prospective thru-hikers ascend Springer Mountain in Georgia, the southern terminus of the AT, hopefully thinking that they will hike all the way to Maine. However, if you look at the chart on this page, a whopping 15 percent quit at Neels Gap, a mere 30 miles into their journey![13]

About 70 percent drop out before the halfway point (Harper's Ferry). Fewer than 20 percent actually complete the entire trail. Moreover, the vast majority of thru-hikers make major changes in

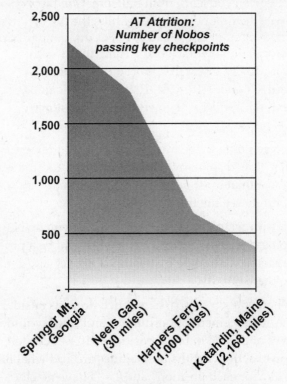

Source: Appalachian Trail Conservancy. This is the average of the 1999-2003 seasons

their gear within the first couple of weeks. What accounts for these dismal statistics? It is what happens when people don't learn from trail lore.

This chapter will explain the importance of the Fourth Principle. It is hard to get the most out of life when you spend the majority of your time unnecessarily suffering from errors that you could have easily avoided. Some of these mistakes are meaningless, but others can devastate your life. To squeeze the most out of life we need to learn from the experience of others. By building on this experience not only can we make progress as individuals, but also as a society.

Trail lore quiz

Let's see how well you learn from trail lore. Don't worry I won't ask you who was the first person to thru-hike the AT.

1. Before you accept a job at a company, do you usually research it thoroughly? Rate yourself on a 1-10 scale, 10 = "I do meticulous research" and 1 = "I go with my gut instinct 100 percent."

2. Before going to the movies, do you read reviews? 10 = "I read so many that I know more about the movie than most people who have seen it" and 1 = "I rarely see the trailer!"

3. How much planning and research do you do before going on a major vacation? 10 = "I could be a professional tour guide by the time I arrive" and 1 = "I go there blindly!"

4. When you job search, how much do you consider the advancement opportunities and the day-to-day lives of people in those positions? 10 = "I can tell you exactly what the possibilities are and what life is like for each position" and 1 = "I have no clue where this job may lead me."

5. When you consider buying or renting a new home/apartment, how much research do you do? 10 = "I teach the realtors lessons" and 1 = "I grab the first thing that feels good."

Scoring: If you scored less than 30, then you need to learn more from trail lore before you make important decisions in life. If you scored 31-45 points, then you should keep learning from trail lore like you've been doing. If you score 46-50, then you might want to relax a little bit—as we'll see later, you don't want to overdose on planning. By the way, in 1948 Earl "The Crazy One" Shaffer was the first person to thru-hike the AT (and he did it again for a third and final time in 1998 when he was almost 80 years old).

What makes humans special?

We were thrilled to leave Connecticut behind, especially because New York was next. The August temperatures were blazing in the high 90s and the next day was supposed to soar past 100 degrees. It was so muggy that we would sweat profusely while we were sleeping and had to pour water over our heads during the night to keep cool. Trying to hike up a mountain was like trying to do a two hour step aerobics class in a steam shower.

We happily escaped the inferno by taking the Harlem Line of the Metro North Railway right into Grand Central Station in Manhattan. This brisk train ride transported us from the woods to the center of civilization. We stayed with a business school friend, whose apartment had air conditioning—a glorious invention.

I was overwhelmed! My senses, now heightened from six weeks of backpacking, were overloaded. For weeks I'd grown hyper-sensitive to the subtle crack of a twig, the gentle song of a bird, the refreshing smell of rain, and the soft colors of sunrise. Now, I was assaulted by the cries of sirens, the screeching of subways, the flashing neon lights of Times Square, and the din of millions of people!

Night Hiking

I enjoy night hiking, even though you miss out on most of the scenery. It's not only romantic to hike by the light of the moon, but your mind also runs wild whenever it hears the strange sounds in the bushes. You feel like Death lurks in every shadow! It's thrilling in a strange way.

Given the heat in Connecticut, we decided to try night hiking, hoping the slightly cooler temps would let us travel more efficiently.

Bad move.

By 10 p.m. Lisa's Photon light was fading. With no place to camp, we slept in the middle of the trail. It was such a hot and humid night that we didn't even bring out our sleeping bag. We hadn't seen many bugs since Maine, so we were caught off guard when they came out in force in Connecticut.

For one hour I stared at the stars and endured the high pitched squeal of mosquitoes, and then I finally asked Lisa, "Have you slept at all?"

"No," she replied.

"How about we hike some more?" I suggested.

"OK."

So from midnight to 5 a.m. we hiked, taking occasional breaks to sleep. Within a few minutes the mosquitoes would find us and wake us up with their bites. The humidity and heat was still atrocious at 2 a.m.

At 5 a.m. we cooked up a meal. We kept hiking until 8 a.m., where we collapsed on the side of the trail. We slept without any pads, on the hard rock. By 10 a.m., we woke up and kept going.

The sad thing is that instead of walking 15 miles that night, we had hardly done five miles because we had only one Photon flashlight that had a dying battery. I was hiking using the pale moonlight that filtered through the trees and Lisa doesn't have great night vision. In short, our hope to hike more efficiently in the cooler temps was a complete disaster.

However, it was thrilling! This was the ultimate One-Time Upgrade! Lisa enjoyed wearing heels, putting on makeup, and feeling like a girl again. I simply enjoyed traveling 30 miles per hour in a taxi.

We ate like royalty. We dined at the famous Union Square Cafe, had Tibetan food, gelato, New York bagels, and of course, pretzels from the charming street vendors.

We went to a couple of museums, Broadway shows, and monuments. We did things we could never do on the trail, like being able to get Ben and Jerry's ice cream at 2 a.m. and sleep in a soft bed. As I lay in bed, I thought about what we had been doing just a few days before on the AT. Then the TV weatherman came on and reported the record breaking temperatures. He advised citizens to "avoid strenuous activity."

I chuckled and mumbled, "That's the understatement of the week." Then I rolled over, turned the AC up a notch, and drifted off to sleep with a big smile on my face.

Manhattan shocked and overwhelmed our senses, but the air conditioning sure was nice.

I was savoring Manhattan and admittedly somewhat reluctant to jump back on the trail, knowing that it had not cooled down that much. Nevertheless, we could not wait forever or else winter would set in before we finished the trail. I knew that August would be a hot and challenging month. No one ever said it would be easy weather the whole way. Before we left, we went into the World Trade Center to feel the aura of New York one last time, not knowing that just a month later it would no longer be standing.

History is a gallery of pictures in which there are few originals and many copies. — *Alexis de Tocqueville*

My pit stop in Manhattan had rejuvenated my spirits and I quickly relished the trail again. We zipped through New Jersey's 72 miles and were eager to tackle the 230 miles of extremely rocky trail ahead of us in Pennsylvania, or as I liked to call it, Rocksylvania. When I wasn't watching my step, I scanned for wildlife. But thruhiking isn't a great way to see animals, because they run away before you ever see them. The best way to see them is to stay put for several hours. But thru-hikers are almost always moving. Therefore, the only bear we saw on the trail was in New Jersey. It was rather small and it hid from us. We saw moose in Maine and Vermont. We saw many birds, squirrels, deer, bats, frogs, lizards, salamanders, and snakes. With the thought of wildlife and New York juxtaposed in my mind, I wondered: "What makes humans so special? Why are we able to construct such vast metropolises? Why don't the squirrels dominate this planet? Why aren't blue jays constructing skyscrapers, subways, and air to ground missiles?"

Weaseling out of things is important to learn. It's what separates us from the animals. Except the weasel.
— *Homer Simpson*

Clearly, our ability to communicate sophisticated concepts, coupled with our amazing capacity to learn, has allowed our species to excel. One of the reasons we have done so well is that we are

Wildlife was usually elusive, but these three goats weren't. They licked the sweat off our legs to get the salt. They had escaped from the back of truck about a year ago and were making a living high in the mountain. They made me wonder what makes humans special.

able to quickly pass an enormous amount of knowledge onto our children. Of course, other animals are also capable of learning. After all, many animals can teach their offspring how to fly, how to create a shelter, or how to act cute and beg those silly humans for food.

However, animals are incapable of transmitting and remembering the *massive* amount of information that we humans are able to. Our brain's ability to communicate and assimilate *petabytes* of data is one of the reasons we're so special. It's a shame when we don't take advantage of it, because when we do we can get the most out of life.

 But though all our knowledge begins with experience, it does not follow that it all arises from experience.
— Immanuel Kant (1724-1804)

What the brilliant German philosopher Immanuel Kant was trying to say was that not all our knowledge must come from our personal experience. Indeed, the more we leverage the experience of others, the better off we will be. That's the key lesson in learning from trail lore.

Those who are not getting the most out of life are usually only learning from their own experience, and ignore the experience of others. What would happen if all humans did this? We would still be living in caves, hiding from our predators, and wondering how we can take over the world. Gee, that sounds like a bunch of Al Qaeda terrorists, but never mind.

The point is that our rapid progress both as a species and as individuals is tightly correlated to how much we learn from others. Think about what you're good at, and ask yourself if you could ever be that good without having learned from the knowledge and experience of others. For example, a benchwarmer on a professional sports team today would have been one of the top players in the league just 50 years ago. That athlete has learned from all the moves, training, and techniques of the previous athletes. Astronomers today are discovering new planets because they're building on all the accumulated human knowledge of the stars. Even the art of making some mouth-watering French bread has been passed down for generations.

Therefore, to live our lives to the fullest, we shouldn't start from the basement; we should start from the highest floor possible. The only way to do that is to diligently study those we would like to emulate and see what they did to get there. Our ability to learn from trail lore is one of our competitive advantages as a species, so let's use it.

No matter what passion you pursue, learn from the accumulated knowledge out there. For example, if you want to be the best mother in the world, then read all the latest books on parenting and see what works. Don't just trust one source. Read multiple opinions to help you get diverse viewpoints and experiences. Your mind will assimilate this knowledge and formulate a solid plan to accomplish your goals. You will diminish the number of missteps and counterproductive actions.

We learn from history that we do not learn from history.
— Georg Friedrich Wilhelm Hegel

When we study history, we see that people repeat the same errors. Indeed, it's impossible to live life without repeating the same silly mistakes that humanity has done over and over again. George Santayana said, "Those who cannot remember the past are condemned to repeat it," but some may question why making a misstep is such a big deal. I questioned that myself as I slipped and nearly broke my ankle on the millionth rock I walked on in Pennsylvania.

The cost of missteps

The cost of missteps can vary from the annoying to the life threatening. After getting through Pennsylvania, we entered Maryland and met a thru-hiker who experienced an annoying mistake because he mistimed his box shipments with his hiking pace. Some towns along the trail are so remote that they have a post office, but no supermarket. Before their hike, many thru-hikers use guidebooks to identify stretches of trail without easy access to a supermarket. For those areas they prepare a re-supply box filled with dried food, band-aids, and other valuable items. Before our AT hike, for example, we prepared a dozen re-supply boxes. My wonderfully supportive mother in California would faithfully take each box to the post office about two weeks before I needed it and shipped it across the country.

This system worked well unless the thru-hiker arrived at the post office on a Saturday afternoon. Most post offices would close around noon on Saturday and would not open again until Monday morning. Therefore, for those thru-hikers who were trying to keep a certain pace (and most were), it was annoying to arrive at the post office on Saturday afternoon because you would be forced to stay there until Monday morning, when the post office reopened.

I met a thru-hiker who mistimed his pace so that for three weeks

Double Stuff

One gray, soggy morning in Maine we groggily woke up to the realization that we had no fuel or matches. Despite all our planning and learning from trail lore, we had accidentally not brought enough fuel for the first leg of our journey. Unfortunately, the only food we had left needed to be cooked. The wet wood surrounding us extinguished any hope that would be able to spark up a fire like our ancestors.

Instead, we resigned ourselves to eating cold, uncooked oatmeal. This disgusting pasty gruel was about as appetizing as eating a soggy newspaper.

Shortly after hitting the trail and listening to my stomach complain as it tried to digest the raw oatmeal, I smelled something delicious: bacon.

Lisa and I both noticed the saliva seeping out of each other's mouths. Close by was a man merrily cooking in the wilderness. He had countless clothes strewn about drying on trees. His accommodations were extravagant: one tent for himself and a palatial tarp for his cooking area. His kitchen was grandiose: pots, pans, and utensils everywhere. The aromas emanating from his gourmet cooking were intoxicating.

"What's your name?" I asked, trying not to stare at his food.

"Double Stuff," he said proudly.

"How did you get that name?" I wondered aloud, suddenly fantasizing about his massive stash of Oreo's Double Stuff cookies that he must have in his enormous backpack.

"They call me Double Stuff because I carry about double the stuff that most thru-hikers carry. Most thru-hikers carry about 35 pounds of gear, but I carry about 70," he explained. "I'd rather section hike the AT and camp in comfort."

We nodded and gave him a strained smile. He cheerfully smiled back, and we grabbed a last whiff of his cuisine, dreaming of Oreo Double Stuffed cookies as we miserably cranked out another 25 miles.

I've never forgotten fuel since then.

in a row he arrived at the post office on a Saturday afternoon. He was frustrated. He needed to either hike faster or slower. But the stubborn man didn't adapt or learn. Sadly, he's not the only man with this shortcoming.

Of course, some people welcomed the 42-hour break, but he did not because he would get in a hiking groove and did not want to lose momentum. Moreover, sometimes a day and a half off did more harm than good—your muscles would tighten up and making them move again was excruciatingly painful. He wanted to keep a rhythm. Because this thru-hiker did not learn from the trail lore of previous thru-hikers (or even his own lore!), he continued to make the same aggravating mistake over and over again. This decreased his enjoyment of the hike, yet he could have easily avoided it had he just learned from trail lore (or listened to his wife).

History never looks like history when you are living through it. — John W. Gardner

Some missteps are not simply annoying, they're life threatening. On the wall of the bookstore at the Pinkham Notch ranger station was a massive list of all the people who had died in the Presidential Mountain Range in New Hampshire. The list described how and where each person died. Many perished in Tuckerman's Ravine. Clearly, some were not learning from the past catastrophes in this dangerous ravine. How many of these deaths could have been prevented had these people learned from trail lore?

Although most of these deaths occurred in the brutal winter, some occurred in the middle of summer. By doing just a little bit of research one can learn about how fast the weather can change in the Presidential Mountain Range and that it can even snow in July! Moreover, because of the infamous winds and unpredictable rainstorms, it doesn't have to get below 50 degrees for someone to die of hypothermia—the number one killer of backpackers. The wind chill robs you of your warmth, and if you set off, like this one doomed hiker did, in just shorts and a T-shirt, you are asking for trouble. I stared at the wall in dismay and saw how some had repeatedly made the same mistakes.

In conclusion, mistakes can certainly be costly. They can be massive Inflection Points that send your life into a tailspin. The trick is learning how to avoid the costly ones.

Backpacking versus thru-hiking

Let's see how to apply the Learn from Trail Lore Principle when hiking the AT.

Imagine kissing your job and your friends goodbye to hike the AT over six months, and then you quit hiking the trail in just two days! As crazy as it sounds, this happens to hundreds of people every season as they are surprised by the reality of a thru-hike. Over 20 percent of wanna-be thru-hikers quit within the first week!

Had they just done some research on it, or gone out one weekend and walked 10 to 30 miles a day over mountains, they would have realized that they weren't up for the task. Instead, they relied on their limited backpacking experience, their gut instinct, or Uncle Harry who supposedly knows everything.

As all those who attempt thru-hiking the AT quickly learn, there

Two friendly brothers, Bear and Tag Along, take a break in the 100-mile Wilderness in Maine. Like many thru-hikers, they started with heavy backpacks. They learned the hard way that they were carrying too much and eventually lightened their load.

PUD

Here's another difference between backpackers and thru-hikers. A typical backpacker doesn't really mind getting to the top of a mountain and discovering that there's nothing noteworthy to see. Who cares if the trees block the view, or that there's no cool plaque or pizza stand on the summit? The backpacker is happy to get some exercise and breathe the fresh air.

Thru-hikers, on the other hand, may throw a fit. They believe that if there's nothing to see on the summit, the trail should take the low road around the mountain. They hate such uninspiring trails so much that they have an acronym for it: PUD, a Pointless Up and Down.

It's hard to imagine how frustrating it can be to climb endless PUDs. By the end of the day you'll usually find thru-hikers making a little voodoo doll of the trail designer and poking him cruelly with a sharp stick.

is a big difference between backpacking and thru-hiking. That explains why a whopping 50 percent quit within the first six weeks of a thru-hike that normally takes six months. For example, compared to a successful thru-hiker, the typical backpacker brings far more items and far heavier items:

What a typical backpacker brings	What a typical thru-hiker brings
Heavy pots and pans to make gourmet meals	One ultra-light titanium pot
Fresh clothes for each day outside	Extra pair of underwear—no extra clothes
Large comfortable tent	Tarp
Full-length deluxe inflatable mattresses	Thin foam pad

What a typical backpacker brings	What a typical thru-hiker brings
Heavy duty sleeping bag	Light sleeping bag and sleep with your clothes if it's cold
Gigantic expedition backpack	Small, lightweight backpack
Camp shoes and lightweight chair	Neither
A radio	Ears to listen to nature

Bringing a sleeping bag that is one pound lighter than the typical sleeping bag may not seem like much, but the differences begin to add up. Even little items, such as taking a minuscule knife versus a heavy Swiss army knife, can have an impact if you do it across the board. Indeed, if you consistently find an item that weighs 25 to 50 percent less than the typical version of that item, then your pack weight will decline 25 to 50 percent. As obvious as that sounds, most of those who plan a thru-hike don't think about this, nor do they heed the lesson of those who have hiked before them. Instead, hikers look at their heavy-duty compass and think, "What's the big deal, it's only an ounce or two heavier." On the other hand, a prepared thru-hiker will search for a lightweight and accurate compass. In my case, for example, the compass was integrated in my watch. In fact, the AT is so well marked that you could even leave the compass at home. Besides, carrying a compass does not guarantee that you will not get lost—I managed to get lost on the AT even with signs all around me.

The paradox of backpacking is that the more distance you walk, the less you should carry. This is counter-intuitive, and so the best way to learn this lesson is through the experience of others. Most people assume that if they're going to embark on a six-month expedition, they should take a ton of gear to prepare for all the possible challenges. However, trail lore teaches us the exact opposite: the longer the backpacking trip, the less you should carry. It's better to carry a light pack and re-supply every four days or so. It's nearly impossible to walk over 2,000 miles in less than six months with 90 pounds on your back. If the simple exhaustion doesn't do you in, the inevitable injuries will. Since it's almost unbearable to carry more than 10 days of food, a long distance backpacker must re-supply along the way. If you don't believe me, just go to the supermarket, buy 10 days of food, put it all in a backpack, and try to make it back to your car without collapsing!

Therefore, thru-hikers either hitchhike into a town that has a supermarket or ship food to a remote post office or hostel. They usually don't carry more than six days of food with them at any point during the journey. Why? Because the less they carry the more miles they can walk. So the smart thru-hiker carries the bare minimum to be safe and walks 10 to 30 miles a day so that he avoids backpacking in the winter (which requires far more gear and is more dangerous than hiking during the other three seasons).

The weekend backpacker, on the other hand, is in no rush and can afford to carry the kitchen sink because he's usually not walking very far. The casual backpacker loves having the pancake griddle and the comfy chair in the middle of nowhere. He walks five miles, sets up camp, and enjoys relaxing with his espresso. Although that is great fun, it can cloud your ability to understand the backpacking paradox that one should carry less the more one travels. We can learn about this paradox either (1) from personal experience or (2) from trail lore. Because this lesson is so counter-intuitive, even the avid weekend backpacker is usually poorly prepared for a thru-hike because he is burdened with preconceived notions of what thru-hiking must be like. And he can't imagine just how many rocks litter the trails of Pennsylvania.

History not used is nothing…and if you don't use the stuff—well, it might as well be dead. — Arnold Toynbee

Before I had ever backpacked, I talked to those who had. One guy told me how he would hike 10 miles a day and carry 70 pounds— this same guy would later tell me about his chronic back problems.

I intuitively knew that carrying that much weight all day must be highly stressful on the body. Moreover, I knew I could walk more than 10 miles a day if I had nothing on my back. Therefore, instead of getting an "expedition" backpack, I examined the "day packs." These packs were not much bigger than your average school backpack. Getting a small backpack was a great way to discipline myself. With so little storage space I had no other choice but to get rid of unnecessary items and to find lighter versions of the necessary ones.

Hundreds of people have completed the AT and a few have written books about what you should bring and how to minimize your pack's weight. Nevertheless, every season over half of the hikers repeat the same errors of the previous year's hikers. For example, when we started in Maine nearly everyone we saw had these gigantic 50+ pound packs! By the end of the journey, nearly everyone had trimmed down their packs to half their starting size. To do this, thru-hikers frequently abandon hundreds of dollars of gear, buy hundreds of dollars of new gear, and get back on the trail again. It's thanks to these discards that Cheapo (whom we met in Chapter Two) was able to hike from Georgia to New York on $20. He didn't have any gear, but he picked up most of it from the castoffs of hikers before him. He acquired almost all the gear he needed in just the first 30 miles!

When I talked with the thru-hikers, they all wished that they had minimized their pack-weight from the start. In other words, they all wished that they had learned from trail lore. This lesson applies to life off the trail too. *The goal is to learn from other people's experiences so that your experience is the best it can be.*

How to follow this Principle

Following this Principle doesn't just apply to thru-hiking. Indeed, you can benefit from it whether you are a father, a factory worker, or a rock star. Let's go through the five steps of how to learn from trail lore.

Step 1: Clearing your mind of assumptions

It's hard to learn from trail lore if you have a closed mind. I asked one backpacker, "Why do you carry such a heavy backpack?" He replied, "Because that's the way I've always backpacked—that's how my dad taught me." This backpacker might have trouble learning from trail lore because he assumes that there was only one way to backpack, and he can't fathom any other way of doing it. *Therefore, Step One is to clear your mind of assumptions; otherwise, you will not consider all the possibilities.*

Step 2: Research meticulously

The more important the decision, the more you should research it. Yes,

---

Trail Lore from a Three-Time AT Thru-Hiker

I enjoyed meeting Spur at the Upper Goose Pond Shelter in Massachusetts. He had thru-hiked the AT three times and had a wealth of wisdom. I asked him what he had learned from trail lore. He wrote me an email that contained this advice:

Walk yourself into shape gradually. Don't try to accomplish too much too fast. Your body will toughen and grow stronger. So will your confidence. Stay in touch with your body. Learn to recognize and respect its limitations even as you stretch and exercise it to become stronger.

Lighten your load. Learn to live with less stuff and your life (and your hike) will be considerably less burdensome.

Start the day early. The world is never more interesting than it is at dawn, especially in the woods. By noon you'll already have accomplished a pretty good day's work.

Don't be in too big of a hurry to finish. There's so much to savor along the way. Conversely, maintain your momentum. Don't allow yourself to get stuck by all the potential distractions.

Good luck,

Spur

---

listening to your gut instinct is important. After all, there's a reason why your instincts are frequently correct. Our senses pick up subtle signs that may be difficult to explain, but they often signal the best way to go. As Steven Pinker points out in his brilliant book *How the Mind Works*, these senses are tuned through millions of years of evolution, and ignoring them is often a bad idea. Nevertheless, our instinct is not always right, and it is often wrong when deciding something that is more cerebral than emotional. So what helps us make a good decision? Relevant information, and lots of it.

Can you imagine if we got all our history from just one source? After World War I, for example, Germany's history books depicted their country as a victim, not as an aggressor. Some students of that era made decisions based on one (erroneous) source. Similarly, people who decide to hike the AT after only talking with one hiker may be ill prepared. Instead, read a few books on whatever subject you're about to engage in, read magazines that take different points of view, and talk with a variety of people (especially those who have substantial experience on the matter). By sampling a broad spectrum, you can synthesize the best lessons from trail lore.

Step 3: Periodically question your assumptions again

The world and technology is not static. Trail lore does not always reveal the right answer. Don't be afraid to ask such seemingly silly questions such as, "Is using a cellular phone without a headset unsafe?" Listen to someone who has an argument to claim that point—keep your mind open and consider the idea no matter how ludicrous it may sound. Copernicus had a "crazy" idea that the Earth revolved around the Sun. This idea was so sacrilegious that he didn't reveal his theory until he was on his death bed. He feared getting killed for arguing such a point. Bruno, another astronomer around the same period, was burned at the stake for espousing similar views. Luckily, nowadays we can ask wacky questions and make silly statements without getting flogged. *In summary, we must question and re-question our beliefs and assumptions in order to keep learning from trail lore, especially recent trail lore.*

Step 4: Plot Your Path

Once you've learned from trail lore, you're ready to apply what you learned. For example, when I would plan my four day backpacking trips I knew my destination, but I had to figure out how to get there. Similarly, after reading Chapter Three, you might know where you want to end up, but you're not sure how to get there. That's when you should leverage the knowledge of previous hikers. Before starting a hike, I would learn the location of the mountains, the springs, the bridges, the trail junctures, and the shelters. Likewise, you should study the common shortcuts, pitfalls, and milestones that those who have gone before you have discovered. By doing that, you'll be taking the most enjoyable path to your destination.

Step 5: Create trail lore

Let's say you've learned from trail lore and you're Plotted Your Path. Now comes the fun part—creating trail lore. In New England I heard about the legendary Barefoot Sisters who did just that. The year before, Isis and Jackrabbit (two sisters) thru-hiked most of the AT *barefoot*. They walked an amazing 1,300 miles barefoot and used sandals for the other 868 miles.

They weren't able to go the whole distance barefoot because it's hard to walk over 10 miles a day without foot protection. So as they slowly headed south, winter caught up to them in Virginia. The icy ground sliced their bare feet into a bloody mess.

This forced the hardy Barefoot Sisters to slap on shoes. With the determination of a bull, they made it to Georgia despite hundreds of miles of freezing temperatures. But their tale doesn't end there.

They rested a couple of months in Georgia, slung on their backpacks, and then hiked right back up to Maine! This is what thru-hikers call a "yo-yo hike." Like a yo-yo, the hiker hits her destination, turns around, and walks back to where she started. A yo-yo hiker can make a proud thru-hiker feel kind of wimpy. Toss in the fact that the sisters walked most of their yo-yo hike barefoot and even macho men start feeling pretty puny.

After hearing about the Barefoot Sisters, I was lucky to run into them at the Upper Goose Pond Cabin in Massachusetts. The rain and the all-you-can-eat pancakes for $3 drew over 40 thru-hikers into this barebones off-the-trail cabin. As a Sobo, it was rare to see so many thru-hikers in one place, but New England is where Sobos and Nobos converge. Sadly, Jackrabbit was feeling lethargic because she had contracted Lyme disease from a tick. She had a fever, muscle pains, a stiff neck, and inflamed joints. This forced her to hike in sandals. Although it was obvious how much she was suffering, she still had that fire in her eyes that told you, without a doubt, that she was going to Maine.

I asked Isis, "So why do you and Jackrabbit hike barefoot?"

"Imagine if you wore gloves all day long for most of your life," Isis explained, "Then one day you took them off. Imagine how incredible that would feel. That's how it is for us—we truly *feel* the trail."

The Barefoot Sisters certainly hiked their own hike. Although they had learned from other barefoot hikers, they were venturing into unknown territory. Nobody had done this before. They were creating trail lore.

The lesson of the Barefoot Sisters is clear. You can't spend all your

The Terrible Ticks

It's hard to avoid ticks when you backpack 2,000 miles. These tiny parasitic arachnids lie in the vegetation and latch onto you when you brush by. They can spend several hours crawling all over your body before finding a nice juicy spot to burrow into.

I've caught a few on me and I've always marveled at how you can't feel them, even when they're digging into your skin to feed off your blood. If you don't pluck them out of your body within 36 hours, then you risk contracting a disease.

Therefore, smart hikers inspect their bodies at least once a day to see if any ticks have moved in without paying the rent.

The legendary Barefoot Sisters, Isis and Jackrabbit, created some amazing trail lore: they did most of their yo-yo hike barefoot.
(Photo by Jeff "Rabbit" Dishman)

life learning from trail lore. At some point, you should summon the courage to create some. I'm not saying that you have to do something as monumental as a barefoot yo-yo thru-hike. *But once you Plot Your Path, walk it.*

Learning from trail lore can help throughout your life. It can help you get into a good university, find your ideal job, make lucrative investments, attract your soul mate, and even avoid an untimely death. Clearly, it's a lesson that can be applied throughout life, not just in backpacking.

Conquer your fears by learning from trail lore

Even after Plotting Your Path, it's hard to summon the courage to walk it. However, one of the big benefits of learning from trail lore is that you learn to overcome your fears. Think about all the things you would do if you had no fear. Probably the number one thing you would do is pursue your passion. You might also skydive without a parachute, but I suppose that's when fearlessness becomes stupidity.

Many of us don't pursue our passions because we're afraid of the unknown. By learning from trail lore, the unknown becomes known. You shed light on the subjects that were dark and mysterious. By understanding the risks and how others overcame them, you will feel more confident taking risks. Your research will help you conquer your fears and let you do what you love. When you Plot Your Path based on trail lore you can walk boldly down that path. Fear paralyzes us and impedes us from squeezing the most out of life. Learning from trail lore will let you crush your fears and take intelligent risks.

 Take calculated risks. This is quite different from being rash. — George S. Patton, United States Army General

Although it's a lifelong dream for many, most don't hike the AT because of fear. Hundreds have told me, "I've always wanted to do that. Someday I will." I would see those who are in their sixties attempting it because they've postponed it all their lives—and those were the brave 60-year-olds. Most 60-year-olds are still not hiking it because of fear of injury, fear of not completing it, or fear of financial difficulties. Learning from trail lore teaches you that there are ways to minimize or eliminate all these fears so that you can complete your lifelong dreams today and not postpone them forever.

 I used to love [playing] all sports, but as I've gotten older I enjoy the outdoors more than anything. For this I thank my wife. I enjoy playing golf, especially with my father-in-law Roy. Most of all I enjoy my wife and dogs. To me, hiking the Appalachian Trail is our first step in starting a simpler life. I have always said that it is a shame to work every day for 65 years in hopes of a retirement when one can enjoy life. I want to do all that I can while I'm young enough and my health is still good. Our plans after the trail are to move back home to Wisconsin near our families, buy some land, and live together a bit simpler. I'm doing this hike for my best friend, my wife. The only time I am truly happy is when I'm with her.
— Zokwakii, AT Sobo 2002

It's now becoming clear how all the Principles that I learned on my odyssey interrelate. Following the Fourth Principle, like following the Second Principle, helps you follow the Third Principle. In other words, it's tough to pursue your passion (Third Principle) if you're financially handicapped, afraid, or not sure how to pursue it; thus, the Second and Fourth Principles show you how to live below your means and learn from others. Respecting these Principles lets you truly hike your own hike and enjoy life to the fullest. Although you can follow one of these Principles and ignore the others, you create a *virtuous cycle* when you follow all of them concurrently.

Common criticisms

I had plenty of time to question the Fourth Principle during the mild Mid-Atlantic States and come up with counterarguments. After all, that's part of questioning your assumptions!

I would have had to postpone such deep thinking had I decided to do the Four State Challenge. This macho challenge involves walking on four states in 24 hours. For a Sobo like myself that meant starting near the Pennsylvania border (1st state), plowing through

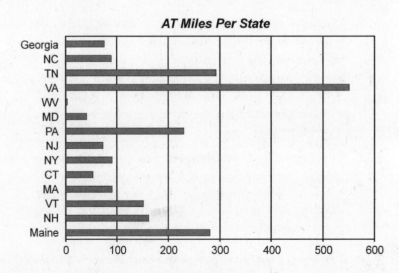

Source: Appalachian Trail Conservancy

33 miles of trail in Maryland (2nd state), blazing over the Potomac River and through Harper's Ferry in West Virginia (3rd state), so that I could cross the Virginia border (4th state). Total mileage: 43 miles.

Walking 43 miles in less than 24 hours is hard. The average thru-hiker walks two miles an hour when you factor in hills and occasional breaks. That means it would take almost 22 hours to hike 43 miles! Most don't want to take so much time, so they simply take fewer breaks to pick up the pace. Most Nobos start near the border of Virginia, leave before the sun rises, and finish around 3 a.m. At that point they enter the 5th state: a state of utter delirium.

This is the only part of the AT that you can pull off this testosterone inspired feat because it's the only place where two adjacent states total less than 43 miles. The next shortest side-by-side states on the AT are Massachusetts and Connecticut. Crossing those two states on the AT means walking 140 miles. You can't cover that much terrain on foot in less than 24 hours no matter how much caffeine you consume.

I didn't do the Four State Challenge for three reasons:

1. **The days were getting shorter, so that would have required more night hiking than the Nobos have to do when they attempt it.** Since they attempt it around June or July, they enjoy 18 hours of daylight; by the time we got there in September, we only had 13 hours of daylight. Night hiking is slower than day hiking.

2. **This trail had challenged me enough.** Some Nobos, on the other hand, are looking for a challenge to prepare them for the hardest part of the trail (New England), whereas the Sobos had already completed it.

3. **I felt sorry for poor Maryland and West Virginia.** These neglected states were a hazy memory for those attempting the Four State Challenge. So many

thru-hikers just blazed by these states without even giving them the honor of a campsite. I figured I'd pay attention to the fine state of Maryland and give it the respect it deserves by sleeping in the middle of it.

During my leisurely stroll through Maryland, I thought of the best criticisms I could muster against the Fourth Principle.

But you're discouraging risk taking!

The purpose of this chapter is not to discourage you from taking risks. The purpose is to demonstrate how learning from trail lore can help you achieve your goals in an efficient and pain-free manner. Life is about taking risks. If it's not clear yet, this book is about taking risks, for without taking risks you're wasting your life. As we saw in the last chapter, you must take some risks to hike with passion. Of course, we will all slip and fall at times in our lives; however, there are plenty of obstacles we can avoid if we just learn from those who have gone before us.

Some may argue that if you spend your life learning from trail lore you'll never do anything. After all, you can always study a bit more and suffer from *analysis paralysis*. That's where the Third Principle comes into play—it's a Principle about action, about hiking with passion.

However, recklessly hiking with passion is dangerous because that route is filled with heartache, disappointment, and regret. Of course, a few get lucky, but most don't. As a result, they get discouraged, and hit such economic hardship that they are forced to abandon their passion and get an unfulfilling job. So go ahead and take big risks, but just remember: *when you ignore trail lore, you increase the odds of failure; when you learn from it, you increase your odds of success.*

But ignorance is bliss!

Some successful people have said, "If I knew what it would take,

I probably would have never done it." In other words, had they learned from trail lore before pursuing their passion they might have never pursued their passion! They would have been paralyzed by fear.

This is a legitimate criticism, because it's true—a few people who have reached the top of their profession might not have pursued their profession if they really knew the odds and the challenges before them. However, for every person who fits that profile, there are far more who did research, had a plan, and executed. Although they probably had to alter their plan, they avoided many mistakes just in their initial planning process. A carefully researched plan, based on the lessons from trail lore, is better than no plan. Obviously, no one can plan perfectly; after all, how many people on their deathbed would tell you that their life turned out exactly like they thought it would? OK, maybe Nostradamus could have said so.

Although ignorance may be bliss, it does not help you improve your odds of success. On the contrary, ignorance hampers your decision making, and makes it more likely that you will fail. Look at the history of the successful individuals and ask yourself how many were ignorant about their area of expertise before they embarked in it. Surely some were, but most weren't. Go with the odds and don't be ignorant of trail lore.

But I'm unique!

Ralph Waldo Emerson said, "All life is an experiment." Similarly, you might think that since life is just one long experiment that there is something unique about your experiment, or that life is just a bunch of random events that you have no control of. Let's analyze this counterargument.

When I'm feeling pretty special, I like to remind myself: "Francis, you're unique. Just like everyone else."

If you had good parents, you probably were told that you are unique. It's a way to build self-esteem, and realize that you are important. This is good for kids (and adults too!). However, we take that logic to the next level when some of us believe that we're so special and unique that there's no point in learning from trail lore since we're so incredibly different from everyone who preceded us!

But that's rarely the case. Any student of history can show that both as a society and as individuals, we repeat history. For example, on a society level, as Paul Kennedy documented in his well researched book, *The Rise and Fall of Great Powers*, there are common ways that empires collapse. We Americans would like to think we're special and different from these other empires, but it's certain that at some point we will repeat the same errors of the empires before us and that our reign at the top will not last forever. Similarly, on an individual level, Stephen Covey and others have shown the common good habits that successful individuals share. I may be unique, but if I repeat those common habits, I will probably be successful. Nobody has written a "self-hamper" book about how to be loser, but I'm sure that there are Principles on how to do that. No matter how unique you are, if you follow those Principles you too can become a complete loser.

Although we believe we can beat the odds and break history's pattern, it rarely happens. We are unique, but the Principles that ensure our success do not change.

But I love spontaneity!

Some worry that if you always focus on learning from trail lore you'll never enjoy spontaneity. *The key is that there is a difference between being spontaneous about Major Trails versus Minor Trails.*

It's rare that there's an advantage of learning from trail lore before getting involved in a Minor Trail. For example, if a friend invites you to learn how to ski, there's no point in trying to figure out how the professionals learned. Enjoy the spontaneity of the event and break a leg like everyone else.

If, on the other hand, you hope to become a professional skier, then it's time to research trail lore and see how others got to the top of that profession. Therefore, the Fourth Principle doesn't kill spontaneity.

There are some free spirits who embark on long-term journeys on a whim. After all, many famous actors drove out to Hollywood hoping to hit the big time. The AT certainly has its share of such free spirits. Indeed, many of my friends and co-workers thought I was a free-spirit for just quitting my job to hike the AT. There is something romantic about just throwing caution to the wind and going off on an adventure, sight unseen. It's similar to getting married to someone you just met a week ago. That strategy rarely works, especially if you're marrying J-Lo.

However, the road of pursing your passion or any long-term objective is hard enough as it is—even with meticulous planning and research. The path of the AT didn't suddenly become easy just because I spent months researching it. Reading and planning didn't flatten any mountains or make the mosquitoes go away. It still was one hard and challenging trail! I just did not want to make it any harder than it needed to be.

Other hikers who chose to "wing it" nearly always fell short. They ended up repeating the same errors and suffering from the same frustrations as thousands of hopeful hikers ran into before them. Party House, the fellow we met at the beginning of this chapter who decided to hike the AT on a whim, never made it to Georgia.

In short, spontaneity is great for short term events, but for the few decisions that really matter, learn from trail lore.

But can't you overdo following this Principle?

Yes. If you scored extremely high on the Trail Lore Quiz earlier in this chapter, then you might be overly zealous in following this Principle. Those who meticulously plan every minutia of most of their lives need to relax.

For example, one Sobo from New Jersey named Paradise (after a Jack Kerouac character) had not only planned every food drop, but could predict exactly to the hour where he would be. "At 2 p.m. in September 22, I will be eating pasta with beans in Tennessee," Paradise assured me.

I met Paradise later on, and he had thrown his detailed plan into a campfire. He was hiking far faster than he had originally planned; by Pennsylvania he was already four days ahead of his schedule, throwing his timing completely off. Moreover, he quickly tired of the food he had painstakingly packed. So he bought new food along the way and left his pre-packed food behind. Eventually, he was so eager to see his girlfriend that he skipped hundreds of miles of trail so he could get to Georgia sooner. He certainly learned from trail lore before embarking on the AT, but probably overdid it.

Clearly, it's better to over-plan than under-plan. Most of us under-plan and fail to learn from trail lore before embarking on an endeavor; as a result, we fall short of squeezing the most out of life. However, if all your close friends accuse you of over-planning, then you probably need to relax a bit on your trail lore research. Be more spontaneous, especially on the little activities in life, and most activities are little.

Summary

We all make mistakes; however, only the great ones learn from them. Those who squeeze the most out of life learn from trail lore. They learn from both those who have done the right moves and the wrong ones. Most of those who successfully completed the AT had not just learned from the mistakes of those who were unable to complete it, but also had studied the common actions of those who did complete it. That combined knowledge gave them an inherent advantage over other hikers—it diminished their suffering, it increased their pleasure, and it let them enjoy the trail (and their lives) to the fullest. And they also knew where all the cool spots were off the trail.

Let's review the key points in this chapter:

- Humans are special because we can share a vast amount of knowledge and history between ourselves—we should leverage that ability.

- To squeeze the most out of life we must develop a strategy to avoid costly mistakes.

- To learn from trail lore, do not assume anything—have an open mind.

- Research multiple sources and periodically re-question your beliefs and conclusions.

- Use trail lore to Plot Your Path to your goal.

- Conquer your fears by following this Principle so you can create trail lore.

As we observed in the last chapter, our time on this planet is short and precious. Our conscious hours are less than we realize, and it's clear why life blazes by for most people. The worst part is that we have no idea when we are going to die. Nevertheless, many people live their lives assuming that they will get the average 80 years. Math says that half of us won't make it that far. Because we have so little time allotted to us, to truly optimize our life we must make every moment count. We should strive to minimize the number of painful and time-consuming errors that millions have done before us.

The more we learn from trail lore, the less likely we will repeat mistakes, and the more we will get out of life. Therefore, deeply research any important decision before you make it by surfing the Internet, talking with experts, and reading voraciously.

 I find television very educating. Every time somebody turns on the set, I go into the other room and read a book.
— Groucho Marx

Pennsylvania isn't as bad as I made it out to be. Yes, there were a lot of rocks, but I got used to them. In fact, Lisa loved Pennsylvania because the pastoral vistas of the Amish farms reminded her of growing up in the agricultural valley of Central California. She deeply inhaled the comforting smells of the freshly tilled earth. She felt at home.

And although it was hot, the oppressive summer heat wave was gone, and the diabolic trails of New Hampshire and Maine were literally a thousand miles away. Indeed, after we crossed the Susquehanna River and neared the southern end of Pennsylvania we reached the emotional halfway point of our odyssey.

We sat under the halfway marker that said we had hiked 1,069 miles. The marker is more symbolic than precise. Every year the AT evolves slightly, as sections are re-routed for a variety of reasons. In our year, for example, the true halfway point would have been 1,083 miles, but what's 14 miles between friends?

It had taken us two months to walk this far. The trek had already taught me four valuable lessons: I had learned that the purpose of life was to enjoy it; that I should live below my means; that I should pursue my passion; and that I should learn from history. I knew these lessons would stay with me for the rest of my days.

I wasn't sure what else I would learn during the second half of my pilgrimage. However, I couldn't imagine that the AT had finished teaching me her lessons. I rose eagerly in anticipation and continued hiking south.

Lisa pondering her next step on a rock filled trail near Lehigh Gap in Pennsylvania. Somehow we never twisted an ankle even after 200 miles of non-stop rocks.

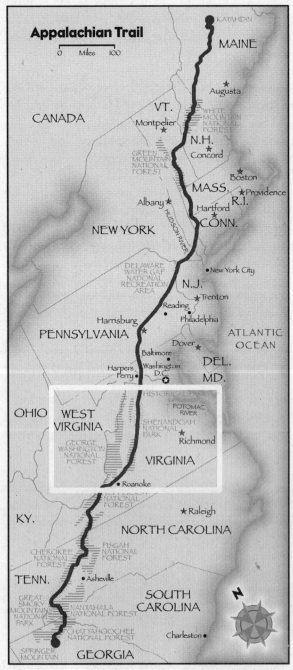

Appalachian Trail

0 — Miles — 100

KATAHDIN

MAINE

CANADA

Augusta ★

VT.

WHITE MOUNTAIN NATIONAL FOREST

Montpelier ★

N.H.

GREEN MOUNTAIN NATIONAL FOREST

Concord ★

Boston ★

MASS.

Providence ★

Albany ★

Hartford ★

R.I.

CONN.

NEW YORK

HUDSON RIVER

DELAWARE WATER GAP NATIONAL RECREATION AREA

New York City •

N.J.

Trenton ★

Reading •

Harrisburg

Philadelphia •

PENNSYLVANIA

★

ATLANTIC OCEAN

Baltimore •

Dover ★

Harpers Ferry

Washington D.C. ✪

DEL.

MD.

HISTORICAL PARK

OHIO

WEST VIRGINIA

POTOMAC RIVER

SHENANDOAH NATIONAL PARK

GEORGE WASHINGTON NATIONAL FOREST

Richmond ★

VIRGINIA

Roanoke •

KY.

NATIONAL FOREST

Raleigh ★

NORTH CAROLINA

PISGAH NATIONAL FOREST

CHEROKEE NATIONAL FOREST

TENN.

Asheville •

SOUTH CAROLINA

N

GREAT SMOKY MOUNTAINS NATIONAL PARK

NANTAHALA NATIONAL FOREST

CHATTAHOOCHEE NATIONAL FOREST

Charleston •

SPRINGER MOUNTAIN

GEORGIA

© Appalachian Trail Conservancy, reprinted with permission

Chapter 5:
Eat Well, Walk Hard, and Sleep Soundly

Near Roan Mountain in Virginia we came across a man whose belly stuck out enough to make me think he was pregnant. He boldly declared that he was a "thru-hiker" and that he had hiked to Virginia from Maine. Lisa gave him a most dubious look and while staring at his gut said, "Oh really?"

It's not that Lisa thought overweight people couldn't hike the trail; on the contrary, most people who hike the whole trail start off overweight. However, everyone gets thinner after walking 1,000 miles. No exceptions. Thru-hiking the trail is such an incredible weight loss program that after meeting hundreds of thru-hikers, we didn't see a single overweight one, no matter what the age. Every once in a while we would meet slim men who said that they had lost over 50 pounds.

This fellow we met in Virginia was clearly stretching the truth further than his tummy for we hadn't heard his name before, and when you thru-hike the AT you tend to know almost everyone ahead of you and behind you. You know nearly all the hikers behind you because you passed them. You know nearly everyone in front of you because every 10 miles there is a shelter along the AT with a journal; thru-hikers write notes in these journals. The notes range from the mundane to the poetic. As a result, usually a

few days before you catch up to someone you've been reading his or her notes in the journals. Once you spot the hiker (who usually looks disheveled and smells like he's carrying a skunk), you already know his name and something about him.

There are about 20,000 white blazes between Maine and Georgia to mark the AT. An AT thru-hiker follows them and is sometimes called a "white blazer." The AT is so well marked that we never carried a map!

Therefore, when we met this so-called thru-hiker in Virginia and didn't recognize his name, we knew he probably wasn't a true thru-hiker. His waist size only confirmed the suspicion. After some cajoling, he finally admitted he had hitchhiked most of the way down.

He's someone thru-hikers call a "yellow blazer." To complete the AT you have to follow white blazes until you get to the end—thru-hikers are called *white blazers*. Trails connected to the AT, but not part of it, are marked with blue blazes. Sometimes AT hikers follow blue blazes for less than a mile to get to a shelter. When I got lost on the AT, I accidentally took a blue blaze trail, thereby becoming, for a moment, a *blue blazer*. Finally, for those who don't like walking, they can get in a car and follow the yellow blazes on the road (the painted yellow rectangles that divide the roads). Such *yellow blazers* are also known as cheaters. If you do enough of it, and you eat like a thru-hiker, you'll probably develop a nice belly to confirm it.

Six out of seven of the Principles I learned during my trek have to do with the mind, whereas only one has to do with the body. It reminds me of what Yogi Berra said about baseball:

Baseball is 90 percent mental, the other half is physical.
— Yogi Berra

This chapter is about taking care of your body. For how can you really squeeze the most out of life if you are so unhealthy that you are abnormally prone to diseases and are unable to do physical tasks you should otherwise be able to do? This chapter explores the brain-body connection and how improving your health can lift your spirits. It shows how the AT revealed the practical steps one should take to follow this Principle.

The soul follows its own laws, and the body likewise follows its own laws... they are all representations of one and the same universe. — Gottfried Leibniz (1646-1716)

Health quiz

Let's see how healthy you are by taking this simple quiz:

1. In a typical 10 day period, how many days do you get at least 30 minutes of rigorous cardiovascular exercise?

2. Over 10 days, how many days do you do stretching exercises for at least 10 minutes per day?

3. Over 10 days, how many 30 minute periods of weightlifting do you have? (For example, if you lift weights every other day for one hour, then give yourself 10 points. If you lift weights every other day for 30 minutes, then give yourself five points.)

4. On a 1-10 scale, how much of your diet consists of fruits and vegetables? (1 = "What's a fruit and vege-table?", 5 = "I eat a little bit every day, as a side dish", 10 = "I eat mostly fruits and vegetables and spend a lot of time on the toilet as a result.")

5. On a 1-10 scale, how often do you have days where you are extremely tired and/or stressed out? (1 = "I am a basket case", 5 = "About half my days are like that", 10 = "Zen Buddhists come to me for advice.")

6. On a 1-10 scale, how much do you smoke? (1 = a pack or more a day, 5 = a couple of cigarettes a day, 10 = never)

7. On a 1-10 scale, how often do you drink alcohol? (1 = "It's better than orange juice in the morning"; 5 = "I usually have a drink with a meal, especially at din-ner"; 10 = "I'm always the designated driver because I never drink.")

8. How many eight ounce glasses of water do you drink a day?

9. How close to bedtime do you eat? (1 = "I eat in bed as I drift into unconsciousness"; 5 = "I usually eat a good sized meal two hours before bedtime"; 10 = "I avoid eating anything four hours before I doze off.")

10. On a 1-10 scale, do you do any illegal drugs (pot, cocaine, speed, ecstasy, etc.)? (1 = "My buddies call me 'Scarface'"; 5 = "I take a hit about once a month"; 10 = "Once again, I'm the designated driver.")

Scoring: If you scored over 80, then you're doing great. If scored between 50 and 80, then you could improve some habits, and this chapter will show you how. If you scored under 50, then not reading this chapter could be hazardous to your health.

The Ultimate Prescription

I can neatly sum up my activities for my 111 days on the AT: wake up, eat a nutritious meal, walk, eat some more healthy food, walk some more, sleep. OK, so there was a bit more eating in there (and it wasn't always healthy), but that was the basic pattern. Life was extraordinarily simple. Just eat, walk, and sleep. It's this simple way of life that taught us how to get the most out of our bodies.

I read thousands of pages of medical studies and reports to try to understand the causes for the myriad of physical aliments that afflict the human body. The more reports I read, the more I detected a distinct pattern. Over and over again doctors and researchers seem to bang on the same drum. There is one preventative solution that solves or prevents over 90 percent of the aliments out there. Simply put, the Ultimate Prescription is:

○ Eat healthily.

○ Exercise regularly.

○ Don't overstress yourself.

Indeed, you don't have to read thousands of reports to figure this out. Even just a few reports will already bear this pattern out. It makes me so happy that all researchers agree on this! Can you imagine if you needed to exercise and eat well to prevent heart disease, but you had to do zero exercise and eat milk chocolate bars to prevent cancer? Talk about a conflicting signals! In that case I would do my best to help my body fight cancer.

Thru-hikers follow this Ultimate Prescription to help them complete their odyssey. You can also follow these steps to live a long and healthy life. But like following the rest of these Principles, it's easier said than done; otherwise, most of us would be quite healthy. This chapter will focus on practical ways you can follow this Principle so you can squeeze the most out of your body so that it operates at its peak performance. We'll start by looking at how we can eat healthily, then we will examine how to exercise and lower your stress.

Eat well

The USDA has tracked our fat intake from 1968 to today and found that it dropped from 40 to 33 percent. So why are we getting fatter? The USDA noted that in 1968 the average American consumed 1,989 calories, but today we consume 10 percent more—2,153

Hanging onto McAfee's Knob in Virginia. It's not a good place to be on a rainy day because you could slip and it's a long way down.

calories.[14] But that's only half the story. The other half is that we are exercising less than before. So when you combine an increase in calorie intake with a decrease in calorie expenditure, you get an expanding waistline.

Many may say "I'd rather be fat and happy than not eat what I want and live the life I want." Yet consider these facts:[15]

- By 2010, 40 percent of America will be obese (overweight by more than 30 pounds).

- 16 percent of children are overweight and another 16 percent are at risk of becoming so.

- Obesity causes about 300,000 deaths a year.

- Obese non-smokers live seven years less than average, obese smokers live 13.5 years less than average.

- Obese folks earn up to 6.1 percent less than average.

- Obesity leads to osteoarthritis, diabetes, heart disease, and cancer.

Percentage of Americans Who Are Obese

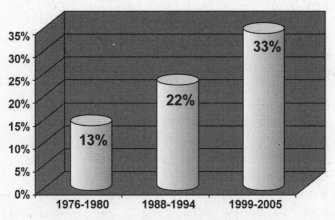

Source: US National Health Examination Survey, CDC

Those who do not take care of their bodies believe they are enjoying themselves by eating what they want and being sedentary. And they are willing to trade off life span for quality of life. After all, who wants to live to 120 if you have to eat raw broccoli all day?

But as the above facts illustrate, the quality of life of an obese person is lower than a normal person. Suffering from diseases and struggling to do everyday physical tasks can put an unnecessary damper on your happiness. Also, by not exercising you're missing out on all the free endorphins your body produces! Who can turn down free drugs?

Weight loss is all about calories

On a bright sunny morning sitting on the impressive overlook at Dragon's Tooth near McAfee's Knob in Virginia I thought of a brilliant way to put Weight Watchers out of business. It's called Club Pilgrim, where you can eat all you want, no restrictions, and you are still guaranteed to lose weight! In fact, you will end up at or below your recommended body fat level. What's the catch? Just walk over 2,000 miles in six months or less.

OK, maybe it wouldn't sell.

However, consider the master's thesis of thru-hiker Karen Lutz. Her 1982 study of hiker nutrition found that *thru-hikers simply cannot carry as much food as they burn*—some 4,000 to 6,000 calories per day. No wonder Club Pilgrim is such an effective weight-loss plan. It's like making someone run marathons, but not letting them stock up their fridge.

The amount of weight hikers lose varies drastically, but they almost all reach their optimal weight. The average thru-hiker loses 23 pounds in body weight and secretes more than 400 liters of sweat. A thru-hiker will generally expend about 400,000 calories and consume 450 liters of water. According to Roland Mueser, a thru-hiker and Harvard trained physicist who researched this issue, heavier hikers tend to lose both more weight and a greater percentage of their body weight than thinner hikers. Another finding: women lose less weight than men, possibly because they build more muscle on the trail relative to men, but also because their bodies retain more fat than men. Sorry ladies. Finally, the constant calorie deficit can cause problems for thru-hikers who were at their ideal weight or underweight to start. They may experience excessive weight loss, loss of muscle mass, and malnutrition.[16] The fascinating lesson is that all thru-hikers attain their optimal weight regardless of what they eat. How many diets can claim that? Finally, there's a diet that's even more decadent than the Atkins Diet!

Thru-hikers eat amazing quantities of food. One day in Vermont we heard about the Blue Ben, a diner in Bennington that serves some legendary breakfasts. We realized that if we maintained our normal pace, we would get to Bennington in the afternoon. However, we wanted to eat breakfast around 9 a.m., so we decided to go for our first 30-mile day. We just barely made it before dark, and we slept way above the trees in a fire tower that night.

PB&J

In southern Pennsylvania we bought a loaf of whole wheat bread, peanut butter, and jelly (or PB&J).

We had eaten a big breakfast, but after two hours of hiking we were lethargic. Although it was warm, we couldn't blame the weather— we had walked through hotter conditions without impact.

Suspecting our bodies simply needed more fuel, we plopped on a rock at 8 a.m. to have a "snack." Lisa made each of us a PB&J sandwich. Overflowing with jelly, it was delicious. So we each had another. Then another. Then yet another.

Before we knew it, we had no more bread. We had swallowed the whole loaf!

We were disappointed that we devoured the food that was supposed to last us through two or three pit stops. We giggled at how easily we could eat endless quantities of food. Eventually, we nibbled on the bread crumbs at the bottom of the plastic bag, licked our peanut butter coated fingers, and energetically set off to hike 23 miles.

The Half-Gallon Challenge

If there were ever any doubt at how easily thru-hikers can consume all they want, there's the "Half Gallon Challenge."

Just north of the halfway point on the trail, the Pine Grove Furnace General Store in Pennsylvania challenges hikers to finish a half gallon of ice cream in one sitting. Although you have to pay $5 for the privilege and you don't get any reward for succeeding except for a silly wooden spoon, many hikers do it just to say they did it.

Although the older hikers do better than the younger ones, one young guy ate *two* half-gallons of chocolate ice cream. He didn't feel so good afterwards.

One half-gallon of chocolate or vanilla contains 2,246 calories. But chocolate has *only* 128 grams of fat versus vanilla's 144 grams. Finally, Moosetracks delivers the biggest punch: 3,520 calories and a colossal 240 grams of fat.

The owner told me that most hikers choose a flavor they don't like because "they know once they do the challenge, they will never eat it again."

The record is nine minutes. The thru-hiker was 66 years old. He was raised in an orphanage and knew how to eat. After polishing it off, he returned to the store to inhale a cheeseburger and a bag of potato chips.

We walked into the Blue Ben around 10 a.m. after walking 10 miles that morning and our eyes widened as our nostrils took in the mouth-watering aromas around us. We ordered two entrees each. The spread included three huge butter topped pancakes dripping with maple syrup, an enormous cheese filled veggie omelet, a generous serving of golden hash browns, two pieces of whole wheat toast, a colossal veggie burger packed with lettuce, tomatoes and a hefty side order of curly fries. Sadly, when we walked out we were still hungry, so we bought a pint of rich chocolate ice cream and devoured it while sitting on the sidewalk. Incredibly, we didn't even feel stuffed. We had simply satisfied our hunger. Three hours later, we would be eating again.

We continued this gluttony for 111 days and managed to lose weight in the process. How is this possible? Contrary to popular belief, we didn't have a tapeworm in our systems.

Instead, the lesson of the AT is simple math: we lost weight because we expended more calories than we took in. It's the secret to weight loss that we can apply to our every day lives.

She got her good looks from her father. He's a plastic surgeon. — Groucho Marx

We've come full circle with diets. A few decades ago, Americans were counting calories to lose weight. Then the diet gurus declared that only fat mattered: eat low-fat foods and you'll lose weight! Next came diet fads that included the Atkins diet (fat is OK, carbohydrates are bad; protein is in, carbs are out) and the sugar-busters diet. Finally today dieticians are returning to the wisdom of long ago—*when it comes to weight loss, calories are everything.*

According to the USDA, we've made minor adjustments to the percentage of our calories from carbohydrates, protein, and fat; however, the most telling statistic is that the total number of calories we eat is higher than ever.[17] It's simple: Americans are getting fatter because we're eating more calories. According to *The Wall Street Journal* women are consuming nine percent more calories than women 20 years ago, while men are wolfing down 13 percent more. This correlates well with the food produced in the US—it's gone up by equal proportion.[18] Combine that with less exercise than ever and it becomes clear why Americans are the fattest people on Earth.

Therefore, if you are looking to lose weight, the secret is so simple: you just want to burn more calories than you take in. That's it. It's nothing fancy. The USDA recommends that moderately active women consume 1,700 calories a day (men need about 2,100). That's good to know, but what's equally important is how many calories you burn. For example, if you consume 2,500 calories a day and expend 3,000 calories, you will lose weight—guaranteed! The same goes if

Learning from the Trees

As far as teachers go, trees are pretty boring. They only move around when the wind is blowing hard, they wear the same outfit everyday, and they don't speak English.

Yet they somehow manage to teach something to those who have a lot of time on their hands—like thru-hikers.

For example, I wondered why some trees are so much bigger and healthier than others of the same species. Answer: good nutrition. The healthiest trees grow in nutrient rich soil, have just the right amount of water and sun, and are hidden from the lumberjacks.

Although a tree can't control its access to nutrition, we can. We choose what we put in our bodies. Therefore, if you want a sharp mind and a strong healthy body that fends off diseases and illnesses, then learn from the trees and feed your body well. Also, avoid running into chainsaws.

you consume 3,500 calories and burn through 4,000 everyday. It doesn't matter: you're in a caloric deficit situation and your body will react in the same way—it will burn off the fat first, and then it will burn off the muscle, and then, unless you change your ways, you will die. *It's not rocket science, although diet pushers make losing weight sound extraordinarily complicated.* The trick is to hit a caloric equilibrium once you've burned off the excess fat.

Hence, the solution to weight loss is amazingly straightforward. Just gauge the amount of calories you burn everyday and make sure you consume fewer calories than that. If you want to consume more food, then just make sure you exercise more.

The single most important issue in nutrition right now is gaining weight, and that's a matter of calories. It doesn't matter if they're healthy calories or unhealthy calories—calories are calories. — Maria Nestle, chairwoman of the department of nutrition and food studies at New York University

Healthy eating is all about fruits and vegetables

I won the food lottery in Hot Springs, North Carolina. We stayed at Elmer's, a famous AT hostel, where the fine cuisine is legendary even among the not-so-picky pilgrims. While I was relaxing in Elmer's back porch admiring the brilliant autumn leaves, I spotted a tattered package lying in a corner. I picked it up and noticed that it was addressed to a thru-hiker and had a shipping date of May 22. It was early October, so this package had been around for a few months. We called the sender to see what he wanted to do with the package. The man said that his son had started the AT in Georgia, but was unable to hike more than 100 miles. He was grateful we called and added, "Feel free to open the package and take whatever's inside. It's just food. No need to send it back."

We hung up the phone and, being hungry thru-hikers, we ravenously attacked the package like a vulture attacks a carcass.

Jackpot.

Out of the package poured Snickers bars, Twix bars, Three Musketeers, Pop Tarts, and other sinful treats. It felt like Halloween. We scored big time! I'd never seen Lisa with a wider smile on her face.

Although we were ecstatic, we were somehow disciplined enough to take several days to consume all the goodies. We were not used to eating so much junk food, so we savored each Snickers bar like it was fine French cuisine.

However, once we left Elmer's behind, I began to wonder why that kid never made it to Hot Springs. Could I learn anything from his experience? Up until that point I figured that a calorie was just a calorie. Although we usually ate healthy calories, I always wondered if that was really necessary. After all, everyone who hiked the AT lost weight, regardless of the type of calories they consumed. The kid's father had just told me that his son had "burnt out." Although that burn out might have been purely mental, could feeding himself that junk food diet contributed to his weakness? Is there a brain-body connection? After hiking 2,168 miles and seeing others trying to do the same, it's hard not to see the brain-body connection. It also became clear that not all calories were created equal.

Eating more calories than you need is unhealthy, but so is eating the wrong kind of calories. In fact, four of the top 10 causes of death in the United States—heart disease, cancer, stroke, and diabetes—are associated with diets that are too high in calories, total fat, saturated fat, cholesterol, or too low in dietary fiber.[19] Diet-related health conditions cost society an estimated $250 billion annually in medical costs and lost productivity. In addition, new research suggests

Lisa is showing off her wide smile when we found an abandoned care package full of goodies at Elmer's Hostel in Hot Springs, North Carolina. The sinful sweets made Lisa bubbly!

that low intake of folic acid—found in many fruits, vegetables, and legumes, as well as in fortified cereals—may increase the risk for heart disease and stroke in adults.[20] *The key to healthy weight loss, therefore, is to cut calories, but not nutrition.*

Although those who attempt to thru-hike the AT can get away with eating anything, those who actually completed it generally watched their nutrition as well as their calories. We needed lots of vitamins, minerals, and protein. They are the basic building blocks that are bodies require to reconstruct themselves each night and prepare for another 25 mile day.

However, we also needed basic fuel which came in the form of complex carbohydrates and fats. Probably 70% of our calories came from carbohydrates. However, we were cautious not to claim that Twix was nutritious just because it supplied carbohydrates and fat. Instead, we favored high calorie complex carbohydrate food that was also highly nutritious in vitamins, minerals, fiber, and protein. Since we could only carry so much food on our back, we couldn't afford to carry empty calories. Every calorie we carried had to supply us with healthy nutrition. If it didn't, it was costing us calories to carry it and was an unnecessary burden. Hence, while chocolate Mars bars were a good reward for a hard day's work, we didn't want to live off them. Carrying a bunch of them would weigh us down with empty calories; albeit really tasty empty calories.

Calorie for calorie, nothing provides as much nutrition as fruits and vegetables. The ratio of nutrients per calorie is far higher than any other food group. You don't need to be a doctor to figure out that 1,000 calories gotten from fruits and vegetables is incredibly more nutritious than 1,000 calories gotten from white bread, pork, and chocolate mouse cake.

Although normal people can eat 1,000 calories from mostly fruits and vegetables, it was nearly impossible for thru-hikers to do that because carrying all that produce would weigh too much. Besides, 1,000 calories was a snack. We needed at least 5,000 calories per day and we wanted it packed in the lightest weight possible. For example, I carried about four days of food for both Lisa and I. That meant carrying almost 50,000 calories on my back, not to mention the other gear. I had a veritable grocery store on my shoulders!

Pound for pound, few foods packed calories like pasta. It was a lot easier to carry 50,000 calories in the form of pasta than in the form of apples and salad. With pasta, my 50,000 calorie pack never weighed more than 30 pounds, and on a typical day it only weighed about 15 pounds even with all my gear (see Appendix 2). Had I carried the 50,000 calories in the form of oranges and lettuce, I would have had to carry over 300 heads of lettuce and 400 oranges!

Although pasta let me carry lots of calories in a small package, not all pastas are created equal. The traditional refined pasta that most people buy in stores lacks nutrition. Even though it packs in the calories via carbohydrates, we also needed protein, fiber, vitamins, and minerals. Learning from trail lore, we discovered that corn pasta offered high calories and high nutrition in a relatively lightweight package. Whole wheat pasta and spinach pasta also works. Sunridge Farms, another sponsor of our trek, donated several boxes of healthy pasta. We tossed in some dehydrated beans and some vegetable broth flavoring, and *voila*, we had a yummy 5,000 calorie soup that we could share.

Fortunately, when we're in the real world we don't have to worry about how many calories we can carry on our backs. Our cars can carry lots of calories, we don't have to empty the entire car in one trip, and (unlike thru-hikers) we don't have to lug the bags over 80 miles.

Therefore, since most people only need about 2,000 calories a day, focus on getting a high percentage of those calories from fruits and vegetables, *especially if you are trying to lose weight*. The rest of the calories can come from whole grains, beans, nuts, fish, chicken, and other nutritious foods. If you are a healthy weight or you do a lot of exercise, then you may need more low-fat complex carbohydrate rich foods.

Thru-hikers love high fat foods, but normal people shouldn't.

How Much Protein Do You Need?

Not as much as you might think.

Most Americans overemphasize the importance of protein; studies show that we don't need that much, unless you're entering a body building competition or running for Governor of California.

If you always exercise rigorously, the easy rule of thumb is for every kilogram you weigh, you should consume one gram's worth of protein a day. For example, if you weigh 68 kilograms, then you should eat 68 grams of protein a day. One kilogram equals 2.2 pounds.

Those Americans too lazy to do the conversion can just take their weight in pounds and divide it in half to get a bit more than their recommended intake. For instance, if you weigh 150 pounds, you don't need more than 75 grams of protein per day. If you're only moderately active, you can have 20 percent less than that.

Another way of looking at it: the US Recommended Daily Allowance of protein is 10 percent of your calories. The United Nation's World Health Organization recommends 10 to 15 percent of your calories should come from protein. So if you eat 2,000 calories a day about 200 of those calories should come from protein, which is easy to do.

Lastly, some obsess about not getting a *complete* protein. A complete protein contains the eight amino acids your body needs. Although all animal proteins are complete, they come with the baggage of saturated fat. Soybeans (and soy products) are the only plant that delivers a complete protein. Other plant proteins are incomplete but by combining them (not necessarily in one meal), you can get complete proteins that have more vitamins and minerals and less saturated fat than you get from most animal proteins.

(Sources: Food and Nutrition Board, Recommended Daily Allowances, *Washington DC: National Academy of Sciences, n.d., and numerous WHO publications. Regen Dennis, "Proteins Are Pro-teens," Seattle Post-Intelligencer, Feb 1, 2005, p. D4.)*

The East Coast had plenty of wild berries to supplement our diet. Lisa was picking them in the spectacular Grayson Highlands in Virginia. Free food was our biggest distraction on the trail.

What makes you feel full? Basically, the heavier the food, the more full you will feel. For example, you will feel fuller if you eat a one pound of spinach than if you eat just a quarter pound of pasta. If you don't believe me, I challenge you to try it, or just ask Popeye.

The reason thru-hikers love fatty food is that it has over twice the calories as a non-fat option that weighs the same. One gram of carbohydrates has four calories. One gram of fat has nine calories. *Do the math: eating a pound of fat fills up your stomach about as much as one pound of carbohydrates, but it delivers more than twice the calories.* Therefore, if your diet is mostly fat, then you can eat twice as much food if you focus on carbohydrates instead. Or you can eat half as much and feel equally full. Bottom line: thru-hikers love fat for a reason—it delivers high calories in a relatively light package. Thru-hikers could get away with it, because they're burning so many calories, but let's face it, most of us don't burn calories like thru-hikers.

To get calories on the trail, sometimes I was tempted to just eat a stick of butter. However, like most high fat foods, butter has few healthy nutrients. Moreover, saturated fats and trans-fats are extremely unhealthy and we should minimize their intake. Monosaturated and essential fatty acids are generally good for you, but we don't need heavy doses to get the nutritional benefits. Eating more fats than we need just means we're eating far more calories than we need. And the more calories we take in, the more we need to burn to stay at a healthy weight. And that means more time on the treadmill.

Being a vegetarian

Although I am not a hyper-strict vegetarian, I nearly always eat like one. I always order a vegetarian option at a restaurant, and I only buy vegetarian food at a grocery store. The only times I make an exception is if I am traveling (I enjoy trying the local cuisine) or I am someone's guest (I don't want to insult the host). I practice these habits because I love animals, and I want to minimize my contribution to the harsh living conditions that most of them face. Also, raising livestock is far more resource intensive than harvesting plants. Lastly, as one person put it, "I'm vegetarian because I hate plants."

 Nothing will benefit human health and increase the chances for survival of life on Earth as much as the evolution to a vegetarian diet. — Albert Einstein

If you choose to become a vegetarian, just make sure you take the following:

- **Vitamin B12:** It is difficult for vegetarians (and especially vegans) to get enough of this critical vitamin; therefore, supplements are the best bet.

- **Omega 3:** It is hard to get enough of this essential fatty acid in by eating a plant-based diet. Although some health food stores carry cereals that have flax seed (which is packed with Omega 3), some may just want to get their Omega 3s via a flax seed supplement, which comes in pill or liquid form.

- **Protein:** If you pay attention to what you eat, it's easy to get plenty of protein as a vegetarian by eating nuts, broccoli, beans, and soy meat substitutes. But for those who do a lot of exercise (especially weight lifters) consider protein powder supplements. Even meat eaters consume protein powder.

○ **Calcium:** Since many plants have plenty of calcium and enriched soy milk has just as much calcium as cow's milk, it's probably not necessary to take a calcium supplement. However, women might consider taking a 500 mg pill everyday.

For vegetarians, the Omega 3s and Vitamin B12 are the two most important supplements, because it's hard to get those nutrients on a strict vegetarian diet. It's not that hard for vegetarians to get enough protein and calcium—as long as they watch what they eat.

Don't Vegetarians Lack Energy?

I'll make you a deal. Come walk the Continental Divide Trail with me. At 3,100 miles, it's a whopping 1,000 miles longer than the AT. You can eat whatever you want, and I'll eat a vegetarian diet. Let's see who makes it.

Most people take 180 days to thru-hike the AT. We took 111 days on our vegetarian diet.

But we're not superstars. Here are just a few of the many superstar vegetarians athletes:

✓ Martina Navratilova, champion tennis player

✓ Desmond Howard, pro football player & Heisman trophy winner

✓ Bill Pearl, four-time Mr. Universe

✓ Paavo Nurmi, long distance runner, nine Olympic medals and 20 world records

Eating vegetarian food gives you plenty of energy. If you lack energy, you usually lack calories and/or sleep.

(*Source: John Robbins,* The Food Revolution, *Red Wheel/Weiser, June 2001, p. 78*)

The flip side of being a vegetarian is that you never have to worry about getting all the other nutrients that the classic meat and potato eaters usually lack. Those who focus on eating mostly fruits and vegetables will get loads of antioxidants (e.g., vitamins A, C, and E). Those who eat the dark leafy greens will get plenty of folic acid, iron, and tons of other vitamins and minerals. These nutrients ward off cancer and other diseases that will ruin your day.

Should you become a vegetarian?

I highly recommend eating most (if not all) of your calories like a vegetarian or a vegan. However, you can be perfectly healthy without being a strict vegetarian. For example, despite my vegetarian tendencies, I recognize that fish is healthy and nutritious. I just don't eat fish because I like these marvelous creatures, and in particular I dislike the conditions that farmed fish are raised in. I also worry that we are over-fishing our waters and that there's

---

Veggie Diet Equals Medicine

Researchers compared individuals who follow a low-fat vegetarian diet versus those who take statins, a cholesterol lowering drug.

The fiber and soy rich diet lowered total and "bad" cholesterol about as much as the expensive drugs. In just one month the average cholesterol plummeted 28.6 percent, compared with 30.9 percent for the statin drug.

They were also monitoring a third group which ate a low fat diet but without the soy and fiber emphasis. Their cholesterol only dropped 8 percent.

We blow a lot of bucks on medicines when cheap and easy solutions are available to anyone who watches what they eat.

Someday I hope they do a study on how much cholesterol drops for thru-hikers.

(Source: Thomas M. Burton, "Strict Diet May Cut Need for Statins," The Wall Street Journal, July 23, 2003, p. D7.)

high mercury content in many fish. However, if those things don't bother you, then you can make fish a key part of your diet. Fish is generally healthier than chicken, pork, lamb, and beef. Fish is usually low in saturated fat and high in good fat, such as essential fatty acids (e.g., omega 3). Fish also has nearly as much protein as meat, without the saturated fat and triglycerides. Just favor wild fish over farmed fish, because wild fish are more nutritious than the farmed ones. And at least those fishermen have to make a bit more of an effort to catch the squirrelly little devils.

If you can't imagine life without meat or poultry, then at least consider making them a side dish to the main course, which should be plant based. Plant based doesn't mean just wimpy salads and fruits; it includes the filling stuff like brown rice and whole wheat pasta. A lot of people think that you can't get full by being a vegetarian; for those skeptics, I invite you to a try a bowl of our Thru-Hiker Special. With 5,000 calories in a bowl, I bet you can't finish it.

Furthermore, it's easier than ever to become a vegetarian. Many regular grocery stores are now stocking meat substitutes. The knee jerk reaction of most meat lovers to a soy based sausage or tofu burger is to run to a farm and slaughter a cow. I understand. Most of the early versions of such foods were pretty bad. And yes, today a few of the meat alternatives still suck; however, most are surprisingly good. Try them. Moreover, they're loaded with protein while avoiding most the saturated fats of real meat.

The Thru-Hiker's #1 Obsession

Thru-hikers spend most of their day thinking about one thing: food.

More specifically, they focus on any kind of food that is not in their packs, and they could never carry. Ice cream is a classic obsession, but so are burgers, pizza, and hot dogs.

Surprisingly, many thru-hikers also fantasize about salads and fresh fruit, because these are also hard to carry into the wilderness.

Lastly, beware of the unhealthy vegetarian diet. Although most vegetarians have a healthy weight, sometimes I meet vegetarians who are overweight. Frequently these vegetarians eat a lot of high calorie foods, such as ice cream, cheese, and cookies; they may also be the same ones who douse their salads with high calorie dressings. Sure, they're vegetarians, but they're eating just as many calories as the guy who eats Big Macs and fries twice a day. Being a vegetarian doesn't automatically make you a healthy eater; it just means that your friends will think you're healthy.

Three dietary mistakes Americans make

Shenandoah National Park in Virginia is one of the three National Parks that the AT cuts across. It was my least favorite (the Whites and the Smokies were better). Perhaps the biggest disappointment is that the AT closely parallels the Blue Ridge Highway which also

What Americans Eat

A survey of 4,760 Americans found that fruits and vegetables make up a paltry 10 percent of the caloric intake.

Meanwhile, almost one third of our calories come from junk foods. Sugary foods, soft drinks, and alcoholic beverages account for nearly 25 percent of all calories consumed each day. Five percent of total calories eaten daily include salty snacks and fruit-flavored drinks.

The largest source of calories was regular soft drinks, making up 7.1 percent of the American daily caloric intake. Those surveyed consumed sweets and desserts more than any other type of food, followed by hamburgers, pizza, and potato chips. Cheese, beer, and French fries were also high on the list.

A thru-hiker would salivate just hearing all those sinful treats. Lisa would tell me to shut up if I said the words "grilled cheese sandwich" too often.

(Source: Block G, et al. "Foods contributing to energy intake in the US: data from NHANES III and NHANES 1999-2000," Journal of Food Chemistry and Analysis June 2004. 17:439-447)

cuts across the National Park. Therefore, for about 100 miles, the highway and the AT are within half a mile of each other—you don't exactly feel like you're in the wilderness.

However, I am grateful for all the human interaction. There were a couple of cafes and I would see people eating at picnic tables. After observing my fellow forest lovers eat throughout the park, I realized that Americans make three dietary mistakes: (1) the ratio of vegetables and fruits to other food groups is backwards; (2) we eat most of our daily calories in one or two meals; and (3) our timing of when we eat our calories is way off.

Mistake #1: Vegetables to non-vegetables ratio is backwards

If you look at the typical American meal, you'll see that meat or poultry dominates the main plate. Meanwhile, there's a tiny little side dish of salad or vegetables that we quickly ignore. Fruits usually don't even factor into the equation. This is completely backwards.

We should start most our dinners with a nice plate of fruit, preferably 20 minutes before the meal to pave the way for the rest of the food to come. Our main course should be a big (but lightly dressed) salad, a variety of vegetables, and perhaps a slice of some

---

Minimize the Salt

We didn't carry salt with us on the AT, so when I returned to civilization I wondered if I could continue living without it.

Americans get heavy doses of salt because we eat a lot of processed food. Also, restaurants use salt liberally. Even if you got rid of your salt shaker, you'd probably still get more salt than you need. Some studies show that the more salt you consume, the more you increase your blood pressure.

Therefore, instead of using salt, try herbs, spices, lemon juice, garlic, or mustard. Use fresh celery, onion, and carrot instead of stock cubes. Make gradual changes to allow your taste buds to adjust. It's just like going from whole milk to nonfat milk.

toasted whole wheat bread. Finally, there should be a side dish, or a small third course, with meat, fish, poultry, pasta, brown rice, or beans. By the time we get to this final course, we won't mind that it's so small because we'd probably be full from all the fruits and vegetables we ate. If we all made this simple change, our medical bills would plummet as fast as our waistlines.

The beauty of this method is that we front-load all our calories with the nutritious food. If we're starving, we'll eat a lot and finish off that first and second course, and maybe even go for seconds before we get to the final plate. It's healthy because we guarantee getting plenty of nutrition with every meal.

Americans make dietary errors, but so do the Europeans. The French, for example, eat their salad after the meal. It's easy to not finish off the salad when you're stuffed with lamb, potatoes, and

Here's the real reason most people go northbound on the AT. The best time to squeeze through this narrow gap in Maine's Mahoosuc Notch is after you've walked 2,000 miles and you've lost all your body fat. Sobos get here after only walking 150 miles, so it's a tighter squeeze. I had to take off my backpack to squish through.

bread. By the time the French get to the salad, they are full and will probably skip it. Although I went to a French school for 12 years and have a French father, I recognize their unhealthy food order. Meanwhile, the British are notorious for boiling their vegetables to death, although Americans inherited this silly practice too. I guess that foolish concept came along with the idea of not using the metric system.

Vegetables lose over half their nutrients when they're cooked. Ideally, you should eat your veggies and fruit raw. If you hate eating them raw, then eat them as close to raw as you can stand. The more you cook veggies and fruits, the more nutrients go into the air and not in your body. As a result, you'd have to eat twice as many veggies to get the same nutrition, and that might be even more torture for some veggie haters than eating the stuff raw.

In conclusion, focus on eating tons of fruits and vegetables in your every day life, particularly if you're aiming to lose weight. They will deliver the nutrition that really matters—fiber, vitamins, and minerals. Serve them on the big plates, and save the small (so-called "salad plates") for the food you used to eat on the big plates. Sprinkle your meals with complex carbohydrates (whole grains, spinach pasta, etc.) and protein (nuts, beans, soy products, egg whites, protein powder, poultry, and fish). Finally, minimize saturated fat from your diet—what little fat you consume should come from mono-saturated fats, such as olive oil and avocado or essential fatty acids, such as omega 3s from salmon or flax seeds. By tilting the balance towards vegetables and fruits, you will begin to eat healthily and your body will function better than ever. The only price is that you may have to buy more toilet paper than before.

Mistake #2: We eat most of our daily calories in two meals

Most Americans consume just two meals a day—lunch and dinner. That's where we get about 85 percent of our calories. On the AT, we learned that such a calorie per meal ratio doesn't work. Processing a lot of food in one sitting is incredibly taxing on the human body. That's why many people go into a food coma after lunch.

The solution: consume slightly fewer calories, but spread them out into five to six meals. The AT made this clear again. We wanted to carry the least amount of food we needed because food is so heavy. We knew that there is a 20 minute delay from when your stomach says you are full and when your brain registers it. Knowing this, we spread out our calories by snacking all day long. We would only cook one big meal a day and that was usually around 4 p.m.—when we needed an extra boost to give us another three to five hours of hiking. By eating six meals a day, we were stretching out those calories for all they were worth.

By spacing out the calories, you make your brain think that it's eating more than it really is. The 20-minute delay makes a seemingly small meal feel like a bigger one. We weren't completely full when we would finish our food, but we knew that 20 minutes later we would feel fine. And if for some reason we were still hungry 30 minutes later, then we'd just eat some trail mix.

Furthermore, one way to boost your metabolism is by eating frequent small meals. Such a technique can boost your metabolism by up to 20 percent for several hours after a meal. Meanwhile, *not* eating for several hours is a great way of *slowing* your metabolism. Think about it: your body realizes that it's not getting food, so it's going to do its best to conserve what little calories it has by slowing down your metabolism, thereby *decreasing* your burn rate. Finally,

Radiation or Vitamin Deficiency?

Would you rather get some radiation or be short on your vitamins? Strangely, your cells look the same in either case.

If you don't feed your cells vitamins and minerals, they look like they've been irradiated. In both cases they have suffered mitochondrial and DNA damage.

That's enough incentive to spend $25 a year on a multivitamin.

(Source: Jean Carper, "Vitamins Are Vital," USA Weekend, Nov 21-23, 2003, p. 6.)

before you conclude that you have a slow metabolism, consider getting it measured—the results may surprise you. Lawrence J. Cheskin, a Johns Hopkins physician and director of the weight management center, told *The Wall Street Journal* that most people are surprised by how high their metabolic rate is. Although that may depress some overweight people, the upside is that it means that nearly everyone can lose weight if they just make behavioral changes.[21] I know it is so much easier to blame your parents for all your problems, but in this case they probably gave you a normal healthy metabolism.

Mistake #3: When we eat our calories is way off

Not only do Americans concentrate about 85 percent of their calories in two meals, we eat the bulk of the calories at the end of the day. We're following the Sumo Diet (see sidebar on the next page). Look at the previous graph, and you'll see how the typical American has two huge calorie spikes during the day (lunch and dinner). What's worse is that they get about half their calories at the very end of the day—exactly when they don't need them! The body stares at these calories, and not knowing what to do with them, just stores them as fat. Instead, we should consume the bulk of our calo-

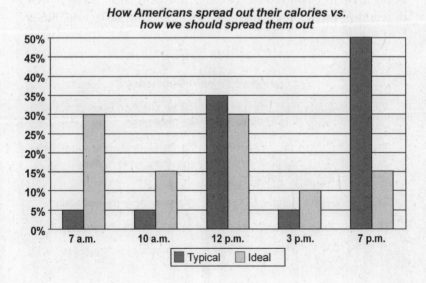

How Americans spread out their calories vs. how we should spread them out

ries by the end of lunch time. As our metabolism slows during the day, so should our caloric intake. We did this on the AT and it really stretched our food supply. If you get the munchies before you go to bed, then eat something light (like fruit or yogurt), wait 20 minutes and your craving will probably go away.

In short, Americans should cut back the amount of calories they consume, focus on eating more fruits and vegetables, spread their daily calories into five to six meals, and eat the bulk of their calories in the first half of the day, not the second half. Just doing that will not only make you feel better, you'll also lose weight! These eating habits were instrumental at helping me complete my odyssey. OK, except for that part about cutting back the calories.

The Secret Sumo Diet

Many people think they're fat because they have cursed genes. Although genes play a role in determining our weight, it's not the only reason we're fat. Otherwise, how did sumo wrestlers get so big? After all, when you think of a Japanese man, don't you immediately think of a thin person?

Clearly, the sumos are fighting an uphill battle against their Japanese genes that favor a lean physique. So what's their secret to getting so fat? For those of us who prefer not weighing 300 pounds, can we learn something from them and make sure we don't end up like them?

Their secret to getting fat is simple: *they go to sleep immediately after eating*. For example, they train from 5 to 11 a.m., eat at noon, and take a nap. Then they save their biggest meal for the end of the day, right before they go to bed. They gorge and then jump in the sack.

By flooding their bodies with calories right before they go to sleep, the body has little choice but to convert them to fat. By following this "eat a ton before going to bed strategy" skinny Japanese men are transformed into obese sumo wrestlers!

Therefore, unless you have sumo ambitions, avoid food three hours before going to sleep.

(Source: T.R Reid, National Geographic Magazine, July 1997, p. 48)

Chew like a cow

It should be clear that one of the goals of a thru-hiker is to stretch their food as much as possible. The more you stretch those calories, the less you have to carry and the easier your journey. Ideally, you could make your stomach think you are gorging, when in reality you may be only eating a medium sized pizza.

I got an idea on how to stretch out those calories from observing the dozens of cows I saw along the AT. These creatures seemed to chew forever before swallowing. Yet they have four stomach compartments! You would think that if any animal could get away with not chewing, it would be one that had four compartments to process the food. But instead the cow chews religiously. Meanwhile, humans have only have one stomach compartment, so we should make the job of digesting as easy as possible for our lonely little organ. *Therefore, try chewing each bite 50 times before swallowing.* Consider the remarkable benefits, for thru-hikers and non-thru-hikers alike:

- **You help your digestive system:** Your stomach and intestines have less work to do if you thoroughly break down the food before it gets there. Your body can easily extract the nutrients it needs and then move out the rest.

- **You eat less food:** It takes about 20 minutes for your stomach to signal to your brain that it is full. This delay makes you eat more food than you need to. By chewing so slowly, you allow your brain to catch up to your stomach.

- **You savor your food more:** I see people inhale a delicious crème brule or a slice of deep dish Chicago pizza. If they chewed 50 times, they would truly appreciate every flavor and let each taste bud enjoy every morsel.

Chewing 50 times is particularly useful to thru-hikers who are short on food. It allows them to stretch out their food supplies. It sure beats inhaling it, which is what most of us do. Some of us eat fast because we're in a hurry. Change your habits. If you're alone, read a magazine or watch TV, as long as you don't lose focus on your chewing. By reading at the same time, you won't feel like you're wasting time while you're chewing like a madman.

Some might complain that if you chew each bite 50 times your food will get cold. You can combat this by heating up your plate before serving food on it. In the worst case, when your meal starts to get cold you can put it in the microwave and nuke it.

Moreover, since one of the keys to weigh loss is minimizing sweets and desserts, don't you really want to savor each morsel? Instead of quickly consuming a cup or two of ice cream, consider just one spoonful to satisfy the craving. By letting that spoonful slowly melt in your mouth you will cherish that spoonful like you once cherished the entire cup. This is what I do now that I am not thru-hiking; tragically, I can't polish off a pint of ice cream without eventually putting on some pounds.

In conclusion, as strange as it sounds, if you eat like a cow, you won't look like a cow.

Combining Second and Fifth Principle

The Second Principle demonstrates the money draining power of subscription expenses. Although I used coffee as an example, our daily lunch is another. Most of the work force buys their lunch at

Here's a rare section of flat trail on the AT. When I passed fields I would observe cows and horses chewing endlessly. That gave me the idea that humans should probably do the same.

the employee cafeteria, the lunch truck, or a fast food joint. We typically spend $5 to $10 and usually twice that if we go out to a restaurant. By packing your own lunch you get two benefits:

1. You save money.

2. You can make sure you eat a healthy meal.

The first benefit is fairly obvious, especially if you're spending over $5 on lunch everyday. The cost of packing some dinner leftovers is minimal. No leftovers? Then the cost of making a lunch is also minimal. Consider filling a huge bowl of Tupperware with romaine lettuce, spinach, avocado, tomatoes, carrots, broccoli, black beans, red and yellow peppers, and whatever else looks good. This salad may be enormous by your usual standards and could last you all day, especially if you have it with a little whole wheat bread or brown rice on the side. The trick is to put minimal dressing on it. These lunches are extremely nutritious and dirt cheap.

If you're spending $5 a day, going down to $3 may not seem like much. After all, "It's just $2!" Remember, the Second Principle—calculate the true costs of a subscription expense. The nominal cost is over $700 a year. If you're spending $7/day, the yearly savings is more dramatic—almost $1,500. Finally, those who eat in restaurants often and spend $10/day could cut $2,550 from their yearly spending. Wouldn't it be great to get a $2,550 bonus?

The second benefit of packing a lunch is less obvious. The main problem is that you have little control over how restaurants prepare your meal. The reason many dishes taste so good is that chefs frequently use significant amounts of butter, salt, and sugar. Few restaurants will display the nutritional value of each meal on their menus. If they did, many would have to close their doors. Once you realize that eating at a reputable steakhouse may be just as, or more, unhealthy than eating at Burger King, you might reconsider eating there. Similarly, perhaps the "healthy" salad option has more calories than the pasta dish because they drown it in fatty dressing. On the other hand, perhaps one of the desserts might not be so bad after all.

If you don't like packing your own lunch, then consider cutting back on restaurant dinners for much of the same reasons. In addition, it will help you avoid the sumo diet.

Lastly, another way to combine the Second and Fifth Principles is by making tap water your standard beverage. This is another way to get a double bonus: both your health and finances will improve. With restaurant wine costing $8/glass and coffee costing $3/cup, you can trim nearly $20 from your restaurant bill (assuming two glasses of wine). That's nearly $1,000 year, assuming you go out once a week. With that much savings you could afford to go out twice as much, or even better, pocket the savings so you can hike with passion.

The power of water and the power of the mind

Lisa and I almost didn't hike the AT. A couple of months before our AT hike, Lisa could barely walk.

Prior to the AT adventure we had hiked almost 500 miles to prepare ourselves psychologically and physically for the pilgrimage. We would go backpacking almost every weekend. Yosemite was our favorite stomping ground—we had hiked over half the National Park. Although we would return somewhat sore after these demanding trips, we never had any major problems. However, just a few months before our departure date, in the middle of a four day trip in Henry Coe State Park in California, Lisa started suffering terribly—her knees were falling apart.

Henry Coe State Park is enormous. It is the largest state park in Northern California with over 87,000 acres and a whopping 250 miles of hiking trail. When we came to the ranger station and submitted our ambitious backpacking plan the ranger said, "Wow, you guys are really going out there."

"Really?" I asked, "When was the last time someone went out that deep in the wilderness?"

The ranger scratched his head, "I'm not sure, but the last time we sent a ranger out there was over a year ago."

"Nobody else has gone back there for over a year?" I asked incredulously.

"Not that I know of," replied the ranger. "So when you return, come back here and tell me how it is back there, OK?"

I nodded and thanked him for the permit. You can get fined if a ranger finds you in the wilderness without a permit. I stared at the permit wondering what good it would do me when there would be no rangers where we were going.

Even though the entrance of Henry Coe State Park is less than an hour drive from Silicon Valley, this ranger's comments give you an idea how deep the park extends. We were right in the middle of that remote wilderness when Lisa's knees started aching more and more. Eventually, they hurt so bad that she broke down and cried.

Lisa felt like knives were piercing and burning her knees. Every step she took made her wince in agony. She looked up at me with teary eyes and wanted to know what we should do.

I scanned the vast wilderness around us. I listened to the wind rustle the leaves. Soft rain was falling. I felt the cool water stream down my face. We were about as far as we could be from any help.

We could either: (1) camp for a day or two and hope her knees feel better; or (2) just push it. As usual, we had not weighed ourselves down with tons of extra food. We figured that if one of us couldn't move, we could set up camp anywhere and just stretch out the food that we carried. If we weren't walking 20 to 30 miles a day, then we would burn (and need) far fewer calories than usual. We could make a couple of days of food last a week if one of us was immobile, so I wasn't worried. On the other hand, Lisa could still walk, albeit in pain. Therefore, I suggested we tough it out and make our way back home. She agreed.

Her backpack was exceptionally light (about eight pounds), but that's eight additional pounds of pressure she was putting on her knees with every step. So I slung her backpack over one my shoulders. One of the advantages of carrying such light packs is that I could easily carry both of them in a pinch. Mine weighed less than 20 pounds. Nevertheless, it would take us two full days of walking to get back to our car.

Lisa limped all the way home. A violent rainstorm assailed us in the final few miles. The winds were some of the fiercest we ever experienced. We finally made it back home, exhausted from the ordeal.

Lisa is incredibly strong, tough, and healthy. I couldn't believe that her knees would suddenly fail her with no apparent cause. This training hike taught me a wise lesson that helped us throughout the AT. After much thought, I concluded that there were probably three causes to her knee problems:

1. **Psychological:** Lisa was worried about quitting her job, selling most of her belongings, and moving out of her place to hike the AT. Her worries manifested themselves in her knee pain; it would be her mind's way of preventing her from taking such a big risk, forcing her to retreat to safety.

2. **Poor hydration:** Although Lisa normally drank a lot of water, in Henry Coe State Park I noticed that she wasn't drinking often. I surmised it was because she had become tired of going into the bushes every 30 minutes. Despite all my encouragement to drink more water, she insisted that she was not thirsty and kept hiking until her knees gave out on her.

3. **Physical:** It was possible that her joints needed additional strengthening and support.

Lisa, on the other hand, was convinced the cause was purely physical. Although I believed there might have been some physical inflammation, I suspected her mind manufactured most of her pain.

She got a MRI. The results were negative—there were no physical signs of knee damage. When she got the results she wept.

She felt the doctors were telling her that she was a crazy hypochondriac. She was positive something physical had happened, but despite numerous tests, there was no evidence of physical trauma.

Nevertheless, Lisa started taking a tablet that had glucosamine, chondroitin, and MSM. The human body produces glucosamine, which is effectively the oil for our joints. Some humans just don't produce enough, especially when they put their body through heavy activity, so they need supplements. It takes one to two months of taking the supplement to detect a difference. Lisa started taking the supplement to help prepare her joints for the AT's steep mountains.

Meanwhile, I was secretly relieved that there was no physical damage, because I was confident that she could overcome the psychological challenge, perhaps with a little help from water.

Guzzling water

Poor hydration is the root cause for many physical problems. Humans are mostly water. Water lubricates our bodies, facilitates digestion, carries nutrients to our cells, improves our skin, helps us maintain a normal body temperature, and gets rid of toxins. *One of the cheapest and easiest ways to improve your health is to guzzle three to four liters of water a day.* It is a natural elixir. Water helps make everything function smoothly. Every body part and every cell craves water. And remember: soft drinks and juice aren't water; tea and coffee aren't water; and despite your old college fraternity beliefs, beer and vodka are definitely not water.

As you can see from the chart, less than 15 percent of the liquids we consume are pure water. This is backwards—*85 percent of what we drink should be water.* Fifteen percent can be some other beverage. There are two exceptions. First, green tea and herbal tea are benign and arguably good for you. Second, if you're doing an endurance

What Americans Drink

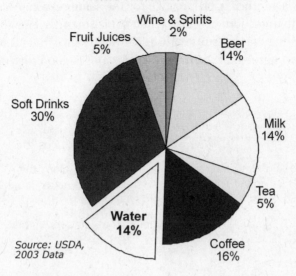

Wine & Spirits 2%
Fruit Juices 5%
Beer 14%
Soft Drinks 30%
Milk 14%
Tea 5%
Water 14%
Coffee 16%

Source: USDA, 2003 Data

sport, you might benefit from a nourishing sports drink. XTerra, one of my sponsors, gave me a sports powder which has no simple sugars, sucrose, fructose, or aspartame. The powder delivered a great energy boost, but we also managed to hike over a thousand miles without it. Others felt they could not have thru-hiked without a sports drink. Try it out and then hike your own hike.

Although drinking cola and beer is better than not drinking any water, it's healthier to keep the unnecessary chemicals and calories out of your system. *Drink when you're not thirsty, because by the time you feel thirsty, you're already dehydrated.* The thirst mechanism is an alarm that you should prevent from going off, even when you're not backpacking 2,000 miles. Anticipate your hydration needs by constantly guzzling water so that you never feel thirsty. And don't worry about overdosing on water. We should drink as much as we can handle. The limiting factor is how many trips to the bathroom you can tolerate before you go absolutely insane.

It's a good idea to drink a large glass of water before even starting a meal. This will fill up a bit of your stomach, so you will feel full faster than normal. We did this frequently on our odyssey to give the illusion of fullness. Similarly, drinking lots of water during the meal is another good practice for the same reason. Also, water helps with digestion. In short, when sometimes it seems that nearly everything you consume causes cancer, it's nice that all scientists can at least agree that drinking lots of water is good for you.

Water Sources on the AT

People always wonder where we got our water along the AT. The answer is simple: any body of water, such as springs, creeks, rivers, and lakes.

The next question is how we purified it. My answer surprises everyone.

We didn't.

We usually didn't purify the water because we were careful to select a good source. We looked for springs, high mountain creeks or rivers. Even in the heavily populated East Coast, we proved that many water sources in the Appalachians are still safe for drinking. We never got sick.

Did some of the water have giardia? Almost certainly, but tap water and even bottled water has trace amounts of giardia. Fortunately, humans evolved to handle small amounts of bacteria in the water. A healthy immune system, supported by vitamins and minerals, can protect us from the harmful effects of these waterborne organisms. Interestingly, there are significant quantities of vitamin B12 in nature's water sources. This B12 vanishes during the purification process of most municipalities.

Despite my experience, I don't recommend drinking straight from streams, at least not until you either study more or gain more experience about picking good water sources. Whenever I had any doubt (about 30 percent of the time), I purified the water.

My favorite purification solution is chlorine dioxide, which takes about 15 minutes to work; however, it doesn't have the bad taste or side effects of iodine, and weighs a fraction of a traditional filter. You can get some from Pristine (www.pristine.ca), another company that sponsored my pilgrimage.

Although some experts advise drinking at least eight large glasses of water a day, I recommend a cruder way of monitoring your water intake that I learned on my trek: just observe the color of your urine. Clear is good; yellow is bad. When our urine was a shade of yellow, we drank more water. Although staying hydrated was tedious because sometimes we would have to go into the bushes every 15 minutes, the benefits far outweighed the annoyance. Drinking copious amounts of water can be a pain for those who work at a desk, but if you're hunched over a computer screen you should give your eyes a break and go for walk every 30 minutes anyway. By the way, Lisa developed a peeing system that made her as fast as I was. One day she'll have to write a book about how she did it, because I'm sure many women are curious.

Lastly, we would generally stop drinking water about three hours before bedtime. If we got thirsty, we would just take a small sip. This made sure we would have an uninterrupted night of sleep. Getting out of a toasty sleeping bag when it's really cold and dark outside is no fun.

Mind over body

I firmly believe that 25 to 50 percent of our physical problems are created in the mind. Since they are created in the mind, they can be fixed using the mind. Why such a high percentage?

Because of a phenomenon called the placebo effect. When scientists want to test a new drug, they frequently have three groups: one takes no drug; one takes the drug; and one takes a sugar tablet that supposedly is the drug. This last group receives the placebo— a tablet without medicine. However, what is fascinating is that usually those who take the placebo do better than those who take no drug; and even more strange, sometimes the placebo takers do just as well as the drug takers. According to *The New York Times*, the placebo effect can help 35 to 75 percent of the patients.[22] If that's the case, that means that these patients are only using their mind to heal them—they are not taking any medicine. Therefore, we could treat a significant number of our physical ailments just using our mind. That's a powerful lesson!

I decided to apply this lesson with Lisa's knee. Having studied Hinduism and Buddhism, I knew the importance of mantras. Mantras are incantations that worshipers repeat often in prayer and other religious activities. Mantras are usually short, such as this ancient Upanishadic Hindu mantra: "From non-being to being lead me, from darkness to light lead me, from death to immortality lead me." However, there's no rule that says you can't make mantras longer, like the Lord's Prayer in Christianity. There is an incredible power in saying a statement aloud over and over again. Religions tap into this power and so can we. Therefore, I wrote a mantra for Lisa to help heal her knee before the journey and give her confidence that she could walk over 2,000 miles.

The key in a mantra is to repeat positive affirmations, to avoid mentioning negative thoughts, and to visualize attaining your goals. Lisa agreed to read her mantra aloud when she woke up, at lunch, and right before she went to sleep. I wanted to include her mantra in this book, but she didn't because her mantra is deeply personal. In fact, when we recorded the audio version of this book,

---

Examples of the Placebo Effect

The placebo effect has been proven in a variety of cases:

- ✓ In one study doctors painted warts with a pretty inert dye and promised the patients the warts would disappear when the color faded. And that's exactly what happened.

- ✓ Patients got the same pain relief from a phony ultrasound as from a real one, provided both the patient and the doctor believed the device was on.

- ✓ In 11 different trials, over half of the colitis patients who received the placebo felt better; moreover, half of the inflamed intestines looked better when viewed via a sigmoidoscope.

- ✓ Researchers discovered they could dilate an asthmatic's airway by simply telling the patients that they were inhaling a bronchiodilator, even when they weren't.

(*Source: Margaret Talbot, "The Placebo Prescription,"* The New York Times Magazine, *January 9, 2000.*)

tears went down her cheeks just looking at her mantra. She wept because this was her special private prayer and it meant so much to her. However, she eventually agreed to share it because she realized that it might help and inspire others to improve their lives too. So here it is:

Lisa's Mantra

- *I am strong, and my body is getting stronger everyday.*

- *I am stronger than 99 percent of the women out there. When I forget this, I will walk into a grocery store or an office building and compare myself with 100 women, and I will see that I am the strongest. How many people do I personally know who could have done the amazing outdoor accomplishments that I have done in my life? None, I alone have done it, and I am the strongest.*

- *I close my eyes and see myself climbing the mountains of Maine, with strength, courage, and determination.*

- *Although the rock faces are terribly steep, I see myself doing them effortlessly and without pain anywhere in my body. My pack feels light as a feather as I pull my body up the mountain, and my iron legs bravely take me down the steep ravines with pleasure. I close my eyes, visualize all this, and I just know it will happen.*

- *Why do I know I will do it easily? Because I can clearly remember the much harder mountains I had to climb in Yosemite where I was dangling from a nylon rope. Although I was scared, I was never in pain, despite the super steep mountains we had to climb. I was strong then, and now I am strong again.*

- *I now realize that the pain I have felt in the past is the pain of fear, not the pain of a physical problem. My joints have never let me down, and they never will. All they ask is that I feed them water—lots of water. I have pushed them up and down the highest mountain in the lower 48 states. Did my body complain? No. I am stronger now than I was then, so there is no reason that I should feel pain. Indeed, I feel my bones, my joints, and my muscles are all strengthening. When I wake up tomorrow, I will feel even more powerful than today.*

- *I have done so much harder than the White Mountains of New Hampshire, whose winds don't compare to the gusts of Henry Coe.*

I see myself standing on the top of the White Mountains in triumph and in strength.

● *I see myself climbing on all fours as I scramble over boulders on the AT. I feel like a child, climbing over sofas and furniture and monkey bars. This will be fun! I see myself laughing with a smile on my face as I amble up the boulders of Pennsylvania. What a joy it will be!*

● *I have always been strong, ever since I was a child. I was one of the strongest in my class. My body was blessed with unusual power, a power that comes from within.*

● *I have hiked the rugged Red Peak Pass, where I went up and down and up and down across brutal and diabolic off-trail terrains. My body never let me down. The next day when we found the trail, I hiked another 20 miles. The next day, another 20 miles. I felt great. I feel great again. I will do it again. And again. I am mighty, I am tough, I am solid. Nothing will stop me.*

Ask anyone who has accomplished a tough goal, and most of the time they have visualized the ending. Professional athletes visualize winning a championship and scoring the winning point. Although Lance Armstrong may not have recited a formal mantra, he filled his mind with positive thoughts as he fought testicular cancer. The mind is a powerful tool; mantras exercise the mind's force and allow humans to achieve extraordinary feats. It doesn't really matter whether you formally write and recite mantras or you simply maintain positive thoughts through more casual means; what's essential is that you fully engage your mind in maintaining your body's health.

Lisa had absolutely no physical problems on the AT. Although we can all guess why that was the case, we will never know for sure. Perhaps it was because of the glucosamine supplements, or because of her efforts to stay well hydrated, or because of her mantra. Most likely it was a combination of the three solutions. Personally, I suspect drinking voluminous amounts of water every day and maintaining a positive attitude were the most important factors. In any case, it should be clear that water is an excellent preventative measure against all sorts of ailments. Similarly, one should not underestimate the healing power of the mind.

Lisa's mantra prepared her for the AT's intense trails which can make you crawl under boulders. Her smile shows how she's enjoying this like a child enjoys an obstacle course.

Finally, for those who still doubt the power of the brain, consider a study reported in the *New England Journal of Medicine*. While Lisa's knees were taking the pounding of five million steps in 111 days, a bunch of patients who had horrible knee problems got a "fake" surgery. A total of 180 patients with osteoarthritis of the knee were randomly assigned to receive either:

○ Arthroscopic débridement – real surgery

○ Arthroscopic lavage — real surgery

○ Placebo surgery — fake surgery

Patients in the placebo group received skin incisions and underwent a simulated débridement without insertion of the arthroscope; so when they woke up, they saw the scars and assumed that the surgery was done, when it really wasn't. The results of this experiment were remarkable. *At no point did either of the groups who had the "real" surgery report less pain or better function than the placebo group.*[23]

Lisa might have felt silly after seeing that her MRI showed no damage to her knees, but can you imagine how silly those guys who had fake knee surgery felt? The doctor sedated them, sliced the skin around the knee to make it look like he did something, and then sewed it up. The doctor told them that he fixed their knee. Hence, they expected to get better and they did. A few months later while playing basketball some of these patients were told that they never had surgery. Imagine how they felt!

While some patients who get a placebo treatment may come out feeling silly, I think it's incredibly empowering! It demonstrates how much power the mind has to heal the body. It proves the brain-body connection, and shows how we can use our brain-power to make ourselves feel better. I'm not suggesting that you stop going to the doctor or taking your medication. I'm simply suggesting that we should combine the two methods—for clearly the human mind is a potent force.

Supplements

Given that we were doing some extraordinary exercise everyday on the AT, we needed some extraordinary nutrition. There was no way to get enough nutrition by just eating food. Every cell in our bodies demanded more than we could get by conventional methods. Therefore, we took at least one strong multivitamin per day. Even now that I'm off the trail, I still take a multivitamin. The downsides are nearly non-existent: if you consume a few more vitamins than your body needs, you will excrete it. The upsides, on the other hand, are numerous, because supplemental vitamins:

- Boost your immune system to prevent sicknesses and infections.
- Deliver the building blocks for your cells to regenerate and grow.
- Increase your life expectancy by lowering risk of heart disease and cancer.
- Regulate your hormones and other bodily functions.

Medical research shows that taking vitamin supplements is a good idea whether you're hiking 2,000 miles or being a couch potato. I've already addressed some of the supplements that vegetarians should take, but non-vegetarians might want to take them too. Perhaps the most important vitamins are antioxidants, which include vitamins A, C, and E. Doctors love to debate the merits of taking mega doses of vitamins, but most agree that taking a multivitamin everyday is smart. For example, in the *Journal of the American Medical Association* two Harvard researchers recommended that adults take a multivitamin daily to help prevent heart disease, stroke, cancer, and osteoporosis. Elderly people should take one multivitamin plus vitamin B-12 and vitamin D supplements.[24] Multivitamins also help in getting enough minerals. The key minerals are calcium, magnesium, potassium, iron, selenium, and zinc. Usually a good multivitamin combined with a healthy diet should cover your mineral needs too. Although it's hard to overdose on vitamins, consult your doctor before taking them.

Lastly, never let multivitamins make up for poor eating habits. It's far better to eat a lot of fruits and vegetables and not take a vitamin, than to eat junk food and hope the multivitamin gives your body enough nutrition. Vitamins obtained via food beats pills any day. A thru-hiker wouldn't complete the AT just eating Pop-Tarts all day, even if he was gulping down 10 multivitamins a day.

Minimize legal drug consumption

We sometimes forget that we are biological creatures. Fundamentally, we're a bunch of chemicals and elements acting in a coordinated fashion. Therefore, it shouldn't surprise us that our bodies are easily addicted to certain chemicals and molecules. To stay healthy and to follow the Fifth Principle, it's best to avoid the harmful drugs, even the ones that are so embedded in our society that we don't think of them as drugs.

The US fights hardcore drugs like marijuana, cocaine, and heroin; however, we do little to stop people from taking legal drugs (e.g., tobacco, alcohol, and caffeine) that sometimes are even more addictive than the illegal drugs. It's obvious to most people why smoking crack or shooting heroin is a destructive activity, so I won't spend any time proving that. The trickier problem is the legal drugs, because they seem rather benign and many use them.

Some people will declare that since we should hike our own hike, it's fine to consume legal drugs if we enjoy them. But do we really need them to be happy? Clearly, there are plenty of people who don't drink alcohol, smoke, or have coffee and live a wonderful life. Therefore, taking such drugs is not a requirement to being happy. But all people are different, so while some people may do just fine without it, others may like it and enjoy it. So as long as it's legal and you enjoy it, go ahead and consume it. However, the key to doing legal drugs is not moderation, it's *minimization*. None of these drugs do you any good, so the less you consume, the healthier you are. Let's review each one.

Stop smoking

Unless you've been living on Mars or some European country, you should know that smoking is bad for you and for those who are around you. *Just quit.* There are plenty of programs out there. You could minimize your habit to a couple of cigarettes a week, but it's best to just quit. It was sad to see the few thru-hikers who smoked coughing and hacking their way up the mountains. Some of these smokers were low on cash, yet could save $1,000 a year by just cutting their stinky habit.

On the other hand, before we berate the 20 percent of Americans who still smoke, just remember that living in a rural area and smoking one cigarette a day is healthier than not smoking and living under the polluted skies of Bangkok or Los Angeles. However, no matter where you live, save your money and your lungs—stop smoking.

Abandon alcohol

AT pilgrims had to live with little alcohol since liquids are heavy. You could re-supply your water at any stream, but if you wanted a glass of wine or a beer, you had to haul it for miles. Without refrigeration, that meant warm beer in the summer months. Cool spring water started looking pretty good.

Since the First Principle states that you should hike your own hike, some are tempted to run to the wine cellar. However, consider the negatives of alcohol:

- It slows down your nervous system that can depress you later on.

- It is a vasodilator, which misleads you into thinking that you're warmer than you are by widening your blood vessels and could lead to hypothermia in cold weather.

- It dehydrates you.

- Alcoholic drinks are packed with worthless calories helping you get fat; they supply zero nutrition—it's like eating a candy bar, but one that impairs your senses.

- It overtaxes your liver—leads to cirrhosis, which prevents you from digesting food properly, which then can lead to edema (swelling/fluid retention) and jaundice (yellowing of skin/eyes).

- It causes accidents—50 percent of auto accidents are alcohol related.

- It's addictive—now you have some real problems.

There are two reasons to eliminate alcohol from your life. First, it's healthy to live without alcoholic drinks. As the list above proves, alcohol causes a host of problems. Second, it's an expensive habit. Avoiding alcohol helps you follow the Second Principle. Consider how much you spend in alcohol at bars, liquor stores, and restaurants. Imagine drinking water instead and retiring a few years earlier, with your liver intact!

On the other hand, there are studies that drinking one glass of red wine is better than not drinking it. If drinking wine makes you feel good, then go ahead and drink that one glass of red wine. *Otherwise, minimize your alcohol intake.*

Cut coffee

I like to hike from sunrise until sunset. Dawn and dusk are my favorite hours of the day. The magical glow of the sun in the multicolored sky, the joyous birds singing, and the cool temperatures all combine to make for a tranquil and enchanting moment in the forest. I do everything I can to walk during those precious moments.

However, I confess that waking up in the first month on the AT was incredibly difficult. At the end of June and late July in Maine, the sun sets at 9 p.m. and gets up at 4 a.m. Getting seven hours of sleep may be enough for the average office worker, but when you just walked 16 hours the day before you want to sleep for 12 hours! When I would wake up I felt like a zombie extra in *The Blair Witch Project Part III*.

Nevertheless, many pilgrims learned to wake up without caffeine assistance. Coffee represented more empty calories—no nutrition, unnecessary weight. Moreover, boiling water for the coffee used up precious fuel. The ritual of waking up is rough for all animals, just observe a dog or cat when they wake up. We all start groggy at the beginning, but eventually the body catches up without caffeine. Frankly, I'm not sure how easy it would have been to wake up at 4 a.m., even with five cups of coffee.

Chapter Two already demonstrated how the coffee habit can be expensive. Although not nearly as destructive as alcohol or tobacco, caffeine offers no benefits to a naturally alert and healthy mind. A good substitute could be brisk morning exercise. *Therefore, aim to minimize your caffeine consumption.*

Walk hard

We've carefully examined our calorie input, now we need to focus on our calorie output. There are three components to being physically fit: (1) cardiovascular fitness; (2) raw strength; and (3) flexibility.

Cardiovascular training

This is arguably the most important of the three types of exercise (weightlifting and stretching being the other two). Fortunately, there are many ways to get into cardiovascular shape. Running, biking, walking, and swimming are just some examples of cardiovascular exercises. Some sports, such as basketball and soccer, emphasize constant movement, with occasional sprints, and so they also help keep your heart in shape. Other sports such as football, volleyball, and tennis are more anaerobic than aerobic, because they emphasize explosive power, not constant movement, so they are not as effective at keeping your heart in shape as more aerobic sports. The key to a cardiovascular exercise is that you elevate your heart rate and maintain it there for 30 minutes at least four days a week. If you want to lose weight (or get into even better shape), then push yourself for 45 to 60 minutes five to seven days a week.

Some may worry that doing cardio five to seven days of week is "too much exercise." On the contrary, your body is a machine. It wasn't meant to sit around all day—that's abnormal. Our ancestors were extremely active and our bodies evolved to handle a high amount of activity. We weren't optimized to be office workers and couch potatoes. Exercising one to two hours a day seven days a week is hardly pushing the limits of your body. I was just beginning to test the limits by walking through mountainous terrain 12 to 16 hours per day, seven days a week. Other humans have done endurance feats that make my odyssey seem like walking in a Thanksgiving parade.

Walking has the best value as gymnastics of the mind.
— Ralph Waldo Emerson, US essayist, 1803—1882

For those who are out of shape you will need to build up to this goal; it's dangerous to embark on an overly ambitious exercise program. You don't want to do what we did and hike 27 miles on your first day on the AT unless you're already in shape and a bit nutty.

On the other hand, a common mistake people make is that their cardio exercise is not sufficiently *vigorous*. For example, some bikers pedal slowly (or just coast)—they are not sweating or breathing hard. Similarly, some swimmers just wade in the pool hardly making an effort. Of course, some of these people are just trying to relax and not exercise. However, others truly believe that they are getting a meaningful workout and wonder why they're not losing weight or becoming more fit. For an effective cardio workout, you must push your body. For some that may mean a slow stroll, for others that may mean running up a steep mountain. The key is gauging your heart rate; there are fitness tables that help you determine your appropriate training level. If you don't have a heart rate monitor, just pay attention to your breathing. If you are breathing quite hard, but can manage a simple conversation, then you're doing great. If you're so out of breath that talking is impossible, then you're pushing yourself too hard. On the other hand, if you're walking 2,000 miles over mountains with backpack, then don't walk too vigorously. Not only do you need to make it through the day, you need to keep a solid pace for several months. And that's vigorous enough.

Either he's dead or my watch has stopped.
— *Groucho Marx*

Finally, there are mental benefits to cardio exercise. In 1981, John Griest and others working at the University of Wisconsin gave patients with a moderate degree of neurotic depression two options: psychotherapy or a running regime. Both groups showed improvement. In fact, those who did the graduated jogging program were still keeping up with it a year later. So if you don't have the money to pay a shrink to improve your mental health, take the cheap option: walk or run a few miles everyday and watch your spirits soar. The key is to monitor your progress and periodically raise the bar.

Weightlifting

One thru-hiker told me she preferred hiking with poles to avoid developing the "kangaroo body." Indeed, thru-hikers exercise their legs far more than their arms, so they can end up looking like a kangaroo. OK, so a thru-hiker has her pouch on her back instead of her stomach, but you get the idea.

Many hikers use poles because they work out your arms, help you keep your balance, take some pressure of your knees, and help you burn more calories. Nevertheless, Lisa and I didn't use hiking poles because we wanted to conserve calories, not burn them; also, our knees were strong and we think kangaroos are quite sexy.

On the other hand, to prepare for the AT we definitely hit the weight room. Weightlifting is a vital way to maintain your health and prevent injury. It strengthens your body to take the pounding of five million steps. And even if you're not walking 2,000 miles, there are many other benefits. For example, it also helps ward off osteoporosis. You're never too old to start weightlifting, studies show elderly people also benefit from weightlifting. Besides, weights are far more effective than cardio at giving your body a toned, sculpted look. You would think that thru-hikers would look amazingly fit, but they don't. They look just like everyday people. I confess it was kind of a downer that my super heroic effort didn't make me look like Superman.

When your body is at rest, one pound of muscle burns 25 times more calories than one pound of fat. Therefore, while you are snoring, five pounds of muscle on your body is burning 25 times more calories than five pounds of fat. No wonder the muscular guys have it so easy! They're burning through calories just sitting on a couch, while the overweight folks are barely making a dent. Therefore, the more fat you replace with muscle, the more fat the muscle helps you burn. It's a virtuous cycle! Each pound of muscle you gain could help you lose over five pounds of fat per year. In conclusion, building muscle through weightlifting helps you lose weight more quickly than just doing cardio. And it might even help get you the starring role in *Terminator V*.

Like cardio, start with an easy weight lifting routine and work your way up. There are plenty of books and magazines with advice, so I will be brief:

- Start with two sets for each major muscle group.

- Do eight to 15 repetitions per set. You will build muscle mass if you do a low number of reps; you will tone and sculpt your muscles when you do a high number of reps.

- You can lift weights everyday of the week as long as you don't do the same muscle group two days in a row.

- To speed up the workout, pick two unrelated muscle groups and alternate sets with them in a circuit. For example, do one set of hamstrings and one set of your back muscles, then return to the hamstring.

- Make sure you work out opposing muscle groups with equal intensity. For example, don't do 200 crunches and nothing for your lower back, nor should you do five sets of bicep curls and one for the triceps. Such a routine sets you up for an injury.

- As you become stronger, start doing three to five sets, depending on how much you want to improve. Continue using the technique of alternating between muscle groups. For example, you can do one set of quads and one set of hamstrings. Then repeat that cycle two to four more times.

- Don't rest more than 30 seconds between sets. Since you're already giving your muscles a mini-break by focusing briefly on another muscle, you don't need a two minute break between sets. Plus, this will make your workout go even faster.

 To get back my youth I would do anything in the world, except take [up] exercise, get up early, or be respectable. — *Oscar Wilde (1854-1900), The Picture of Dorian Gray, 1891*

Combining weightlifting and cardio

Most of us are short on time, so doing 30 minutes of cardio and 30 minutes of weightlifting may seem daunting when you have too much to do. Although I don't recommend doing this too often, you can combine both workouts by doing 30 to 45 minutes of cardio weightlifting. Here's how you do it:

1. **Do a three way circuit:** Instead of alternating between two muscle groups, target three muscle groups (e.g., chest, quads, and lower back) and do three sets of each in a circuit. For example, do 10 reps of chest, then 10 of quads, and then 10 of lower back; that is a one circuit. Repeat two more times, so that you do each muscle group three times.

2. **Absolutely no resting:** To make sure this is a cardio workout, do not take breaks. In a normal weightlifting session you may rest up to 30 seconds between your alternating muscle groups. However, since your circuit now involves three muscle groups instead of two, your muscles have extra rest time. While you're working out one muscle group, your other two muscle groups are recuperating.

3. **Reduce the weight you normally lift:** Since you're pushing your body so hard in this cardio-type workout, you'll probably find that you can't lift as much as you normally could.

Another way to speed up your weightlifting workout is to do *supersets*. A superset is when you pick one muscle and do three sets in rapid succession, with 10 second breaks between sets. You can either decrease the weight or the number of reps with each successive set.

You may not strive to have arms like Madonna or a chest like Arnold, but weightlifting has numerous benefits. Not only does weightlifting improve your posture, prevent injuries, and burn mega calories, it can even fool people into thinking that you're in good shape.

Stretching

People neglect to stretch regularly, and then wonder why they get injured, have back problems, and can't reach the remote.

There is plenty of information on how to stretch, but the key points are:

- Hold each position for at least 30 seconds—breathe throughout the stretch.
- Do not bounce.
- Hold each stretch so that you're at the threshold of pain, but not in pain.

Stretching is a great exercise because you can do it nearly anywhere. You can stretch in your cubicle, while waiting in line, while watching TV, while talking on the phone, or even in your cramped airline seat (OK, that's a bit tough).

Stretch at least 10 minutes a day. The best times to stretch are before and after a cardio workout, or preparing for a weightlifting session. However, it also helps to stretch after waking up or before going to sleep. Pilates and yoga are two wonderful exercises that increase your flexibility. By stretching regularly you'll have fewer aches and prevent debilitating injuries; and, if nothing else, you'll truly appreciate *Cirque du Soleil*.

Discovering your natural body weight

Isn't it frustrating that some people can eat like pigs, not exercise, and still be skinny as a pole? Meanwhile, if you glance at a chocolate bar you instantly put on five pounds!

Clearly, some folks gain weight more easily than others. Genes account for such a difference. Some people were simply born with faster metabolisms than others. And some really do put on weight by just looking at food.

However, while our genes may determine our *tendencies*, they do not determine our *fate.* Your body may tend to be skinny, but you can get obese if you want (think of the sumo wrestlers). Similarly, your body may tend to easily put on the weight, but you can have a thin (or at least average) physique if you really want to. Therefore, although your genes influence you, they do not decide your ultimate figure. Only you decide how your body looks like.

Less than one percent of the population is cursed with an out of control fat gene. The overwhelming majority of overweight people are big by choice, not because of a cursed gene. They are overweight because there is an imbalance in the number of calories consumed and expended. That's it. If you're still not convinced, consider that most thru-hikers start their journey with extra pounds, but they all end up being thin. If 10 percent of the population had an uncontrollable fat gene, then you would expect about 10 percent of the thru-hikers to still be overweight by the end of the pilgrimage. I met hundreds of thru-hikers at the end of their journey and couldn't find a fat one, even though many said they started that way. Although some may find it harder to shed pounds than others, the natural body weight of most humans is healthy. To discover your natural body weight, do what I call the Pilgrim's Regime, because it's inspired from my pilgrimage:

- Get at least 30 minutes of vigorous cardiovascular exercise five days a week.

- Lift weights for at least 30 intense minutes three or more days a week.

- Make fruits and vegetables a huge part of your diet—keep your caloric intake at a reasonable level for your height.

Be self aware during your workouts. For example, many people who think they lift weights 30 minutes a day are actually talking most of the time! Also, beware of the leisurely 30 minute bike ride through the park; if you're not breathing hard, you probably aren't pushing yourself. Similarly, you may eat mostly fruits and vegetables, but if you pack in a pint of ice cream everyday, you won't achieve your natural body weight.

If you follow the Pilgrim's Regime for six months, your body will reach its natural state. Let's say you're 5'8" and 200 pounds today. Six months later you might find that you weigh 150 pounds, or as much as 170, or as little as 130. Whatever weight you stabilize at, that is your natural bodyweight. Dramatically losing more weight would be unhealthy, as would adding any more weight. *The key is learning to accept your body at whatever weight it stabilizes at, and to not accept it if it is over (or under) that natural weight.*

Chances are, if you follow this regime, you will end up looking like most thru-hikers: thin and in shape. If not, then start counting calories to make sure you're not sneaking some in (e.g., overdoing the salad dressing, late night snacks, or high calorie drinks). Also, consider making your workouts more intense: do cardio for one hour at least six days a week and weight lift an hour a day (alternate muscle groups to recuperate). These actions should help you achieve your goals. However, if you're still obese after all this, then ask your doctor about medical solutions.

There's no need for Americans to be so overweight. We're not cursed. We just eat too much and exercise too little. It's that simple. If Americans were to eat the same amount of calories as the typical African and also be as physically active as the typical African, we would be a nation of skinny people. If Africans had our lousy habits, they would also be chubby.

Lean doesn't always mean healthy

Just because you're thin doesn't mean that you're fit or healthy. Some people are thin, but starve themselves and never exercise. This is stupid. It's better to have a few extra pounds, eat well, exercise often, and simply accept your natural body weight. *The Wall Street Journal reported that lean individuals who are unfit have death rates two or three times higher than obese people who are moderately fit.*[25] One eight year study examined 22,000 men and concluded that an unfit lean man was twice as likely to die as the fit, including the obese fit. The doctors concluded that doing regular exercise was more important than how you look.[26] If you follow the regime I recommend you will probably have a good physique, but if you don't, do not be discouraged. It's more important to be healthy than to fit into a size 4 dress—especially if you're a guy.

> *When you have worn out your shoes, the strength of the shoe leather has passed into the fiber of your body. I measure your health by the number of shoes and hats and clothes you have worn out. He is the richest man who pays the largest debt to his shoemaker.*
> — *Ralph Waldo Emerson*

How someone looks can give you an idea how healthy he is, but it's not a perfect system. For example, some declare all models (or thin women) are anorexic. However, you can starve yourself and be overweight, or you can be razor thin and eat like a horse. Those who are extremely thin may do a lot of exercise and eat plenty of healthy calories; they probably have some genetic assistance as well. Meanwhile, those who look normal or overweight may be starving themselves, never doing any exercise, and eating unhealthy calories. In conclusion, pay attention to your habits, and don't waste your time speculating on the habits of the supermodels in Victoria's Secret.

Sleep soundly

I had an epiphany while making camp just south of McAfee's Knob in Virginia. Lisa and I had a running joke during our thru-hike of who could fall asleep faster. Lisa always won, except for that one time when a snake attacked her and we had to sleep nearby. But that's another story.

Although we usually slept in the open air so we could see the stars, some nights I brought out the tarp if I thought it might rain. Lisa would get the sleeping bag ready more quickly than I could get the tarp up. I usually told her to not worry about the tarp and to go to sleep. Incredibly, even though it would only take me two minutes to plunge the last few stakes in the ground, by the time I crawled under the tarp Lisa was usually fast asleep.

Our sleeping bag was more like a blanket. If we didn't expect rain, we usually slept without the tarp so we could admire the stars for 3.7 seconds before falling into a deep coma.

That one evening in Virginia, I had not yet slinked into the sleeping bag. Instead, I crouched down and listened to Lisa breathing deeply and rhythmically as she plunged in her deep coma state. I knew she would not wake up until my watch alarm went off at dawn. I often told her the next day, "I doubt you would wake up even if a bear were nibbling on your toes."

We ate well and walked hard on the AT. I figured that was enough to take care of the body, but I was wrong.

That night I smiled as I looked at the heavens, admiring the celestial lightshow. I began to realize just how peaceful and stress-free our lives were. Our calming daily marches nourished our souls while our deep sleep delighted our bodies. Eating right and exercising often are two key elements to squeezing the most out of your body; the third and final element is simply to relax and meditate.

After all, you can be super buff and doing an Ironman every Sunday, but if you're a ball of nerves, you're still somewhat unhealthy. Stress leads to depression, heart disease, asthma, and other complications. You need to learn how to relax, let your mind and body recuperate. Meditate and practice deep breathing exercises everyday. Chapter Seven explains other practical steps on living a stress-free life.

Common criticisms

There are certainly a host of criticisms out there. Although I will not address all of them, I will address the most common ones.

But do you really need to be healthy to squeeze the most out of life?

There are a lot of fat and happy people out there. There are others who take all sorts of medications and maintain a jolly disposition (sometimes because of the medications). So do you really need to eat well and exercise regularly to enjoy life? No, not really.

However, this book isn't about just enjoying life; it's about squeezing the most out of life. It's not about just being content or satisfied. It's for people who want to maximize their enjoyment and really savor life for all it's worth. The goal is to achieve profound and absolute fulfillment. Thus, if you're happy just being satisfied and fairly content, then feel free to skip the Fifth Principle. Just remember that neglecting your body means neglecting your mind. Both are intimately tied together. You are a biological creature at heart. Ignoring your body's needs will ultimately affect your mind and impede your ability to get the most out of life. That's why this Principle and this chapter are so important.

But I know so many exceptions!

Some people refuse to accept a consistent pattern. They adore pointing out their old Grandma Lucy who never exercised in her life, never ate vegetables or fruits, and lived to 102. Or there's famous Uncle Harry, who is 92 years old and watches TV all day, smokes, eats hamburgers and French fries, and yet is thin as a stick and in the winter does tricks on his snowboard.

Fiber's Importance

Strolling through Virginia's Grayson Highlands (one of the most beautiful sections on the AT) I realized how important fiber is to a diet. It's funny how these random thoughts cross your mind, but it would happen to you too if you walked 12 to 16 hours a day through the woods.

Thru-hikers need more calories than they can consume. Their digestive systems are the bottleneck. If they could eat more, they would.

The trick is to get food in, absorb all the nutrients, and then move it out—and do this as fast as possible. It's not healthy or efficient to have the food lingering when your system can either be light and clean or getting more nutrients in.

Therefore, the fiber we got from dehydrated fruits and corn pasta helped keep our digestive systems running smoothly throughout the journey.

It's important to look for high fiber foods even when you're not try-ing to walk 2,000 miles.

Why do some like mentioning these examples? For the same rea-son we admire movie stars, hall of fame athletes, and Nobel Prize winners—they are the exceptions, the anomalies who beat the odds. They stick out above the crowd because they are *exception*al.

Exceptions attract us. Our eyes gravitate to things that break a pattern. When I was in the woods, I could easily spot animal be-cause it broke the pattern. Yet animals are small percentage of the biomass in the woods. Similarly, we like to think of ourselves as exceptions. Remember in the last chapter how some people refuse to learn from trail lore because they think they are so unique that the lessons from history do not apply to them? In the same way, some believe that the Principles of good health do not apply to them. Or else they declare that there is no pattern and they point to the exceptions as proof that no pattern exists. Although this thinking may comfort some, it ignores the wealth of evidence that supports the Fifth Principle. Although it's nice to know that Uncle

Harry and Grandma Lucy can have unhealthy habits and still live forever, it's more useful to look at what happens when the average person has such poor habits.

But I don't have time to exercise!

Most Americans focus on dieting to lose weight because we are short on time. We all have to eat, so people will try to create short-cuts to weight loss by eliminating the time consuming exercise component and simply cutting back the calories. In fact, by skipping meals they are giving themselves even more valuable time. Although this may lead to thin body, it won't be a healthy one.

I am constantly busy and I am obsessed with efficiency. Although I enjoy exercising, many times it feels like a chore. There are several tricks on how to exercise and not lose time. *First, integrate exercise in all your activities.* For example, avoid taking elevators. In a two-story building where I used to work, I would always see people taking the elevator instead of the steps. Sadly, those were usually the people who needed exercise the most. Then there were the ones who I saw regularly at the gym on the Stairmaster machines. They would take the elevator and then climb up 300 steps in the gym. Go figure.

Then again, some people think I'm nuts because I frequently take the stairs even when my hotel room is on the 11th floor. I especially like to take them going up because it's a good workout. There are other ways to micro-exercise throughout your day:

- Instead of running errands in a car, put on a backpack and take a bike.
- Walk briskly or jog to the store.
- While waiting in line do calf raises or repeatedly tighten your stomach muscles.
- Pass up on the gas powered lawn mower and do it manually.
- Instead of meeting someone for lunch at the restaurant, suggest meeting them at the gym.

A Surprising Physical Change on the AT

Most people aren't surprised to hear that people lose a lot of weight on the AT, or that your resting heart rate plummets due to the incredible amount of cardiovascular exercise.

However, what does surprise most people is that a thru-hiker's foot expands 1-3 shoe sizes!

For example, Lisa started in Maine wearing a shoe that was a size 9 in women's, but by the time she got to Georgia she was wearing a size 9 in men's!

I began the trail with a size 10, and ended wearing a size 13! Granted, the size 13 was a bit big (a 12 would have been better), but you get the idea.

Lisa's biggest fear was that her foot would not shrink back and that she would not be able to fit into all her shoes back home.

Fortunately, your feet do return to their original size within a couple of weeks. *Whew!*

○ Run up and down the soccer field cheering your kid on instead of sitting on your duff. You may look silly, but your kid will love you; unless, of course, he's a teenager, in which case he'll think you're an embarrassing dork.

It's funny how many claim to not have time to exercise, yet according to the A.C. Nielsen Co. the average American watches 3 hours and 46 minutes of TV everyday (more than 52 days of nonstop TV-watching per year). By age 65 the average American will have spent nearly 9 years glued to the tube.[27] So I propose a simple solution: *the TV does not go on unless you are exercising at the same time!* If you have an exercise machine, put it in front of the TV. If your ceilings are high enough, consider buying a jump rope. Do sit ups, push ups, and dips. Bring out the dumbbells while watching the news or a reality TV show. Of course, part of watching TV is being able to lay back and relax, especially if you've had a hard and stressful day. However, this is just a habit that most of us have developed. Other people use exercise to relax after a hard and stressful day. The least you can do is stretch every muscle in your body while watching TV; stretching is fairly mellow and might be good for those who really can't give up being a couch potato. If nothing else, forcing yourself to do some exercise while watching TV may diminish your appetite for TV.

I favor parking a few miles from the office and walking to work. You get the benefit of exercise and besides it is easier to get a parking space. — Dr. Paul Dudley White, Cardiologist, 1886-1973

Another key technique is simply making exercise a priority. You don't hear people saying, "I don't have time to go to work," or "I don't have time to take my dying child to the hospital," or "I don't have time to pick up the $3 million reward."

It's not that we don't have enough time, it's just that we have to rearrange our priorities. Treat exercise like an important appointment. If your boss asks you to come to a meeting, you will be there. Hence, if you make exercise a priority, you find the time in your schedule. Finally, consider this. The President of the United States is pretty busy. If anyone has an excuse of not having enough time to exercise due to a busy schedule, it would be him. However, most US Presidents have made a point to exercise regularly. So if they can find the time, so can you.

But most doctors say three days of exercise is good enough!

True, if you just want an adequate level of fitness. However, this book is about *optimizing* your life and your body. If you want to optimize your body, you need more than three hours of rigorous exercise a week.

I encourage everyone to exercise everyday because I know most people won't. However, those who try to exercise seven days a week frequently end up doing it four to six days a week—which is good. On the other hand, if you only try to exercise three times a week, it's easy to miss one day and your fitness starts to slip. Finally, if you're one of those rare individuals who have such incredible self-discipline that you do indeed exercise seven days a week, then congratulations, you're ready to become a thru-hiker.

Here's how I make sure I exercise everyday: I tell myself that the only way I can earn a shower is to exercise for it. No exercise, no shower. The incentive works for me, although I'll confess that a couple of days of month I have that not-so-fresh feeling.

But I can lose weight by going on this fad diet!

There are always wacky diets out there. Some advocate minimizing carbohydrates. Others say eliminate fats. Others proclaim that a liquid diet is best. Others declare that eating raw foods is the way to go. Others suggest eating only pineapples. I figure it's only a matter of time before some diet guru declares you can lose weight by eating pastries and donuts all day long.

Why do some diets work and others don't?

The main reason *any* diet leads to weight loss is that the individual spends more calories than she takes in. Some people, for example, get on a low carbohydrate diet and follow the regime which advises regular exercise. These people may not have exercised before and were consuming 3,000 calories a day, while burning only 2,600. Now they eat high fat (and high calorie) foods, but because they eat the recommended portions, only consume 2,700 calories a day. Moreover, they start to exercise whereas before they weren't exercising, so they burn an extra 500 calories a day, so their daily calorie burn is now 3,100. As a result, they send their body into a calorie deficit, so it begins to consume their fat stores, and the pounds come off. This result would happen no matter what they would be putting in their mouths (as long as the caloric intake and expenditure were the same). Yet they erroneously credit the *type* of food they are eating, rather than the *amount of calories* they are eating and the level of exercise they are doing.

Carbohydrates are not evil. One common misconception is that carbohydrates are particularly good at boosting insulin levels. Not so say Harvard, Michigan State, and University of Alabama researchers who studied 12,000 individuals. They found insulin levels were the same in those eating 60 percent of their calories as carbohydrates, and those eating 40 percent. According to researcher Dr. Jean Kerver, "insulin does not squirrel away food into fat cells. Only eating more calories than you burn does that."[28]

Judith Wurtman, an M.I.T. brain researcher, proved that carbohydrates help regulate the brain's level of serotonin which makes us feel full and happy. On the anti-carb craze, she told *Time Magazine* that someday we'll realize that we were being pretty "stupid."[29]

Since weight loss is all about controlling your calorie input and output, a good diet must recommend nutritious calories and frequent exercise. Therefore, when evaluating a hip, new diet:

- **Beware of diets that don't emphasize fruits and vegetables:** they are the healthiest food groups you can consume, so don't avoid them.

- **Be cautious about diets that encourage you to eat high fat foods:** they are packed with calories, so it's easy to consume a lot of calories.

- **Avoid diets that promise that you won't need to exercise:** although you can lose weight without exercise, working out is a key element to being healthy.

It's helpful to learn from trail lore on this debate. Who lives the longest? Presumably, they must have a healthy diet, right? Japanese live the longest—and they hardly eschew carbohydrates, they eat rice with nearly every meal. Those who live near the Mediterranean also have long life spans, and they eat plenty of fruits and vegetables, along with breads and pastas. Both societies eat healthy calories. Let's learn from them.

We can also learn from the National Weight Control Registry, which studied 5,000 people who had lost weight and kept it off for at least six years. What did the 5,000 people have in common? On average they consumed 1,800 calories a day and walked four miles.

Fad diets come and go, but calories are calories. If the diet emphasizes eating lots of fruits and vegetables and also stresses the importance of exercise, then it's hard to go wrong.

But counting calories is too hard!

When I make a salad at home or a pasta dish, I have only a vague idea of how many calories are in there. Even if I follow a recipe that tells me how many calories there are, I may pour more oil on the salad than asked for, but perhaps I won't suck up the oil with a piece of bread. Restaurants rarely advertise how many calories are in a selection. All this makes counting calories a tricky proposition. However, there is a solution:

1. **Start reading labels and pay attention to how many calories each serving has.** Eventually you will have an intuitive feel of how many calories are in a peanut butter and jelly sandwich.

2. **Log your calories on a notepad.** Although you may not be 100 percent accurate, measuring your caloric intake will be extremely revealing. For instance, you might be sneaking in a few hundred calories when your coworkers offer you a piece of cake.

3. **Pay attention to your waistline and scale.** If you don't notice an improvement after several weeks of watching your calorie intake and output, then start looking for ways to cut back on the calories and exercise more often and more rigorously.

Although you may never have an extremely accurate estimate on your daily caloric intake, these three steps will help you get a better sense of what you're really consuming.

But water is such a boring beverage!

Although humans are mostly water and can't live without it, some just don't enjoy drinking it straight. One simple way to change this habit is to dilute your drink of choice with water. If you enjoy

Spider Runs Out of Calories

I met him in the Bigelows of Maine. We bonded because he was also from the San Francisco Bay Area. He always had a smile on his face, and he hiked with an incredible amount of passion. His secret: go slow, but take few breaks. As a result, he hiked the whole trail in under five months.

However, by the end of the trail his calorie deficit was starting to sap his energy. Later he wrote me an email:

"I really should have done more research on which foods supplied the calories that I needed on the trail…. By the end of the trip, I had lost so much weight that I could no longer count on my own stores and the 6-7 days of food that I normally carried was getting way too heavy and still didn't supply all that I needed."

Although he completed the AT, his dietary choices left him exhausted.

drinking juice, for example, start diluting it with water. At first, add just a bit of water, so that it tastes basically the same. Once you get used to it, add some more. Keep this up until you're drinking mostly water, and you're only adding a tiny amount of juice. By then it just tastes like flavored water, and perhaps you'll summon the courage to eliminate the flavoring. At that point, you'll hardly miss it. Whether you minimize the juice or eliminate it, you will have pulled out at least a few hundred calories from your diet. Also, consider just throwing a slice of lemon in the water to give it some flavor. Many alcoholics learn to wean themselves from wine by diluting it. Although this is sacrilegious to a wine aficionado, it may work for you.

If nothing else, just remind yourself how much money you're saving by drinking water. For some, that will be motivation enough!

But you didn't practice this diet on your thru-hike!

You're right, I did not eat mainly fruits and vegetables when I thru-hiked the AT. Although I would have loved to do that, as I explained earlier, carrying four days of fresh fruits and vegetables is extremely heavy, and under hot, humid conditions they spoil quickly. The only thing that works is eating dehydrated fruits and vegetables, which I did as much as I could.

However, even if I could somehow eat nothing but fruits and vegetables during a thru-hike (let's say I had a personal chef like Alice Waters tagging along with a kitchen at each campsite), I wouldn't want to. Fruits and vegetables don't have a lot of carbohydrates, and when you do over 12 hours of exercise a day, you need mega-fuel—and the best fuel is carbohydrates. Fruits and vegetables just don't pack many calories, which is fine when we only exercise an hour a day, but it's just not enough for a highly active person.

Therefore, the more active you are, the more low-fat complex carbohydrates (e.g., whole grain pastas, whole wheat breads, beans, etc.) you should add to your diet. These will boost your healthy calories and give you the energy you need to accomplish your physical objectives.

So when I got a ride with some nice folk and a very friendly dog and I realized that it would be an obnoxious hitch back, I decided to get a room. Actually what I got was a hiker bunkhouse to myself, with kitchen, sauna, game room, the works. 3 stories. So I had an entire cheesecake (3,000 calories!) and stayed up late watching bad movies on TV. Even with all that, I think I would have preferred the old mac and cheese and rat-infested shelter. — Mary Poppins, AT Nobo, Trail Journal, August 23, 2001

But life is too short to give up bacon!

For many, a meal is just not a meal without steak. Others simply can't imagine life without chocolate or Jelly Bellies.

Let's be clear: *I am not advocating complete abstinence from any type of food.* Remember, hike your own hike! So if you truly love a particular type of food, eat it. But if it's unhealthy, consider eating smaller portions of it and chew it very slowly. That way your level of enjoyment remains the same. If I just inserted a Hershey's chocolate bar in your stomach, you wouldn't really notice the difference between that and some potatoes. The taste buds are on your tongue, not in your stomach, so when you're eating a treat, keep chewing the food and keep it on your tongue to savor it fully. Make those strips of bacon last.

But small dinners diminish family time!

Dinners are important reunion times for families. My Chilean mother always cooked a feast for dinner and our family of four treasured this ritual. It was the one time during the day when the whole family sat at a table together. It was almost a sacred time that we would rarely miss. My mom still cooks up a storm for dinner, but it's always light—soup and salads. These are foods that are low in calories and easily digested. However, one thing hasn't changed: we still have arguments and endless debates!

Small, low calorie dinners do not mean short dinners. You can still bond with your family. One advantage of eating salads for dinner is that since the food doesn't get cold, no one is rushed to wolf down the food before it gets cold. Therefore, people can take more time to have conversations in a leisurely fashion. Similarly, thorough chewing extends the meal, giving plenty of time to connect—as long as your family allows talking with food in your mouth.

But I need to get into a bathing suit next week!

Crash low-calorie diets can be disastrous. Once you understand that the secret to losing weight is to create a calorie deficit, many lazy and impatient people will impulsively try to circumvent the lesson of the AT in two ways:

1. The lazy will think, "I don't have time for exercise, so I'll just eat 1,000 calories a day and that will put my body in a calorie deficit and I'll lose weight!"

2. The impatient will go one step further, "I need to lose weight in a month, so I'll exercise like a maniac, and only consume 500 calories a day—that'll give me a massive calorie deficit and I'll be skinny in no time!"

Unfortunately, both of these techniques are terribly wrong, and even life threatening. Consider this:

○ According to the Center for Disease Control, 60 people died in one year as a result of ventricular arrhythmias (irregular heartbeats) due to liquid protein diets that supplied a pathetic 400 calories a day.

○ Overweight individuals that jump on diets that deliver 400 to 800 calories suffer a multitude of problems: hair loss; muscle cramps; fatigue; intolerance to cold; and menstrual problems.

○ Studies in the *Archives of Internal Medicine* showed one out of three who lose weight extremely fast develop gallbladder disease.

Our cells need fuel to survive. Starving them of their nutrients just punishes your body and makes it more vulnerable to diseases and other ailments.

What human organ consumes 20 percent of your calories? Your brain.[30] The brain-body connection is clear once you realize that your brain craves 20 percent of the nutrients and energy that you consume. When you deprive it of those nutrients, your brain is weak or must steal the fuel that would have otherwise helped your liver cells, your skin cells, or your heart cells. If they could, these cells would love to hit you upside the head for depriving them.

Lastly, many people who try these radical ultra-low calorie diets do not lose any weight. The body reacts to the calorie crisis by clinging desperately to what little body fat remains. It goes into a protective mode and does everything it can to hold onto fat by slowing down the metabolism. Therefore, there is a point of diminishing returns when you create a calorie deficit. If the deficit is too large, your body rebels and no longer loses weight. That's why it's key to eat at least 1,500 calories a day, it's the minimum you need to keep the lights on.

Summary

One of life's great mysteries is how a two pound box of candy can make you gain five pounds. However, my thru-hike solved this conundrum. You can eat that two pound box of candy and lose weight if you just do enough exercise!

Nevertheless, most of us don't have the time to do 12 to 16 hours of exercise a day. Moreover, as the AT showed, eating candy all day can lead to burnout. Therefore, we have to watch what we eat and how often (and intensely) we exercise.

Let's sum up this chapter and the highlights of the Pilgrim's Regime:

- You can't squeeze the most out of life if you ignore your body.

- Weight loss is all about calories—burn more than you take in and you will lose weight.

- Consume nutritious calories—focus on fruits and vegetables because they're loaded with vitamins, minerals, and fiber.

- Spread your daily calories over five or more meals, focus on eating most of your calories in your first eight hours of your day, and have a light dinner.

- Chew 50 times before swallowing or at least as much as you can stand.

- Drink at least three liters of pure water a day—make water your main beverage.

- Take a multivitamin everyday, and consider taking other supplements if your doctor recommends it.

- Minimize your consumption of all drugs, including tobacco, alcohol, and caffeine.

- Exercise at least five hours a week and include the three key elements: cardiovascular training; weightlifting; and stretching.

- Relaxing and meditating are the final elements to a healthy body.

We were still not through the great state of Virginia. Although the AT goes through 14 states, 25 percent of the trail is in Virginia. After blasting through the Mid-Atlantic States, Virginia seemed to take forever. Similarly, this was a long chapter, but like Virginia, it's necessary to complete the pilgrimage. By Virginia our odyssey had taught us to eat well, walk hard, and sleep soundly. Doing so not only allowed us to squeeze the most out of bodies and minds, but also life itself.

Unbeknownst to me, the trail had another lesson to teach me. I would learn that lesson by hearing one amazing story and by suffering through a national tragedy.

By noon Lisa was exhausted in the balds of Tennessee. She clung onto a Butterfinger candy bar for comfort. Although we don't gorge on them, such treats sure were a nice reward after a long day. At this point we had walked roughly 1,800 miles and had about 370 to go.

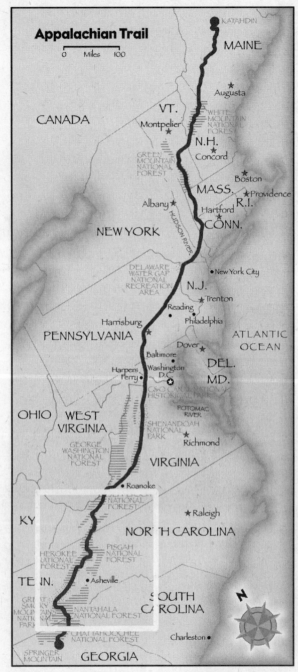

© *Appalachian Trail Conservancy, reprinted with permission*

Chapter 6:
Perform Trail Magic

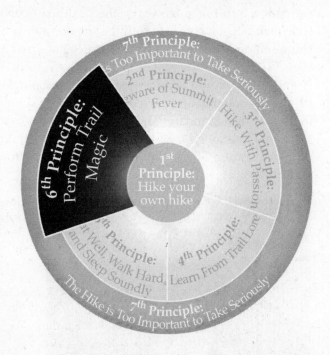

One of the most amazing stories I brought back from my odyssey was told by a thru-hiker named Gander. It's a story about the unbelievable generosity on the trail. I met Gander in the Great Smoky Mountains National Park, about 100 miles from the end of our journey. It was a beautiful autumn day and the multicolored leaves in the Smokies framed our shelter as the sun set. Normally I didn't stay in shelters, but regulations required it because of the prevalence of bears. It's the opposite of a zoo, as humans put themselves in a cage while the bears roam free outside. A weekend backpacker told us that the temperature would dip below freezing that night. So we huddled by a camp fire as Gander told us his tale.

But before Gander shared his tale, he admitted he wasn't a true thru-hiker because he started on Mount Washington in New Hampshire and hiked south to Georgia. Many people might just write off that he skipped one and a half states out of 14 and still call him a thru-hiker. However, the thru-hiker community is not so lenient when it comes to calling someone a thru-hiker. It would be one thing if those one and half states had been Maryland and West Virginia. Missing half of Maryland's AT miles is only missing 20 miles; if you add West Virginia's paltry 2.6 miles, you would be missing roughly one percent of the trail by skipping those 22.6 miles. Besides, Maryland and West Virginia are cakewalks by AT standards. Although thru-hiker purists would still frown sternly on such cheating, at least some thru-hikers would forgive you over

Gander and Lisa chat at the Silers Bald Shelter in the Smoky Mountains. Later we huddled next to a campfire as Gander shared his trail magic story.

a beer, and say, "Hey, that's close enough buddy, you're a thru-hiker in my book."

Gander, however, hadn't skipped the humble AT trails in Maryland and West Virginia. No, he had skipped the toughest state of all, Maine, and missed half of the second hardest state, New Hampshire. Indeed, the terrain in New Hampshire and Maine is without question the most brutal on the AT. Many Northbounders seriously underestimate the difficulty, believing their hardened bodies can hike through it with minimal trouble. We met and heard of countless thru-hikers who had to abandon their journey in New England because the diabolical trail and rough weather broke them down. It's quite common to have to grab the roots of trees to pull yourself up the trail, or slide on your butt down some steep, slick rock. Throw in some lightening storms and snow and you can understand why so many thru-hikers give up in New England.

By skipping those two states, Gander managed to avoid a whopping 360 miles, or 17 percent, of the trail. On the other hand, Gander never declared he was a thru-hiker, so nobody had a beef with him. I liked calling him the "Benton MacKaye thru-hiker." In 1921 MacKaye, a dreamy Harvard graduate, had a bright idea when he was sitting on top of a mountain in Vermont, overlooking the Long Trail, the first 100+ mile trail in America. MacKaye thought it would be wonderful if we had an even longer trail

Hitching With a Cop

Hitchhiking is safer than you might expect. For example, in Pallmerton, Pennsylvania I was sticking out my thumb when a police officer pulled up. I expected him to give us a ticket for trying to hitchhike, but instead he offered us a ride!

Turns out that the Pallmerton police station lets AT thru-hikers stay in their barracks for free.

It's just one of the many examples of the overwhelming generosity and support along the AT.

stretch the length of the Appalachian Mountain Range. Hence, MacKaye hatched the idea of the AT and in 1927 hooked up with another Harvard graduate, Myron Avery, an intense, no-nonsense, action oriented man.

MacKaye had to decide where the AT would start and end. He declared that the southern terminus would be Mount Oglethorpe, in Georgia. However, by the 1950s chicken farmers had encroached on the trail by the terminus, thereby detracting from the wilderness experience. The AT planners thought it would just be easier to re-route the trail to a new and nearby southern terminus, Springer Mountain, than to fight with a bunch of chickens.

MacKaye argued that the northern terminus should be Mount Washington in New Hampshire. Therefore, by hiking from Mount Washington to Georgia, Gander was hiking the AT as MacKaye envisioned it. That's why I call him the Benton MacKaye thru-hiker.

However, once the Mainers found out that they would be left out of the fun, they demanded that the AT include their state. In my version of the story (which has absolutely no basis in fact), MacKaye laughed at Maine's face when they suggested they had some noteworthy mountains to climb.

"Give me a break," MacKaye chuckled, "You guys have a bunch of puny little hills."

But eventually the Mainers got their way and they took their ultimate revenge on MacKaye. They wanted to show him (and world) that their mountains are significant. To display just how tough they are, they made sure to go over every single peak they had (whether it had a view or not) and to ban all switchbacks from their state. The *coup de grace* was Katahdin—the toughest mountain on the AT. This would leave all thru-hikers with a lasting vision in their minds: Maine's mountains kick your ass.

This imaginary tale is the only explanation I could come up with to explain the sadistic trails of Maine.

No act of kindness, no matter how small, is ever wasted.
— Aesop, the Lion and the Mouse

So Gander missed out on some rough trail. However, as he explained by the campfire, he had some incredibly good fortune. One day he was hitchhiking, needing to re-supply. An old lady picked him up and offered to take him into town. After hearing how far he had walked, the lady invited him to stay one night at her house so he could shower, eat a home cooked meal, do laundry, and sleep in a real bed. Although such a generous offer was rare and much appreciated, it was not unheard of. As we listened to the crackling fire, we knew there was more to the story.

The next day she dropped him off back on the trail. He thanked her a million times for her generosity, but then she told him, "Here, take $40. You'll need it."

"No," he smiled, stunned by her selflessness, "You've been so good to me, I can't take any more."

"C'mon, just take it," she insisted.

"No thank you," he said. "I'm not poor, I really don't need it, and you've already been so wonderful to me."

Dismayed, she said, "Fine."

He got out of the car and bid his final farewell to an elderly lady who yesterday was a complete stranger. With a warm smile, she wished him the best of luck on his journey to Georgia. Then, as she started to drive away, she flung the $40 out of her car in his direction and drove away. The two $20 bills tumbled to his feet. By the time he registered what had just happened, her car was far in the distance, leaving only rustling leaves behind.

You have not lived today until you have done something for someone who cannot pay you back. — John Bunyan in
Pilgrim's Progress

Thru-hikers have a name for what Gander experienced: *Trail Magic*. Trail magic is a selfless act that an individual does for a random thru-hiker. Thru-hikers call these generous individuals *Trail Angels*. Trail Angels perform all sorts of trail magic, including:

- Picking up a hitchhiking thru-hiker to take her into town (or back to the trail).

- Feeding a thru-hiker, no matter how little food.

- Leaving behind soft drinks in a cool stream for thru-hikers to drink.

- Helping a thru-hiker make a phone call or deliver a package.

- Welcoming a thru-hiker into their home.

- Giving a thru-hiker a foot massage.

Gander's extraordinary experience illustrates how so many people who live along the AT practice trail magic. As one pilgrim told me, "Trail magic happens so often, you have to believe that it's not magic, it's just the way people are around the AT." Indeed, the mountain towns along the AT are tight knit communities that don't just serve the AT, they take care of each other.

As Gander finished his story, I stared at the golden embers in the fire and marveled at the wispy smoke reaching out towards the Milky Way. The AT had taught me yet another lesson. *On that cold night in the Smoky Mountains I learned that performing trail magic was the Sixth Principle of squeezing the most out of life.*

Trail magic quiz

Be honest with yourself when you take this quiz.

1. When you see someone struggling with a package in a parking lot, do you offer to help? (Yes/No)

2. When an elderly person walks onto a crowded bus, do you offer your seat? (Yes/No)

3. When someone is signaling to change lanes on the freeway, do you nearly always let them in? (Yes/No)

4. What percentage of your wealth do you donate?

5. How many hours a month do you volunteer for a cause?

6. Before making a decision, how often do you consider how it might impact someone else? (1 = "Never, screw the world, 5 = "Sometimes I put my interest in front of others, sometimes I make a sacrifice for others, 10 = "Always, I'm a saint.")

Scoring: Give yourself eight points for every "Yes." Add up your points and if it's over 40, then you're a generous soul. Otherwise, read on.

Sacred texts shed light on the Sixth Principle

As I said from the beginning, the Principles I learned on my trek are not new. Many wise men have practiced trail magic long before the AT ever existed. Religions agree that following this Principle can lead to profound fulfillment. For example, back in the first century, someone asked Rabbi Hillel to summarize the Talmud, the holy Jewish text. He said that whatever would make you unhappy, do not do to anyone else. In other words, *find happiness by making others happy.* This is similar to Jesus Christ's message of doing unto others like you would like them to do unto you. The Koran also instructs its followers to be selfless and generous. Similarly, the Buddha taught that altruism and self-renunciation was a way of overcoming life's miseries.[31] Clearly, the Buddha would approve of those who practice trail magic. It's no wonder why we tend to feel better when we give.

When Oprah Winfrey asked the Dalai Lama what was the one thing that he knew for sure, he replied, "Altruism is the best source of happiness. There is no doubt about that."[32]

When religions agree with each other it's a good sign that there is universal wisdom in that belief.

Practicing trail magic extends your life

Researchers have discovered that those with an altruistic spirit stay healthier and live longer than others. According to the Medical Research Institute of San Francisco self-centered people are much more likely to die of a heart attack than less self-centered people.[33] Moreover, Dr. David Sobel's research discovered that selfless pleasures improve one's health. Examples of such trail magic include caring for a pet, protecting the environment, helping a loved one, or sheltering the homeless (or a thru-hiker).[34] *It's trail magic's strange paradox: when you do something that has absolutely no benefit for yourself, you help yourself.*

Trail magic stories

There are a number of trail magic stories that I accumulated during my 111 day trek. I will share the best ones with you, hoping it inspires you to practice trail magic in your life.

Staring at a house in New Hampshire

The first good trail magic story I heard was in New Hampshire, when we were staying at the dorms of Dartmouth College. A thru-hiker couple was admiring the colonial architecture of a beautiful house in Hanover on a hot, humid summer day. In less than a minute, the front door opened and a warm, smiling lady said, "You guys look thirsty, would you like a drink of water?"

Surprised by the offer, the pilgrims said, "Thanks, but we're OK."

"How about a Coke?" she offered.

The thru-hikers looked at each other, noticing the sweat drip down their foreheads, and then with a big wide smile said, "That sounds good."

I'm enjoying the bald mountains of Tennessee. It was a chilly, but clear October day. Scientists aren't sure why these hills are bald, but some people believe that it's because UFOs landed here. That's clearly the most likely explanation.

Before they knew it, they were invited to the backyard barbeque, allowed to do laundry, take a shower, and stay in a comfy bed. Although they were invited to stay a couple of days, they began to feel guilty, so they left after just one night. I was mesmerized by the story because it was my first concrete example that trail magic did indeed happen. Little did I know that over the 111 days, Lisa and I would be invited to 12 different houses and enjoy the same selfless generosity.

Only on the Trail would you meet someone who would go out of their way to help you in the ways she helped us. I will really miss that spirit when we return to real life. As we make the transition back to life away from the Trail, we will always look back on this time of our lives as one of the greatest experiences. We may never be as free as we were on the trail, though I think we will always strive to live a life as close to that as possible.

I want to give a special thanks to a group of ladies we met at Kincora Hostel in Tennessee. Get this, I talked to them for no more than five minutes and in that time they

*offered us a ride to Georgia when we got done. They gave
us their phone numbers and off we went. When we were
almost done we called one of them, Sherry, and she picked
up our Greyhound tickets and even told us we could stay
with her until the bus came. We got in a day earlier than
planned and she came right over and picked us up. She
drove many miles to pick us up, then she brings us into
her house like we were family. We stayed with her for
two days. She then brought us to the bus station that was
again many miles away. These are the type of things that
happen on the trail, no where else on Earth I think that
would happen. I want to thank her from the bottom of my
heart, she is a living angel.*
— *Budder Ball and Zokwakii, AT Sobos 2002*[35]

Trail magic in the Mid-Atlantic

Churches are known for their generosity, and they exemplify it
along the AT. For instance, in Vernon, New Jersey, the St. Thomas
Episcopal Church demonstrates its amazing generosity: they have
a hiker box full of food donations, shower, laundry, internet connection, and a carpeted floor to sleep on. It's all free, although most
pilgrims donate something.

In Pennsylvania, Pastor Karen of the Presbyterian Church (which
let us shower at their church) warned us about an upcoming wa-
terless stretch. By the time we got to Pennsylvania our number one
concern was no longer the heat, but the lack of water. Most of the
springs were dry, so there were long stretches without water from
Pennsylvania to Virginia. One day, for example, we walked over 20
miles and there was not one drop of water available.

Therefore, right before the dry zone began we stopped at a mobile
home at Wind Gap, Pennsylvania and asked a lady if she would be
willing to fill up our water bottles. Not only did she fill them up,
but she came back with a liter of raspberry-flavored seltzer water,
four organic peaches, and a pack of Bubble Yum (which she said
would "help ward off the dehydration").

We talked with her for a few minutes. She was going to visit her mom who had a stroke and could not walk. She had cancer (and still had not told her mom) and was undergoing chemotherapy. She was obviously not wealthy. Clearly, she was not in the best of situations, yet she graciously gave to us, even though we were complete strangers.

Our first big trail magic experience

There are different degrees of trail magic. From the simple, like handing someone some extra water when they need it, to the ultra generous, like Gander's experience.

A funny thing happened to us on the way to Duncannon, Pennsylvania. Lisa had commented the other day that while we have received some amazing trail magic, we have not been so lucky to experience mega trail magic. We'd heard of tales of strangers offering hikers a place to stay in their homes, feeding them, letting them take showers and do laundry. Indeed, three hikers asked for water at one house, and the owner replied, "Sure! And how many hamburgers would you like?"

Next thing you know, they were each eating countless hamburgers, taking well deserved showers, and happily sleeping in his garage. Thru-hikers are easy to please. How often does your guest thank you profusely for letting them sleep on your garage floor? Although some may not find that offer generous, thru-hikers do. It was incredible trail magic, and we wondered why we hadn't gotten such good fortune. As always, the AT surprised us and fulfilled our wishes.

We were walking along in Pennsylvania when we spotted a family of four heading toward us on the trail. They gave us a friendly hello, and of course we reciprocated.

Kris (dad), Lara (mom), Ben (their son), and Zachary (Ben's cousin) began to ask about our AT experience. Before we knew it, these generous souls invited us to their home so we could sleep in a real bed, have some food, and relax!

The AT has many hostels along the way, and Kinkora's hostel in Tennessee is one of the best. The incredibly generous Bob Peoples and his wife will let you stay in their rustic hostel for free, although nearly everyone donates at least $5. Bob not only made us a fire to keep us warm during the chilly night, but he also selflessly drove us down the mountain to the grocery store so we could re-supply. While Lisa packed up the next morning, Bob told us that it had just stopped snowing and that we would have clear weather for a week. His warm spirit was unforgettable.

Here we were, dirty and smelly, and yet these total strangers were opening their homes to us. It was truly a magical moment and we felt so blessed to have met them.

We told Kris that Andy Jones (a business school classmate of mine) had already offered to shack us up for a couple of nights, so Kris quickly said that he would happily drive us into town to Andy's house. We gratefully accepted his company and his ride. Before we knew it, we met up with Andy and Kara (his wife) to have a fantastic dinner at a Dutch family style restaurant. Our large group, united by the AT, had a wonderful time. Although we never stayed with Kris and his family, we were forever grateful for his altruistic offer. It was the first time any one offered us mega-trail magic.

Hitchhiking trail magic

At Harper's Ferry we visited the headquarters of the Appalachian Trail Conservancy, the governing body of the AT. A woman interviewed us about our AT experience, and the next day she let us hitch a 40-mile ride with her to DC. This was our second longest hitch. Our longest was also our first. David was a gracious salesman who drove us over 100 miles to the Baxter State Park entrance in Maine. This foreshadowed the enormous generosity that we would experience throughout the adventure.

Corporate trail magic

Corporations perform trail magic too. Cynics tend to associate corporations as evil, self-centered entities. They forget that the folks who work there are normal everyday people. For example, a friend of Lisa's had her company (which specializes in temporary corporate housing) put us up in this beautiful apartment in the middle of DC. It was amazing! Thanks to Oakwood Worldwide we were living in luxury. We spent a whole day just hanging out in the apartment, admiring indoor plumbing, the plush bed, the TV, and the air conditioning. Oakwood had little to gain from this offer, but like many corporations throughout America, gave selflessly.

> *The true measure of a man is how he treats someone who can do him absolutely no good.* — Samuel Johnson

Ten different companies sponsored our trek in a variety of ways. GoLite, for example, donated hundreds of dollars of gear to support us. I believe they have the best and lightest backpacking gear and so I was thrilled when they responded generously when I asked for their support. Canon loaned us a video camera to record the experience and replaced it when we broke it (twice!). Pristine, REI, Sunridge Farms, X-Terra QE3, Cascade Designs, and Aquavie all charitably donated in one way or another.

Although it is easy to focus on some of the negative actions that corporations throughout the world do, there are many companies who donate massive amounts of money and time to all sorts of causes, frequently for little direct benefit. Corporate trail magic is more common than you think.

Visiting Monticello

One of my goals on my trek was to savor some of the off-the-trail sites. It would be a shame to pass up some of the major cities and attractions that are just a short distance away. For example, we made side treks to New York City and Washington, DC. These pit stops were useful for recharging our batteries and to see what the real world was up to.

My favorite US President is Thomas Jefferson, so visiting his home and grave at Monticello was a delight. We hitched to Charlottesville, Virginia and along the way met Jim Morgan, who drove us on a quick tour of the University of Virginia, introduced us to our first Waffle House restaurant, and dropped us off at Monticello. After all this generosity and trail magic, Jim gave us his home phone number and offered to help us out just in case the need would arise. Little did any of us know that we would call on his aid later.

Jim Morgan is a Trail Angel who delivered some incredible trail magic.

Lisa is relishing a break with Jim Morgan's dogs on his 20 acre house in Virginia. Jim let us stay in his cozy guesthouse. Trail magic rarely felt so good.

Generosity and interest are so common in most towns near the trail that when you find a community that just doesn't care, it seems surprising.
— Dan R. Smith, a thru-hiker[36]

After touring Monticello, we hitched back to Waynesboro to pick up our re-supplies. We did not want to miss this package. The Waynesboro re-supply had five days of food, our third new pair of shoes, and the section of the guidebook that described the upcoming 100 miles of trail. We could survive without all these things by hitching to a supermarket, hiking in our worn out sneakers, and just walking blindly along the trail without a guidebook; however, we preferred not having to do all that.

The problem was that we couldn't remember where we shipped our package! So we called the two nearby hotels, and both said they didn't have the package. A third hotel had permanently closed, and we feared that maybe the package went there. We also thought that maybe the package went to the post office somehow. It wouldn't be the first time that the post office did something strange. What exactly happens behind the doors of the US post office is a perplexing mystery, especially for those who work there.

It was Saturday afternoon, and the post office didn't open until Monday. We called Jim, because he had offered to let us crash at his place if we were caught in a tough situation. We left a message. While waiting for Jim to call us back, a kind couple spotted us, and said, "How's the hike going?"

We told them our sob story and they offered to drive us to the two hotels nearby to make sure the package wasn't there. It wasn't. Then they offered to drive us close to Jim's place. We graciously accepted their generosity and traded trail tales in the car ride. The gentleman who drove us was a pastor who had hiked over 1,000 miles of the trail; his trail name was "Wild Bill."

Wild Bill dropped us off in Charlottesville, because we thought that was near Jim's place. It wasn't. When we finally got a hold of Jim, we found out that we were now over 30 minutes from his house, and that we would have been better off staying put. To top it off, Jim had already gone looking for us near the trail at 9 p.m.

Despite being so far away, Jim picked us up and took us to his charming guest house on his beautiful 20 acre ranch!

We met his wonderful wife, Cathy, and spent all day Sunday with them and their two dogs. It was genuine trail magic at its best. Jim's warmth and altruism were unforgettable.

The irony is that we never did find out what happened to that package. The new pair of shoes, guidebook, and food were all lost somewhere in the mystifying void of the US post office.

The day hikers we've met, the Trail Angels, the hostel owners who have been patient and kind, the postal workers who laugh with us when taping all our boxes— you impact our journey more than you'll ever know. We've learned more about human nature by merely observing the kindness of strangers than we ever will by watching the calculated behavior of 'civilized' folk. It has been eye-opening and heart warming to need you, all of you. — FeatherWeight, Nobo 2001 AT Thru-Hiker

Will barter shelter, food, shower, and laundry for a good story

We met Jim Chester in North Carolina while he was out on a day hike. He said, "I'm inviting you to my house, and all I ask in exchange is that you share with me some of your stories." We had a nice bed in his lovely summer home, showers, and a warm meal: the works.

Some not-so-Bland trail magic

We were approaching a town called Bland in Virginia. I wonder what inspired the town's founders to call their town "Bland." They should have talked with the Amish folks in Pennsylvania who named their town Intercourse. Now that's good marketing.

At the shelter just north of Bland, we found a note that said that thru-hikers are welcome to stay in Bland with two former Lutheran pastors named George and his wife Murray. George invited us to watch TV, do laundry, and sleep on the carpeted floor of their living room. Meanwhile, Murray cooked a delicious dinner. Although we repeatedly offered to pay for all this, they adamantly refused. George, who had thru-hiked the AT one and half times with only one lung, felt he was simply giving back for all the trail magic he had received. What we didn't know was that George wasn't finished showering us with trail magic.

Over dinner we had told him of how we had made the mistake of packing laundry detergent in our re-supply packages. Despite putting it in a tightly sealed plastic bag, the pungent odor of detergent permeated all our food. As a result, for a couple of weeks all our food tasted like Tide.

We were so hungry we would eat it anyway.

The next day we hugged George and Murray good bye, thanking them profusely, believing we would never see them again. However, about 20 miles south of Bland we saw something tied around a tree. It was a package with a note for "Cartwheel and Mr. Magoo." It was quite a surprise to walk along the AT, hours away from any town, and run into a strange bag hanging in the middle of nowhere, addressed to us! It was a kind note from George wish-

Jim Chester was a day hiker who invited us to his vacation home. All he asked in exchange was that we share our stories.

ing us the best and that we should enjoy the special trail mix he had wrapped around the tree. It was indeed the best trail mix we had on the trail and the way we received it made it even more special.

The next day, as we were about to cross an obscure road in the Appalachian Mountains, we saw George waiting for us by his truck. He handed us some cold Gatorade, fresh bananas, and other home made goodies. Most of all, he had driven out there to cheer us on some more. I believe many thru-hikers abandon their trek because they don't receive the encouragement that other athletes receive in their sporting events. The AT can be a lonely place. Although you may receive an upbeat email from your family and friends every time you re-supply, there's nothing like having them physically on the sidelines cheering you on. George understood this and was there to do just that. With all of George's selflessness, is there any doubt that he was squeezing the most out of life?

The AT hugs the North Carolina and Tennessee border for many miles. It was October which meant that hunting season was starting. Suddenly, many people we saw on the trail had guns, bows, and camouflaged outfits. I tried to not look like a deer.

> *If I made it, it's half because I was game enough to take a lot of punishment along the way and half because there were a lot of people who cared enough to help me.* — Althea Gibson, first black person to play in Wimbledon's tennis tournament (1951)

George and I talked about hiking the Pacific Crest Trail, the 2,650 mile trail that goes from Canada to Mexico via the mountains of California, Oregon, and Washington. Sadly, he figured that at his age and with just one lung, he would never hike that trail which is longer and tougher than the AT. Therefore, when I finally got home after the AT, I mailed George a beautiful coffee table book on the Pacific Crest Trail. It was the least I could do after everything he had done for me.

September 11, 2001

When the four planes exploded, I was busy looking for water.

I was completely oblivious to what was going on in the world. I had no cell phone, radio, or TV. I was completely disconnected. And I was completely out of water.

All the streams and springs were dry. It was ironic that I was out of water near the town of *Troutville*, Virginia. Of all places you figure would have water, it would be a place called Troutville. I imagined my family seeing me on the news, "Man dies of thirst in Troutville, news at 11."

As I entertained myself with that morbid thought, every channel was carrying the tragic news across the world.

About six hours after the first plane struck, we came to a point where the trail crossed a paved road. Lisa and I were relieved when we saw a gas station a quarter of a mile away.

"Water," I uttered through my cotton balled mouth.

We staggered to the gas station, eager to take advantage of their plumbing. When I walked in the radio was blaring. Although I found that odd, I wasn't listening to it and I just concluded that people in Troutville are deaf.

The woman at the cashier said, "You hikin' the AT?"

"Yes," I replied.

"Then you probably haven't heard the news."

"No, what happened?"

Her eyes widened and she said, "Both of the towers in the World Trade Center have been destroyed, they are gone! GONE! A plane has flown into the Pentagon! Another plane has crashed in Pennsylvania! The President's flyin' on Air Force One, nobody knows where he is! We're under terrorist attack!"

I dryly replied, "Oh sure, and I bet California has fallen into the ocean too."

This was the most farfetched story I have ever heard, so clearly it must be a cruel joke that she plays on every disconnected thru-hiker that walks into her store.

"I'm serious," she assured me. "Listen to the radio."

I finally turned my attention to the loud radio and heard Tom Brokaw say, "...it's a sad day for America."

I realized that this was no joke.

We rushed to a TV at a nearby hotel, and saw the horror, albeit much later than most of the world. We were incredulous. We had just been in the Twin Towers about a month before that day; we were near the Pentagon just a week before the attacks. Lisa, who had never traveled east of the Mississippi, cherished seeing and touching those symbols for the first time in her life; now, she cried as she saw those very symbols crumble.

Before the AT, Lisa had never been east of the Mississippi. In August we went into New York's World Trade Center and in September we recharged our batteries in Washington, DC. We left just days before September 11, 2001.

As we watched the surreal replays over and over again, the feeling of dread sunk into me. Although Troutville was hardly a metropolis, I didn't feel safe there. After all, at that moment it seemed that all civilization was threatened. I looked at Lisa and said, "Let's get back on the trail. We have a tarp and plenty of food. Frankly, the last place the terrorists will strike is the Appalachian Trail."

The wilderness never felt so safe. The woods offered protection while the pillars of civilization were under attack. Nature was oblivious: the squirrels continued their busy work; the stars continued to shine; the clouds continued to come and go. The only clue that something was wrong was that there were no planes flying overhead for the rest of our journey.

For the next few weeks we got the news the way people did hundreds of years ago—word of mouth. When we saw a day hiker on the trail (anyone without a large backpack), we would usually ask him about the latest news. About every four days we re-supplied our food at a small town where we could catch some TV news directly. We were probably the most productive people in the US during September 2001. Most of the nation was glued to the TV for several weeks, learning little bits of news as it trickled in. It was nice that when we heard the news we would get a wealth of new information. Nonetheless, speculating on the events of that day became our number one topic of conversation during our daily walks.

The irony is that when I set off to Maine, I told all my friends, "Even though we will be disconnected for four months, I'm sure nothing will have changed in the world. There will still be war in the Middle East, the Democrats and Republicans will still be taxing and spending like crazy, and we'll all be wondering what Clinton ever saw in Monica Lewinsky."

Performing trail magic off the trail

I mention September 11 because there is only one way to describe what happened afterwards: massive trail magic. The big lesson for me was that trail magic should continue when you get off the trail. Before I was not sure if practicing trail magic was a prerequisite to squeezing the most out of life, but after September 11 it became abundantly clear that it is.

The world poured forth so much love and selflessness that the Red Cross did not know what to do with all the donations. Individuals of all religions, races, ages, and wealth gave in various ways. Some gave money, others donated their time, and many did both. This is similar to what we saw the Trail Angels do, except on a much grander scale.

The key is that all the individuals who gave one way or another after September 11 made their lives richer by giving it deeper meaning and connectedness. *It is one of the great paradoxes that religions understand: the more you give, the more you get.*

How do you perform trail magic?

I confess it's easier for me to be selfish than generous. Performing trail magic doesn't come naturally for me. It takes practice. Therefore, as I was closing in on Georgia I thought of six practical steps to encourage everyone to perform trail magic more often.

Step 1: Talk to strangers

Our parents taught us to not talk to strangers and that's good advice for a child. However, many of us continue to obey this command even when we join a retirement community. It is hard to give to strangers if you don't make eye contact and refuse to engage in friendly banter. Be cheerful and welcoming to people wherever you go, even to the ones who seem pretty useless. They may think you're pretty useless too, so show them why you're not and they may do the same.

Step 2: Learn from everyone

Trail Angels are curious about thru-hikers. Perhaps they feel thru-hikers are those harmless members of society who nearly ended up in an insane asylum before escaping to the wilderness. This makes pilgrims odd human specimens. Therefore, Trail Angels were happy to give us a ride, food, or lodging in exchange for something simple: our story.

Thru-hikers aren't the only curious creatures who roam the planet. Even the dullest homo sapien has something he can teach you. The trick is to stay open-minded and inquisitive. When you are, you'll be more willing to give generously to strangers in exchange for their unique knowledge. An old woman can teach you about what life was really like 60 years ago. A middle aged businessman can explain to you the intricacies of his industry. A teenager can educate you on how to be hip.

 Every man I meet is my superior in some way. In that, I learn of him. — Ralph Waldo Emerson

Therefore, if you are debating whether to volunteer to paint a school, help an old man with his groceries, or assist a teenager with her homework, remind yourself that they might teach you a valuable lesson.

Step 3: Think of your epitaph

Do you want people to remember you as a generous soul or as a stingy little bastard? OK, perhaps you don't even care how you're remembered, but people won't wait until you're dead to form an opinion of you. They already have one now. If it's negative today, perform trail magic to change your reputation and you'll be surprised how much your life will improve.

Step 4: Don't just donate money

Although donating money to charities is an excellent way to perform trail magic, some of us are short on cash. Nevertheless, don't avoid giving just because you're broke. For example, you can donate your time by tutoring students, cleaning up a beach, or working the phones at a charity fundraiser. Moreover, even if you are poor, small donations are better than no donation.

Step 5: Build up good karma

The concept of karma is that your actions and conduct today will impact your luck (or misfortune) in the future. You don't have to be Hindu, Buddhist, or even religious to believe in karma. Therefore, if you believe in it, then remind yourself that tossing a few coins to a street performer may be like placing some money in your karma bank account.

Step 6: Follow your religious teachings

Nearly everyone believes in God and most affiliate themselves with a religion. I studied many faiths to get my degree in religion at Amherst College. I learned that all sacred texts instruct their followers to give generously. Many warn that if you live a selfish life your prospects in the afterlife aren't so hot. Perhaps all the motivation you need to give selflessly is the prospect of being re-incarnated as a slug.

Therefore, if you consider yourself a member of a religion, follow its teachings and be altruistic. Otherwise, quit telling people you're religious. On the other hand, if you're selfish and a Satanist, then you're certainly staying true to your principles and you might want to disregard this entire chapter.

Common criticisms

Few would argue against this Principle, but let's consider a couple of objections.

But I don't feel comfortable giving to strangers!

You can perform trail magic on anyone, not just smelly pilgrims. There are many ways to give to those you know:

- Help a co-worker move.
- Baby-sit your friend's children.
- Drop off a surprise gift to your parents.
- Take your daughter to an event she's always wanted to see.
- Help an acquaintance paint his house.

If your relationship with a loved one is suffering, then consider dumping a ton of trail magic on the relationship. You'll be amazed how quickly it repairs itself. In short, don't just perform trail magic on strangers, give to those you know too.

But does this really deserve being a Principle?

Almost nobody would dispute whether performing trail magic is good idea or not. The question is whether performing trail magic is a requirement to get the most out of life.

When I set off on my pilgrimage, I sought to discover the fundamental Principles that we have to follow to squeeze the most out of life. I wasn't interested in the "it's a good idea if you do this" principle. For example, it's a good idea if you make a lot of money or marry well or have children without health problems. These are nice, but they're not vital. You can squeeze the most out of life without much money, without marrying, and with an autistic child.

Therefore, I wanted to cut out the "it helps if you do this" principles, and distill everything down to the essentials. Everyday the AT would teach me something, and everyday I questioned over and over again whether the lesson is a Principle that is truly universal and necessary if you want to optimize your life. There was no Principle that I questioned more than the Sixth Principle. Although my odyssey showed me the importance of trail magic, I

Our spirits were riding high knowing that Georgia was our next and final state. Autumn was in full swing as multicolored leaves adorned the trees and the trail.

wondered whether performing trail magic was a Principle that had the same stature as the other six Principles. After all, can't someone maximize his life by being selfish, or at least not overly generous? Let's say that someone pursues his passion, practices fiscal discipline, maintains good health, learns from history, doesn't take life too seriously, and just enjoys life. Wouldn't most people agree that he has squeezed the most out life?

In fact, perhaps his very selfishness *helped* him squeeze the most out of life. Had he been more giving, he might have been unable to pursue his passion because he would have sacrificed his career for the good of kids, for example. If he could squeeze the most out of life without practicing trail magic, then performing random acts of kindness is not an indispensable Principle.

Post September 11, the AT revealed why one must perform trail magic to squeeze the most out of life. When someone lies on their deathbed, what do they think about? They think about their family and friends. They think about the community that they are leaving behind. The more that they have given to those loved ones, the more fulfilled they feel. It's hard to feel good about your life if you've spent a lifetime putting your needs consistently before others. It took him a while, but even Ebenezer Scrooge learned this lesson.

Human life is about community. Unlike some animals, we are extremely social creatures. We derive satisfaction and fulfillment by interacting with others. Why else is it rare to find someone who vacations solo? Even those who go solo make friends and interact with the locals along the way. Indeed, about 70 percent of those who thru-hike the AT are officially hiking alone, but nearly all find hiking partners along the way. To truly enjoy participating in a community one should give to that community; such generosity is a key ingredient to squeezing the most out of life.

Finally, I don't care what the ancient Egyptians say; you can't take anything with you when you die so you might as well start giving some of it away now.

Summary

I hiked the AT to learn about Mother Nature; instead; I learned about human nature. I thought that I would get in touch with the natural world and the cycle of life. Of course, the AT did bind me to the rhythms of the natural world, but its most surprising revelation was what it showed me about the human world. Let's summarize the key points in this chapter:

- Sacred texts emphasize the importance of performing trail magic.

- Performing trail magic extends your life and improves your happiness.

- Talk to strangers, help them, and then learn from them.

- Think of your epitaph, your karma, and your religious teachings.

Trail magic is one of the most amazing experiences on the trail, and what makes it more amazing is just how often it happens. I never expected such an outpouring of generosity from random strangers. Yet these givers were happier and more fulfilled than the average person. This fact forced me to pay attention to the lesson they were teaching me through their actions. They were getting more out of life by helping others, including filthy pilgrims like us.

We hiked the AT during an interesting time. September 11, 2001 marked a major change to our global society. We felt the shock waves even on the AT, demonstrating how interconnected we have all become; even the AT could not shelter us from this world changing event. It was a pleasure to witness, albeit from a distance, the way Americans rallied together. We were thrilled to see that the trail magic that we encountered was not limited to the trail. However, it was sad that a tragedy had to happen for the rest of the world to show that it was capable of the same selfless acts of generosity that happen everyday on the AT.

Many people are cynical about humans. They say we are simply self-interested and selfish creatures. However, if an alien landed on this planet, and the only thing it did was hike the Appalachian Trail, it would conclude that humans are one of the most generous and selfless species in the Solar System. The alien would also conclude that our species is pretty smelly.

I began this chapter with Gander's tale by the fire ring in the magical Smoky Mountains. I bid farewell to Gander early the next morning. We smiled at each other, knowing that we were less than 100 miles from Springer Mountain—the end of our pilgrimage. The Smokies were my second favorite section of the AT (the White Mountains of New Hampshire was my favorite). It was October and autumn was displaying its marvelous kaleidoscope of colors throughout the leaves of the Smoky Mountains. Nevertheless, I was excited to enter Georgia, our 14th and final state on the AT. Though it lay 100 miles away, over the tranquil zephyr I could hear the sound of Springer Mountain beckoning me.

Around 6 a.m. high in the Smoky Mountains Lisa yelled out, "It's COOOOOOLD!!!!!!" It was October 9 and the temperatures were below freezing. Luckily, we had just received our warm weather clothes for the final push to Georgia.

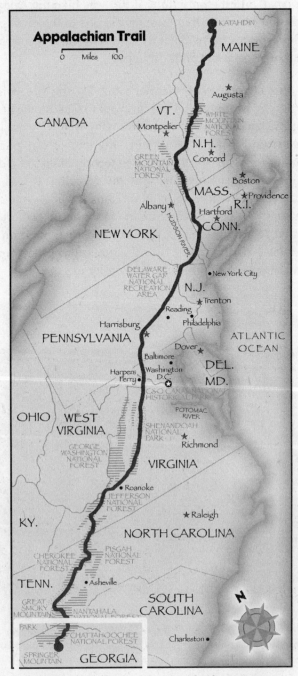

© *Appalachian Trail Conservancy, reprinted with permission*

Chapter 7:
The Hike Is Too Important
To Take Seriously

The AT does not let Northbounders off easy. After hiking 80 percent of the miles, the Nobos run into the toughest part, with the most treacherous weather, as fall merges with winter. It was October 10, and I thought of the straggling Nobos who must be battling the icy conditions of Baxter State Park to make their final climb up the mighty Mount Katahdin. Nobos had warned us about Georgia, but we knew it was nothing compared to Maine. In short, we thought we would get off easy.

We were wrong.

We had smoked through Smoky Mountain National Park in just three days, largely because we followed a 25 mile hike with a 29 mile hike. Those autumn days were crisp and clear, allowing for easy hiking, and giving us spectacular vistas of the multicolored trees in this unforgettable park. We arrived at Fontana Dam thrilled to know that Georgia was just a few days away.

Georgia: our final state. We had been walking from Maine to get to this one last state. Throughout my odyssey people always asked, "So, where are you hiking from?" Now when I responded, "Maine," the reactions were more extreme than ever.

But dark clouds loomed on the horizon. I noted in my journal that the weather forecast predicted rain. Little did I know how much we would get.

A couple of days later, after Jim Chester (a Trail Angel who let us stay at his house) dropped us off, we walked up and down the steep hills of North Carolina's Nantahala mountain range. The rain started coming down that afternoon. It rained while we set up camp, it rained hard that night, and it was raining when we woke up.

That next day it rained nonstop. Rain. Rain. Rain.

After slogging all day through the muddy and slippery trails, we came upon a solitary twisted old oak tree, which marks the famous Bly Gap, the northern border of Georgia. We knew we only had

Taking it all in at Three Miles per Hour

Some may wonder how anyone could possible enjoy a wilderness when one is "zipping through it" at 25 miles a day. The reality is that even at 25 miles a day, we're rarely walking more than three miles an hour.

Think about how much scenery you can take in when you're in a national park driving at 15 miles per hour in a traffic jam. Now imagine going at *one-fifth* of that speed! Now that's slow!

As I liked to joke, "No matter how fast we walk, we can't make the scenery blur."

Other hikers would frequently pass us, so we clearly weren't walking fast. The main difference is that we would spend less time in camp. We would keep hiking until we could no longer see the trail without flashlights.

So while our fellow thru-hikers were hanging out at camp, we would be seeing the scenery they would see the next day.

While they were sleeping in the early morning hours, we would already be enjoying the terrain that they would encounter hours later.

In short, we saw the same things as other hikers. We just slept a bit less and spent less time at camp than other pilgrims. Some may not appreciate our hiking style, but everyone's gotta hike their own hike.

76 miles to go, less than four days. I jumped up and down with excitement as the drizzle continued under the dark skies. We set up our tarp in the light rain and drank from the cool piped spring nearby. The wind really started picking up that night. Fortunately, we were dry in our tarp—at least as dry as we could be. I don't care what method of rain protection you use, if it rains for more than 72 hours straight, you and your gear are bound to get wet.

We awoke the next morning to the beating sound of the rain against our tarp. Tired and bit moist, we crawled out into the rain, packed up, and moved on. This wasn't the easy stroll through

Georgia that I had envisioned. Although the terrain was relatively easy, the weather conditions made it challenging. However, our obsession with Springer Mountain, the end of our pilgrimage, pushed us on.

That day, the third day of rain, was like a monsoon. Although I had experienced incessant precipitation in a rain forest in Costa Rica, this was truly impressive. Nature was letting us have it. The violent winds tested our GoLite umbrellas. Lisa's favorite childhood movie was *Mary Poppins*, and if the winds got any stronger she would become like Ms. Poppins and be carried off into the air.

The storm beat down hard on us, but it didn't dent our spirits. We stayed upbeat. Nevertheless, with our feet constantly wet, we started developing blisters. We stopped hiking at 6 p.m.—abnormally early for us. We wanted to rest our feet so that the blisters didn't get any worse. Before setting up camp, I suggested to Lisa, "Hey, maybe we should go by the stream and 'take a shower.' Oh wait. I'm sorry, there's no need: we've been taking a shower for the past three days!" We burst out in laughter and ignored our aromas.

 You don't stop laughing because you grow old. You grow old because you stop laughing. — Michael Pritchard

That night, however, I didn't want to get wetter than I already was. Therefore, I focused on setting up the tarp as best as I could. As I thrust the final stake into the ground, I couldn't help but admire my masterpiece. I set it up with one side flush to the ground, to make it impossible for water to sneak in. After admiring the aerodynamic shelter, I crawled in for a good night sleep at 7 p.m.

As I drifted to sleep I had visions that Al Capone and his cronies were standing outside the tarp, armed with machine guns. All night long the cankerous machine gun-like rattle of rain battered against our thin tarp. The last time we were pelted so hard by rain was in Maine. For twelve hours we lay huddled in our dry home as nature unleashed its fury upon our surroundings.

The rapid fire rain hammered the tarp all night, but I felt safe. Never mind that the next day we awoke with fallen branches all around us. It would have been rough if one of those hefty branches (or a tree) had fallen on us during the night.

I awoke and soon had an epiphany in the pre-dawn darkness. I was cooking breakfast as the rain continued to slam us for the fourth day in a row. I thought about how I had handled life in the last four days. Whereas the constant rain frustrated me in Maine, in Georgia it just rolled off my back. Instead of feeling depressed about the weather, it was fun to laugh about it. For example, normally we would skip off the rocks to cross a stream, but in those last few days we giggled as we sloshed straight through the streams. Our feet were soaked anyway, so what's the difference? In short, on that unassuming, rainy morning, the AT taught me her final lesson: *the hike is too important to take seriously.*

Oprah Winfrey: "You seem to have a lot of joy. What makes you so happy?"
Dalai Lama: "I don't take myself too seriously! That makes me happy."[37]

I peered out of the tarp and drops of rain greeted my face. During the night I had somehow rolled over my glasses, so now I couldn't see. I chuckled at my misfortune.

Fortunately, Lisa, ever the handywoman, used carefully cut bits of Band Aids to patch the glasses back together again. We packed up our soaked gear and continued walking to Springer Mountain in the driving rain.

Branches and trees had fallen all over the trail, making it a veritable obstacle course. We had only seen a couple of people each rainy day, and nearly all were huddled under the shelters. Aliens must think humans are funny because we run from a drizzle as if it were acid falling from the sky, but we insist on pouring water all over are bodies everyday and washing our clothes in water.

After hiking until midday we pulled aside under a pathetic roof (a trailhead sign with a two foot wide roof). The idea was that this tiny roof would protect us while we cooked. It probably stopped 20 percent of the rain drops from hitting us. However, it wasn't a big deal because by now we were used to cooking and eating in a downpour.

Suddenly a section hiker we had met earlier came by and offered us a ton of food. That trail magic turned the tide. By the time we put the last morsel of food in our mouths, the rain had stopped! Even though the clouds lingered for a few hours, by late afternoon we felt the warmth of the sun's rays. To celebrate, we found a nice open space off the trail and unpacked everything we owned. After four days of incessant rain, everything gets wet, and wetness means weight. Our equipment had picked up about five pounds of water weight. We lounged around for a couple of hours and ate a satisfying meal. Meanwhile, all our gear and clothing dried quickly. We slapped our (once again) light packs on our backs and set off to Springer, with only two days to go.

A serious quiz

Rate how upset you would get on a 1-10 scale (1 = Huh? Something noteworthy happened?; 5 = You curse and your blood boils for a little bit, but then goes down in a couple of minutes; 10 = You pull out your shotgun and take no prisoners):

1. You're on a subway train that's stalled in a tunnel and you're told to exit and take a bus because of a "mechanical problem."

2. You have to make an important call when your cell phone battery dies.

3. You're remodeling your kitchen when the contractor makes an error that sets you back two weeks and $500.

4. You need cash fast and there are 10 people in line at the ATM.

5. You're going out to a nice dinner, all dressed up, when a taxi cab hits a puddle of water and drenches you.

6. You're waiting in line to buy a ticket and someone darts in front of you.

7. You wait to meet a friend at a restaurant, but he never shows.

8. You get a flat tire in the middle of nowhere and it's freezing outside.

9. You and your spouse are finally going to take a vacation when a storm delays all flights for 24 hours.

10. You're watching the climax of a TV program you love when there's a power outage.

Scoring: 10-30 = You will live a long happy life; 31-70 = You could learn ways to brush off these little events in life; 70-100 = Take a deep breath, count to 10, walk around the block, and read the rest of this chapter.

Stressing out sucks

For many people life is serious business. Nearly every event is a big deal. The problem with this perspective is that it decreases your enjoyment and is hazardous to your health. People who are overly serious are easily stressed.[38] There are two types of stress: acute and chronic. They're both bad news.

Acute stress isn't all that bad, as long as it doesn't happen too often and your body has a chance to return to normal. For instance, when a threatening event occurs your body immediately releases chemicals that make you tense, alert, and ready for action. This is known as the stress response or the fight-or-flight response. Your body stays alert until your mind declares that the coast is clear. Your body then stops producing the chemicals that caused the physical reaction and you gradually return to normal. The chemi-

Like this little dog, Lisa learned to not take the hike too seriously. For example, since we only had one outfit, we would have to strip down to the essentials in laundromats. We looked funny, but it worked. Luckily, others in the laundromat weren't taking life too seriously either and didn't give us dirty looks. And these animals just loved us no matter what.

cals take 30 to 60 minutes to leave your system, so if you become stressed again within that time, your body won't recover between the two stressful events. If you keep getting acute stress, you may trigger an abnormal heartbeat or even a heart attack, which will make you feel some seriously acute stress.

Chronic stress can result from frequent bouts of acute stress or a life condition, such as a difficult job situation, a chronic disease, or a lousy landlord. The worse your chronic stress, the longer those nasty chemicals linger in your body and eventually cause physical stress. That's when stress starts pounding your cardiovascular system, your nervous system, and your immune system and the

Wrong Way, an 18-year-old man who lost his wallet on the AT, helped me discover the value of a Pilgrim's Perspective. We were reunited at a restaurant near the trail where he shared his story.

real fun begins. This leads to amusing conditions like getting high blood pressure or becoming susceptible to infections. But that's not all! You become a leading candidate for all sorts of diseases, such as depression, heart disease, and asthma. Fortunately, chronic stress may also result in memory loss, so you can quickly forget about the stressful and miserable life you've had.[39]

How to laugh at life

Along my trek I met an 18-year-old Sobo named Wrong Way. Hiking the AT southbound is so unusual that many people will tell us that we're hiking the trail "the wrong way." To poke fun at that comment, Wrong Way adopted that trail name.

However, one drizzly day in New Jersey, I ran into Wrong Way and he was hiking *north*. I declared, "Hey Wrong Way, you're hiking the wrong way!"

He strained a smile. I asked him what was wrong.

"I lost my wallet," he spat, clearly frustrated. "I think it might have fallen out of my pack when I hitched a ride into town 20 miles ago. I gotta walk back, somehow find the guy who drove me, and get it back."

Wrong Way was understandably upset. This was a big deal for him. We have a tendency to believe that whatever is happening right now is extremely important. Could Wrong Way have taken the loss of his wallet less seriously? What could he have done differently? There are three key skills I learned on my trek that can help you take life a bit less seriously.

Skill #1: Developing a Pilgrim's Perspective

Developing a Pilgrim's Perspective is perhaps the best skill you can work on, and there are two ways we can exercise it. Together you gain a broad perspective of space and time. Oh no, I sound like some guy on Star Trek.

What Do Astronomers and Religious Mystics Have in Common?

An incredible sense of perspective. Both are capable of grasping the concepts of infinity, eternity, and forever. Most humans find it impossible to comprehend these larger than life concepts. Therefore, we have a lot to learn from these wise guys.

Many religious people don't bother reading their sacred texts. Try it. Read passages on the afterlife to help you recalibrate your perspective. Read sections that describe ancient history to get a sense of time.

For those who prefer secular reading, read books on astronomy. Learn what's in our universe and how much real estate is out there.

Think about those books next time you get stressed out and you may find that your problems aren't as big as you originally thought.

Perspective of space

Let's say I just accidentally dropped a Reese's Peanut Butter Cup into a fast moving river. This is about as serious as it gets on the AT. We're talking precious food going to waste. If anything is worth getting worked up about, it's losing sweet treats on the trail.

The second I would feel myself getting stressed I would step out of my body and imagine I was filming myself at that very moment. I would begin to slowly pull back the camera, so that I no longer filled up the screen, but there were others around, perhaps fellow pilgrims at a shelter. I'd pull back further, so now I could see the entire mountain I was standing on, with the shelter being a blip in the forest of trees. Next I would pull back even more, so I could observe the entire AT, then the entire country, and perhaps even the Earth itself. At some point during this process I would start to realize that whatever just happened is really not that important. It may seem important at the time, but in the grand scheme of things, it's really not important.

However, if I still felt upset, I would simply continue pulling back the camera. I'd see the Moon, with the Earth in the background, then Mars with the Earth as a little blue globe, then out past Pluto where the Earth would be a speck of sapphire against a black canvas.

If I was really having a bad moment, I would pull back to our celestial neighbor, Proxima Centuri, and realize that I couldn't see any planets, and that the Sun was simply a bright star in the sky. And just for fun I would pull back to our neighboring galaxy, Andromeda, where there was no hint that our solar system was dangling near the edge of a spiral arm of the Milky Way Galaxy. It was usually at that moment that I would realize that surely someone from the Andromeda Galaxy really cared that I lost my Reese's Peanut Butter Cup in the river.

The thrill of trampling alone and unafraid through a wilderness of lakes, creeks, alpine meadows, and glaciers is not known to many. A civilization can be built around the machine but it is doubtful that a meaningful life can be produced by it…. When man worships at the feet of

> *avalanche lilies or discovers the delicacies of the pasque flower or finds the faint perfume of the phlox on rocky ridges, he will come to know that the real glories are God's creations. When he feels the wind blowing through him on a high peak or sleeps under a closely matte white bark pine in an exposed basin, he is apt to find his relationship to the universe. — Supreme Court Justice William O. Douglas, an avid hiker*

I endured my share of tests during my pilgrimage. By the time I had hiked over 2,000 miles I had mastered the Pilgrim's Perspective technique. Countless times it helped me overcome the adversities of wicked weather, pesky gnats, nasty slips, and lost wallets.

Try having a Pilgrim's Perspective of Space next time something gets your goat. Someone may have cut you off while you're driving, but the world continues to function. You may not have closed the sale, but your country will probably survive and frankly doesn't care. You may have broken a nail, but the planet Earth will pull through, barely.

> *Interestingly, according to modern astronomers, space is finite. This is a very comforting thought—particularly for people who can never remember where they have left things. — Woody Allen*

Perspective of time

The second technique is similar to gaining a Pilgrim's Perspective of Space, but instead puts you in relationship with time. Let's return to poor Wrong Way and see how he could have used this technique to put some perspective on losing his wallet.

The moment Wrong Way realized that he had lost his wallet he should have caught himself before becoming overly stressed out. He needed to freeze that moment in time—just stop. Next he should have begun to fast forward his life and see what kind of impact this event would have on the very next day. In this case, it might still be stressful, so Wrong Way needs to fast forward to the next week. Chances are this event will begin to fade in importance, although it's possible that he'll still be putting up with the hassle of canceling his credit cards, dealing with fraudulent charges, and possibly recuperating from the financial bite of losing some cash. To gain some more perspective, he should fast forward to the next month or the next year. By then having lost his wallet will no longer be a traumatic event; on the contrary, he might even be laughing about it with his buddies. It would become a quasi-tragic trail story that's fun for the whole family.

However, let's assume that Wrong Way has a propensity of envisioning some pretty dire scenarios. A year from now, he imagines he's still reeling from his lost wallet because the fraudulent charges managed to somehow ruin his credit and livelihood. So maybe he needs to jump five, 10, or 20 years ahead and see himself having overcome this fiscal disaster. He finally clears his credit rating, manages to buy a house, and live happily ever after.

The most happy man is he who knows how to bring into relation the end and beginning of his life.
— *Johann Wolfgang von Goethe*

However, Wrong Way is really feeling pretty negative. He imagines losing his wallet to some Al-Qaeda terrorists who use his credit card to provide the seed funds for their nefarious operations that lead to the destruction of the United States and the domination of the entire planet.

Yes, because Wrong Way lost his wallet, 50 years from now we'll all be worshipping Saint Osama Bin Laden.

This is when Wrong Way needs to hold the fast forward button for a while. Maybe 500 years from now St. Bin Laden's unholy kingdom will finally be overthrown when the power shifts to the Eskimos thanks to some serious global warming, which makes the Desert Terrorist Empire to shrivel up and die.

Finally, if that doesn't make Wrong Way feel better, there's always the ultimate fast forward—jump five billion years ahead. Our Sun will run out of fuel, expand, consume the Earth, and then fizzle out. End of wallet story.

One hopes that at some point during the fast forward, Wrong Way would realize that losing his wallet really is not a big deal in the infinite stream of time.

As absurd has this exercise may seem to some, it can truly help place any event in context, giving you perspective to deal with it in a calm, stress-free manner. *Practice using both of these Pilgrim's Perspective techniques by retaking the quiz at the beginning of this chapter.* You will quickly realize that most events that occur today will have little or no impact on the rest of your life, let alone the world at large, unless you're an Al-Qaeda terrorist searching for lost wallets on the Appalachian Trail.

Skill #2: Minimizing what you care about

During our trek, Lisa would frequently ask me what type of dehydrated mix she should put in our Thru-Hiker Special Soup. I usually replied, "I don't care." This would sometimes disappoint her, because she wanted me to care (especially when she didn't have a

---

Family Trees Sum It Up

My dad once showed me our family tree when I was a little boy.

I remember him observing, "It's funny that when I was putting this family tree together, I really just cared about four things: when someone was born; when and who they married; if they had children; and when they died. Their profession, how much money they made, where they lived, and all sorts of other details were unimportant.

"It's as if the only things that matter in life are those four things."

Yes, even my pilgrimage won't show up under my name.

preference either). However, as insensitive as it may seem to not care, it's frequently the most healthy attitude you can have.

Wait a second. Isn't it good to care? After all, it's such a compliment, "Oh, Sandy is such a great girl; she really cares so much about her job and her friends."

There's nothing wrong with caring. In fact, you should care about certain things. However, most people care too much about too many things. Put another way, most people care about things that really don't matter.

Let's say there are 1,000 things you have an option to care about. For example, you can care about the weather, the way your food is served, whether your spouse is faithful, the clothes your spouse wears, whether you make every green light, the way your waiter treats you, the manner in which your spouse squeezes the toothpaste, and whether the Cubs will ever win the World Series.

With everything you have a *choice:* you can choose to care or you can choose not to care. Nobody is forcing you to care (or not care) about something. Caring about anything takes emotional, intellectual, and sometimes physical energy. Hence, it's important to pick your battles wisely. In the list above, only one thing is worth caring about, but many of us waste time worrying and getting stressed out about all the other things. If you have trouble with caring too much, put on your Pilgrim Perspective glasses and see if that helps. Given enough perspective you won't be concerned about all those fleeting things, and you'll focus all your energy on the important stuff—like making sure the Cubs win the Pennant.

Should you care if someone cuts you off while you're driving? Traffic school taught me the proper techniques of flipping people off when they did that. But after I spent three weeks in Mexico's capital I learned not to get worked up about it. Taxis negotiated the horrendous and chaotic traffic. Imagine the worse experience you have ever had of someone cutting you off; that was the standard way most Mexican drivers would use to go from lane to lane. What impressed me was how the cab drivers reacted when someone cut them off. They didn't flinch. They didn't blurt out a profanity or even shake their head in disappointment. If they were talking with me, they didn't skip a beat and they kept on chatting. In short, they didn't care if someone cut them off. Of course, every region has its own driving etiquette, but the point is that there is no fundamental, universal reason to care whether someone cuts you off. It really does not matter.

 Great man is always at ease; petty man is always on edge.
— *Confucius*

However, there is universal agreement on a few things. For example, all humans agree that it's good to care when your father dies or when your wife gives birth. These rare events do matter and are worth spending emotional energy on.

I was talking about being happy on the AT with Ted Tobiason, who is an avid outdoorsman, investment guru, and a close friend. He summed up our conversation well when he said: "The key to being happy is minimizing the things you really care about. If you have a large circle of things that are really important to you, you're bound to be frustrated." It's true. *The more things that you care about, the more expectations you have, the more likely you will be disappointed.*

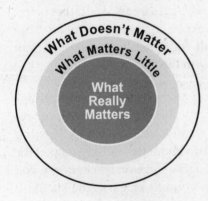

Before
following the 7th Principle

After
following the 7th Principle

Therefore, the goal is to shrink the size of the circle of things that you care about. Chip away at it until you're down to the essentials. Ask yourself whenever you get worked up about anything: does this really matter? In the grand scheme of things, does this make any difference whatsoever? If you're truly being honest and giving it proper perspective, you'll realize that 99.9 percent of things out there aren't that big of a deal. Once you do this, suddenly the great big circle of things you thought mattered starts to shrink dramatically. Even the things that you thought were moderately important also shrink. You've boiled away the unimportant stuff, and you're down to the essentials.

Returning to our friend Wrong Way, should he have placed his wallet in the "What Really Matters" circle? No, probably it would be acceptable if he put it in the "What Matters Little" circle or, even better, in the "What Doesn't Matter" circle.

Write down things you care about and see how much you can pare down the list. This exercise is similar to what thru-hikers do when they are selecting their gear for their journey. There are lots of things that would be "nice to have," but very few items that are absolute "must haves." It took one Nobo 20 miles of hiking to figure out that his antique Russian army helmet wasn't exactly in the "must have" category. The postmaster shipped it back to his house and informed him that the monster weighed an insane 22 pounds.[40]

Skill #3: Decoding events positively

It's crazy how many newlyweds decide to make a thru-hike their honeymoon. What are these couples thinking? What's wrong with Hawaii?

When I was taking a break at a shelter along the AT, I overheard this one newlywed yell at his spouse, "You make me feel so frustrated!"

I almost intervened to calmly say, "She can't *make* you feel anything. Only *you* decide how you feel. She can influence, but in the end you interpret what she does and decide how you will feel." Of course, this

Ways to Tame Stress

For some people laughing at life doesn't come so easily, because they just don't have a sense of humor. So they may need other ways to conquer stress. Consider:

- ✓ Taking a yoga class—yogis have low stress levels.

- ✓ Getting a massage.

- ✓ Going for a run or swift walk around the neighborhood.

- ✓ Checking in with your body every 15 minutes to see if you're slouching, tense, breathing short, etc.

- ✓ Talking about it with a friend.

- ✓ Asking: Is this really important to me? Would a pilgrim be this upset? Is there anything I can do to fix the situation—and would that be worth it? If you answered "yes" three times do something; otherwise, forget about it.

response would have just made him more frustrated. Besides, he was much bigger than me and would have kicked my puny little ass.

So I kept my mouth shut. But however frustrating my observation may have been, it was still valid. *By the end of my long trek I learned that there is no such thing as a great or lousy event; there are just events.* How we decode the event is up to us. For example, when it rains, one pilgrim may become melancholy, whereas a thirsty one might rejoice. Humans might cheer to see rain in a desert because of all the life that springs forth. But if a cactus gets too much water it dies. There's nothing inherently negative or positive about rain. It just is.

Have you ever watched a sports game and not cared who won? In the end, one team loses and the other wins. It's an event. However, the winners interpret this event by joyously jumping around and overturning cars, while the losers come out angrily swinging baseball bats. It's the same event, decoded in completely opposite ways. OK, maybe I shouldn't have used New York fans as an example.

The company I used to work for laid off a bunch of employees. Some decoded the event with sorrow or anger. But a few shrugged it off, appreciated the small severance package, and looked forward to the new opportunities. The company didn't force anyone to feel any particular way. Each employee decided for herself how she would feel.

Just like we have the power to take events that depress most humans and decode them into positive experiences, we also have the power to turn events that thrill most folks into negative experiences. For example, a good friend of mine ran a marathon in three hours and one minute. Although far from a record, this is an extremely fast time, considering most people are quite proud if they can run a marathon in under four hours (or do it at all!). Yet he was disappointed. While people who finished behind him were celebrating, he had a long face. He wanted to run it in under three hours. Since he fell short of this goal, he decided to feel bad about it. Many of those who finished after him felt elated, even if they also wished to do it in less than three hours. After all, three hours and one minute is a great time. In fact, if you kept up that pace and you didn't need any sleep, you could run the entire AT in about ten days. Now that would be worth celebrating.

There is nothing either good or bad, but thinking makes it so. — Shakespeare

As we approached Blood Mountain, the final mountain before Springer, I remembered that I had wanted to hike the AT in under 100 days. Linguini, a fellow Sobo, who was twice Lisa's age, had the same goal. Even though he started after us, he passed us and finished in 96 days. That day was our 110th day on the trail. I could have felt rotten about it, but considering that 85 percent of those who try to thru-hike the AT don't even finish it (let alone do it in less than four months), I was thrilled! To celebrate I did a dance on Blood Mountain that would rival Justin Timberlake's moves.

Yeah, my moves weren't that good.

Although we never met Linguini, we were lucky to talk with him over the phone in Hot Springs, North Carolina. He had been reading our journal entries in the shelters for months until he finally caught up to us and passed us. Unfortunately, we never had a face-to-face meeting because we were re-supplying off the trail, but he sent this photo to us for Christmas. He was in his 50s and his goal was to walk the AT in less than 100 days. He did it in 96 days! We had a similar goal, but we spent an extra 11 days goofing off. Others spend a few extra months goofing off. In the end, we all hiked our own hike.
(Photo by Linguini)

I realized that I had learned a key skill in my odyssey. *Whenever I felt a tinge of a negative emotion coming on, my new habit kicked in: I reminded myself that only I could decide how I felt.* Events happened all around me. People said and did stuff that could rattle me if I wanted it to. How I decoded the events was up to me, and only me. If that newlywed had punched me in the face, I could decide how I would feel. I could exclaim, "That makes me mad!" But that would be inaccurate. His blow didn't *force* me to do or feel anything. "I am deciding to get mad," is a more accurate statement. After all, I could say, "I am deciding to brush this off." Or in my case, "I am deciding to brush this off because you are twice my size."

You have to develop this level of self-control to survive the AT. Thru-hikers are faced with constant challenges and adversities. If you don't learn to decode them in a positive fashion, you will eventually become miserable and quit. Indeed, a thru-hiker's self-control is similar to what Tibetan monks learn to develop. Sometimes instructors beat monks who are not focusing. The beaten monks do not get angry. They choose to stay solemn. It's only later, when the chief monk is not looking, that they spit in his food.

I am using these extreme examples to illustrate a point. If we can decide how we feel when someone smacks us, we can certainly decide how we feel when the waiter brings the wrong entrée to the table. I'm not suggesting that you start celebrating when you find out your spouse has cheated on you, or start laughing at funerals (although some cultures do celebrate at funerals). *Simply recognize that you have the power to decide how you feel every moment of the day; the way you decode the event is up to you.*

Some would say the solution is not to have expectations, but that's hard to do. After all, having and visualizing ambitious goals is essential to achieving great success in anything. So go ahead and have expectations, but at the same time *expect that things won't always go the way you expected.*

Oprah: "What is a perfect day for you?"
Dalai Lama: "There's never a perfect day. There is no perfection in the world."

Pericles, the brilliant general of the ancient Athenians, ended the last speech of his life with a piece of advice that is still valid 2,500 years later:

…They whose minds are least sensitive to calamity, and whose hands are most quick to meet it, are the greatest men and the great communities.
— Pericles, according to Thucydides's account in The Peloponnesian War in 429 BC.

In other words, those of us who brush off misfortune and quickly do something to fix it are the greatest ones. However, this is easier said than done, especially if you're not Pericles. How do we reprogram our brains to decode events positively?

Learning from children

We can learn a lot from children. Jesus said that to enter heaven we must become like children. Do you think children take life too seriously? Well, perhaps they do when you steal their toy truck, but overall their resilience is admirable.

Their ability to shrug off a lousy event is fantastic. It's fun playing with two year olds and seeing how they decode the world. One might suddenly slip and fall, and for a second looks at me, almost asking "Should I just burst out crying now?" Without wasting a second, I distract the boy, "Hey look at that cool bird over there!" Just like that, the kid forgets the silly reason he was about to get so upset and has moved on. Instead of breaking down and crying, he breaks out a smile. In short, he *decided* not to get upset. He faced a choice, thought about it, and then decided to decode the event as insignificant, and brushed it off.

A child of five could understand this. Fetch me a child of five. — Groucho Marx

Somehow we adults forget about this ability we all have because at some point in our childhood *we start consistently deciding to react the same way whenever a certain event happens; as a result, that behavior becomes a habit*. It becomes so ingrained that we think there's no way to change it. "What do you mean I shouldn't get upset when the bus is late?"

More strongly correlated with happiness than anything else is personality, how easy you find it to enjoy other people's company, or how easily bothered you are by life's irritations. — Stuart McCready, The Discovery of Happiness [41]

Start questioning the way you decode events all around you. *Just for fun, try to decode events in abnormal ways.* Let's say you always get mad when the person at the coffee shop doesn't follow your directions precisely. Next time it happens decode the event in the opposite way than you normally would: "Gee, thanks! I've never tried the coffee this way, this should be interesting!"

Conversely, try decoding events that you would typically see as positives and make them negative. Next time your favorite sports team wins, decode the event negatively: "Damn, I could have made some money by betting on that game!"

The purpose of this odd exercise is to prove to yourself that you haven't given up control of how you decode events in your life. You still have the control and the options you had when you were a child. You are empowered to decode events any way you want.

Decoding events in a positive way

The AT lesson of decoding events in a positive way is extremely useful off the trail. At first it may seem a bit odd, but it's a key ability to have to get you through life's challenges. Few periods of life challenge you as much as the AT, and pilgrims have to find inventive ways to stay upbeat. After talking with hundreds of successful thru-hikers, it became clear that those who walked over 2,000 miles had an incredible sense of humor, an ability to not take themselves too seriously, high self-esteem, and, perhaps most of all, unflagging optimism.

The AT is a brutal tester of one's optimism. Probably most who start the AT would consider themselves an optimist, but within a few days, weeks, or months, they are beaten down by the incessant challenges of the AT. It's usually not just one thing that beats down one's spirit, it's the combination of factors that can wear you down—the heat, humidity, mosquitoes, long periods of rain, lack of water, diabolically steep trails, monotonous food, lack of showers, freezing cold, and the post office.

Even the eternal optimist will begin to wonder if she can complete the trail. To finish the trail, the thru-hiker must develop a resolute resistance to misfortune. The thru-hiker must constantly deflect hardship and embrace good fortune. It's a key part of not taking the hike too seriously, and savoring the good moments. Let's see how thru-hikers do it.

When you're good, you're good

When good events happen or when you perform well at an activity, you should attribute it to your inherent skill. Do not attribute it to luck. It's possible that a thru-hiker may believe she's lucky to have hiked 20 miles of trail. Indeed, it's possible that she was lucky. Maybe she was blessed with great weather, or a friendly Trail Angel who gave her some food and encouragement to press on. On the other hand, walking 200 miles of trail isn't about luck—it's skill and determination. Finally, when a thru-hiker has walked over 2,000 miles, clearly luck had little to do with her success—she accomplished that feat because of her pure will.

Some hikers may credit their ability to hike 20 miles because "I was feeling strong that morning." Some may even credit hiking 200 miles because "I'm lucky that my knees have be holding up this far." However, the successful thru-hiker doesn't think like that. She says, "I've hiked 20 miles because *I am strong.*" Or, "I've hiked 200 miles because my knees *are made of iron.*"

It may seem trivial, but this is an important distinction. The doomed hiker attributes any success to luck and a temporary triumph over the normal pattern of failure or underperformance. Meanwhile, the successful pilgrim attributes all her success to just being good, strong, and determined. This is a powerful difference that can be applied to our everyday lives.

When you pass a test with good grades, do you say, "Whew, I got lucky that time—that jolt of coffee did me good that morning." Or do you say, "I'm smart, that's why I did well." When you see an attractive picture of yourself do you think, "That's a good photographer," or "I had some good clothes and makeup that day," or do you say, "I'm beautiful" or "I'm photogenic." By attributing *permanence* to your successes and qualities, you boost your self-esteem and optimism. This improves your chance of success, and your ability to get the most out of life.

Therefore, remind yourself that successes are the norm, whereas bad times are fleeting abnormalities.

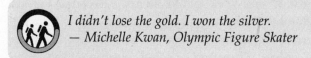

I didn't lose the gold. I won the silver.
— *Michelle Kwan, Olympic Figure Skater*

When you're bad, you're unlucky

When bad events happen or when you perform poorly at an activity, you should attribute it to bad luck. Do not attribute it to being incompetent. When something goes wrong, successful thru-hikers don't assume that they are inept. When bad news happens, they do not blame some permanent shortcoming in themselves—they keep it external and blame circumstances instead. For example, if their back hurts, they conclude, "I must have slept on a rock last night," and not, "I have a weak back." Instead of thinking, "I'm a terrible cook," they conclude, "The altitude must be affecting my cooking." When they lose their wallet they tell themselves, "I can't believe I lost my wallet today," versus, "I have a terrible memory."

Notice how positive interpretations emphasize the *circumstances of the moment*. It is a way to point out the *transient* nature of the negative situation. In other words, when misfortune strikes, it is a brief abnormality, not a permanent problem.

Using this technique doesn't absolve us of responsibility. After all, you're still admitting that your back hurts, that you cooked a bad meal, and that you lost your wallet. It's just that you don't view those issues as reoccurring problems, because you know you're better than that. You'll learn and adjust so it doesn't happen again.

Language is a powerful tool and we can use it to uplift our spirits or crush them. The way we communicate to ourselves and decode the world around us can almost determine our level of happiness. Therefore, do what pilgrims do, and use it to your advantage.[42]

We are not retreating. We are advancing in another direction. — General Douglas MacArthur

Lastly, let's revisit Wrong Way. Could he have decoded his lost wallet event differently? Of course! He needed to realize how this event is not terribly important because wallets are not in "What Really Matters" circle. Therefore, it's not worth getting upset about. Should he have put an effort into retrieving it? Yes, but he needed to do it in a calm, relaxed manner, knowing that the worst case scenario wouldn't doom him. Finally, he shouldn't call himself stupid or even forgetful, but rather he should observe that he must have just had a lot on his mind that day.

Three days later I ran into Wrong Way again, this time he was going "the right way" (south), and he told me what had happened. Of course, he had ransacked his backpack, but could not find his wallet there. He did get a hold of the person who gave him a ride because the driver had given Wrong Way his phone number, "In case you need any help." Unfortunately, Wrong Way's wallet wasn't in the truck either. Wrong Way went back to last restaurant he had a meal and the last hostel he stayed at—nothing. Dismayed, Wrong Way canceled his credit cards and got back on the trail. Two days later, while looking for some matches in a small pouch in his backpack Wrong Way pulled out his missing wallet.

How to make decisions

The Seventh Principle gives you such a broad perspective that it also helps you make decisions. Those who truly understand that the hike is too important to take seriously begin to make wiser decisions. We're faced with choices everyday, and making decisions can be so agonizing that you almost wish Communism was back in style.

Some decisions could be as simple as debating whether to study an extra hour for an exam or go out with some friends. Other decisions may be more significant, like deciding whether to change careers or to get married. Whether the decision you face is a big deal or a little one, try this exercise if you're indecisive:

Paradox: Think Death, Be Happy

It's strange, but those who think about their death everyday are some of the happiest people on the planet.

Although the AT is one of the safest places you can be, your primordial instincts tell you otherwise. You fear death at any moment: hypothermia; bear or snake attack; crazy humans.

As a result, thru-hikers get the most out of their lives. When I returned to the "real world" I practiced this habit of thinking that I might die at any moment.

As morbid and as paradoxical as it sounds, thinking about your mortality may be the best thing you can do to brighten your spirits and get you back on a positive track.

Close your eyes and imagine that you are crossing a street, and suddenly a car goes through a red light and hits you. You fly through the air, and your body slams on the pavement. The pangs rip through your body and you feel your life rapidly leaving you. You realize that, without a doubt, you will die in a few minutes.

As you lie on the pavement, you think back on your life. You hardly hear the sirens and the people yelling around you. Strangely, you are at peace. Thinking back on your life, you ask yourself, "Overall, how was it?"

Listen to your answers.

Then you start narrowing down on sections of your life. How were your 20s? Your 30s? Had you known you would die at such a young age, would you have done things differently?

Then begin to focus in more closely. How was this last year? Would you have done things differently? What about this last month? Were there people you would have seen, things you would have said? What about yesterday? Did you enjoy it? Did you do things you regretted?

And what about that little decision you're facing today, how would you have liked to have handled it?

Perhaps it's a gruesome exercise for some, but it drives home the main point: you can die at any moment and so you should make decisions that you will be happy with when you die. It's a shame that God didn't put expiration dates on our bodies, because it would certainly make life planning simple.

Alas, we have no idea how long we have on this planet. That has spurred the popularity of this wise saying: "Live this day as if it is your last." However, I've always struggled with that saying, because if I followed its advice I'd probably do lots of things that wouldn't go over too well with some folks if it turns out that it's not my last day. Also, I wouldn't have too much left in my bank account either.

Nevertheless, there is wisdom in the saying. Don't bank on living 85 years. If after going through this exercise you realize that's not the way you want to spend the last few months of your life, then you should question whether you're making the right decision.

 Too many people are thinking of security instead of opportunity; they seem more afraid of life than of death.
— *James F. Byrnes*

For those who prefer not visualizing a car accident, project yourself into the far future when you're very old and gray. You're lying on your deathbed. You're looking back at your life, and thinking of all the good and bad times you've had. Then backtrack to this year, this month, this week, and this very moment. What would you tell your younger self while you are lying on your deathbed? What would you advise yourself to do at this very moment?

Looking at your life from the perspective of your last breaths can help you make wise decisions today. If you're debating whether to take a two week vacation or to work so you can get some kudos from your boss for not taking any time off, then perhaps your debate will be a quick one after this exercise. If you're wondering if you should yell at your spouse for being late, then perhaps imagining your untimely death will make you think twice about yelling. Unfortunately, this technique may not help you decide whether to get the light blue shirt or the dark blue one.

A Good Joke: Harvard MBA Meets a Mexican Fisherman

Many Harvard grads take life a bit too seriously. That's why I love this joke.

An American businessman was on the pier of a small coastal Mexican village when a small boat with just one fisherman docked. The American complimented the fisherman on the quality of his fish and asked how long it took to catch them. The Mexican replied, "Only a little while."

The American then asked, "Why don't you stay out longer and catch more fish?" The Mexican said he had enough to support his family's immediate needs.

The American then asked, "But what do you do with the rest of your time?"

The Mexican fisherman said, "I sleep late, fish a little, play with my children, take siesta with my wife, stroll into the village each evening where I sip wine and play guitar with my amigos. I have a full and busy life."

The American scoffed, "I am a Harvard MBA and I can help you. You should spend more time fishing and with the proceeds buy a bigger boat. With the profits from the bigger boat you could buy several boats, eventually you would have a fleet of fishing boats. Instead of selling to a middleman, you would sell directly to a processor, eventually opening your own cannery. You would control the product, processing, and distribution. You would need to leave this small coastal fishing village and move to Mexico City, then Los Angeles, and eventually New York City where you will run your expanding enterprise."

The Mexican fisherman asked, "But *señor*, how long will this all take?""

To which the American replied, "Fifteen to twenty years."

"But what then, *señor*?"

The American laughed and said "That's the best part. When the time is right, you would announce an IPO and sell your company stock to the public and become very rich—you would make millions."

"Millions, *señor*? And then what?"

The Harvard MBA said, "Then you would retire. Move to a small coastal fishing village where you would sleep late, fish a little, play with your kids, take siesta with your wife, stroll to the village in the evenings where you could sip wine and play guitar with your amigos."

Common criticisms

As we've done throughout this journey, it's healthy to question every Principle before accepting it. I did this during my long trek not only because I wanted to uncover the truth, but also because I really had nothing better to do while I was walking 2,168 miles.

But this Principle is a paradox!

If life is so important, shouldn't we take it seriously? No, because as we saw in the beginning of this chapter, those who take the hike seriously end up with acute or chronic stress. How can you squeeze the most out of life if you're wasting emotional, intellectual, and physical energy on things that don't matter? Why not channel that energy into hiking with passion?

But my "What Matters Little" circle is full!

Congratulations, you've managed to move a bunch of useless things that you used to believe really mattered into the "What Matters Little" category. The only problem is that you're caring about so many things that matter little that you're still short on energy to devote to the few things that really matter. There are two solutions.

One solution is that you can scrutinize everything that you put in the "What Matters Little" circle and use the Pilgrim Perspective to push most of them into the "What Doesn't Matter" circle. For example, you may be placing whether your son plays football in the "What Matters Little" circle, when it really does not matter. Perhaps you would prefer he played a less violent sport like tennis, but let him hike his own hike. Get some perspective and you'll see that his sport choice is not worth taking too seriously.

If you still find yourself caring about too many things that matter little, then consider doing something radical: get rid of the "What Matters Little" circle! That's right, just look at life in two categories: what matters and what doesn't. In the case above, you wouldn't debate whether your son's sport choice really matters. With no gray area available, figuring out what matters may be easier than ever: his life matters, his sport choice doesn't; whether he takes drugs matters, his fashion sense does not. If you're taking advantage of the gray area and filling it with unimportant stuff, get rid of the grey area. With a bit of perspective, you'll realize most of those things are not vital and you'll quickly put most of them in the only other circle available: "What Doesn't Matter."

But I don't want to be a pushover!

If you see someone leaving trash behind in a shelter, you could shrug it off and forget about it, because the hike is too important to take seriously. There's no point in getting worked up about something that trivial. Just pick up the trash and you've solved your problem. But if we all did this, we would let these inconsiderate backpackers make a mess of the wilderness. Clearly, we need to reprimand the backpacker who leaves behind trash or washes himself with soap (even biodegradable soap) in a lake. He is ruining the environment, so we shouldn't ignore it. Otherwise, we all would become pushovers and idiots would rule the world. Oh wait, that's already happened. Darn.

Speaking of idiots, there are rare moments in life when we run into something that is truly a serious matter, and it's no time to shrug an event off. For example, it would have been wrong to ignore Hitler by saying, "Oh, don't take the hike so seriously, it's just a few Jews." The policy of appeasement clearly wasn't the right answer. Then again, it's not everyday that we run into someone committing genocide.

Returning to our thoughtless polluting backpacker, you might not want to just quietly clean up for him and let him walk all over nature with no consideration. That's being a pushover. So in a friendly and polite way tell the backpacker that he should change his habits. However, it's also not worth getting overly stressed out about it, especially if he's a jerk and unwilling to change his habits. Unlike genocide, this is not that serious. Save your precious emotional energy and then calmly remind yourself that this idiot's trash doesn't really matter. Do your part to clean up, and then when he turns his back, flip him off.

But I can't help but worry!

Would your friends describe you as a worrywart? Worrywarts tend to care about too many things, and need to work on their Pilgrim Perspective skills.

Worrying is not necessarily a bad thing. If General Eisenhower had not worried so much about the D-Day invasion, it probably would not have been as successful as it was. On the other hand, worrying if your plane will depart on time is clearly a waste of time. It either will happen or it won't. Worrying about it will not change the outcome. Nor will yelling at the folks behind the ticket counters.

When you find yourself worrying about something, ask yourself if you have any control over the situation. If you don't, then there is absolutely no benefit to worrying. Not only will it waste your time, but it will detract from your health and prevent you from doing more productive endeavors.

 If you are going to doubt something, doubt your limits.
— Don Ward

But I'm a realist—I can't delude myself!

Decoding the world in a positive fashion may strike some as being unrealistic. After all, if you can't hit a baseball after 1,000 swings with a bat, then maybe you really do suck at baseball—permanently.

Likewise, if you've played baseball all your life and you've hit your first homerun, you might conclude that you were lucky, not that you're great. However, if you've played that long, you probably are pretty good. That first homerun may be the turning point where you begin to hit many more. A lifetime of practice has finally paid off and you are now entering a new stage of success.

What if you hit a homerun at your first at bat? Isn't that lucky? No, you're a natural; you have inherent skill that if you develop will make you an amazing player.

Decoding life events in a positive fashion is not a delusion; it's just consistently saying that the glass is half full. With the baseball examples above, one could legitimately argue a negative or positive interpretation of the events. The pilgrim always picks the positive one. Yes, a realist may simply waffle forever, but why not just make a choice, especially if it's a positive one? Some may feel such decoding is delusional, but those people are probably the same ones who scoff at the placebo effect and who never hit homeruns.

But nothing matters!

If you're one of those rare individuals who spend most of their time looking at the world from the perspective of the Andromeda Galaxy and thinking about the Sun running out of gas five billion years from now, then you need to come back to the planet Earth.

Although using the Pilgrim's Perspective when you need it is useful, it's not useful to have that perspective all the time. If you do, you'll probably end up feeling powerless, depressed, and directionless. You'll have no friends as most people will classify you as a complete loser.

What you need to do is hang out with those folks who get pissed off if someone in the supermarket's Express Lane has more than 10 items.

Over-philosophizing

There are dangers of over philosophizing and over analyzing life.

Pontificating metaphysical mumbo-jumbo may be interesting for a while, but those who indulge in it are taking life too seriously.

In the end of Voltaire's 18th century satirical novel *Candide*, the character Pangloss is philosophizing endlessly until Candide shuts him up by simply saying, "That's true enough, but we must go and work in the garden."

Summary

People who take life too seriously suffer from acute and/or chronic stress. It's hard to get the most out of life when you're a pile of nerves. It's no fun to lose your wallet, but there are positive ways to deal with such challenging events. Therefore, let's summarize how to take life less seriously:

- Develop a Pilgrim's Perspective of space and time, especially when you're faced with adversity.

- Minimize the size of your "What Really Matters" circle.

- Realize that life is just a bunch of events and that you have the power to decode them positively.

- Keep the meaning of your life in perspective by thinking about the end of your life so you make the wisest decisions today.

The rain had stopped, our gear was dry, and Springer Mountain was in our sights. We walked with the determination of a bull-dozer.

We flew over Blood Mountain, the tallest mountain in Georgia. Although many Nobos had warned us about it, we almost didn't even notice it. Maybe that's because the store at Neels Gap, right before Blood Mountain, gave us a free pint of Ben and Jerry's ice cream as our reward for making it within 30 miles of the end. It was a deeply meaningful, proud, and somewhat sad moment for me; however, not because we were so close to completing our pilgrimage, but rather because at that moment I realized that I had tried every possible flavor of Ben and Jerry's ice cream.

All I could do was hope—hope that B&J would invent some new flavors for my next thru-hike.

On October 16, we woke up at 3 a.m., just like we had 111 days before at the base of Mount Katahdin. This day would be an unforgettable day—it would be the day we finished the Appalachian Trail.

We built a fire (something we avoided throughout the journey to preserve nature's resources) to celebrate this great day. We set off infected with a serious bout of *summit fever*. Summit Fever afflicts most thru-hikers as they near their final destination. We first learned about it when we met Nobos in the 100-mile wilderness in Maine. They would come around the corner with a fire in their eyes and a determination in their stride that just screamed, "Get out of my way, I am about to finish the AT!"

Now we had that same fire and resolve burning within us. Nothing was going to stop us: not the incessant rain; not the imposing mountains; not the monotonous food. We were on a mission. The only thing that could possibly distract us was a well placed Snickers bar.

The day before we had met a wonderful couple: Doug and Evelyn. These day hikers were astounded after hearing our tale of walking over 2,100 miles. They offered to pick us up at Springer Mountain, take us to their home, and then drop us off to the Atlanta airport. It was destiny perhaps, but trail magic blessed us the whole way: from the very first hitchhike in Maine (a two hour hitch from the airport to Baxter State Park) to our very last step on the trail.

I'm holding a map of the AT. These kids were impressed that we had walked from Maine, but they soon became disenchanted once they smelled us. In this picnic ground a family offered us some munchies. We were polite and only ate six donuts.

Hike Your Own Hike

> *Remote for detachment, narrow for chosen company,*
> *winding for leisure, lonely for contemplation, it beckons*
> *not merely north and south, but upward to the body,*
> *mind, and soul of man.* — *Written on a plaque at*
> *Amicalola State Park, the southern tip of the Appalachian*
> *Trail*

Everywhere we went we felt like superheroes. Everyone who learned about our journey during those last miles congratulated us to no end. We felt blessed. Families told their children, "Those two smelly people over there have walked from Maine to get here!"

The children looked at us with awe and admiration, and then said, "Mommy, they stink, can we go now?"

They took our pictures, and we never felt so wonderful. We were superstars in this little part of the world.

Before we knew it, the summit of Springer Mountain was just one mile away. We had hiked 2,167 miles; just one more would complete our pilgrimage. I just stood there while every possible emotion I could have flooded my system. I was glum, blissful, worried, tired, nervous, giddy, enthralled, energized, depressed, silly, pensive, and a bit hungry too.

I took a deep breath. I pulled my backpack tight against my back, shrugged my shoulders, and began walking that final mile. All my senses were on overdrive. My eyes focused on the industrious ants, my ears listened to the rustling leaves, my hands caressed the rough tree bark, my nose smelled the subtle aroma of the crushed leaves, and my tongue savored the trail mix in my mouth, grateful that I wouldn't have to eat that crap again for a long time.

I treasured that final mile, yet it ended so quickly. I turned a corner and there it was: the famous plaque marking the southern terminus of the Appalachian Trail.

I turned to Lisa. We hugged each other for a long time.

I'm climbing Springer Mountain and holding up three fingers to represent 111 days on the trail. Interestingly, those three fingers also represent three months and three weeks—it was an auspicious day!

We also came out here to learn about ourselves. The biggest prize in long-distance hiking is the gift of time. Time to look. Time to think. Time to feel. All those hours you spend with your thoughts. You don't solve all of your problems, but you come to understand and accept yourself.
— *Cindy Ross from* Journey on the Crest, *1987*

I read the plaque on the summit of Springer: "Appalachian Trail: A Footpath for Those who seek Fellowship with the Wilderness." Indeed, I sought such a fellowship. Not only did the wilderness welcome me, but it also shared with me its wisdom. When I stood on Mount Katahdin I knew I was hiking to Georgia, but in many ways I didn't really know where the trail would take me. That day, I assembled the pieces together. I sat on the rock on top of Springer and thought of the seven lessons this trail had taught me. This pilgrimage was important, yet I had learned not to take it too seriously.

We had walked 2,168 miles to rest next to this plaque on Springer Mountain. Sure there were easier ways to get here, but this adventure was more about the journey than the destination.

I had learned to take care of my body and to heed trail lore. I had learned to hike with passion, but not rush to the summit. I was surprised to learn how important performing trail magic is to achieving true happiness. And above all, I learned to hike my own hike.

 I did it. I said I'll do it, and I've done it. — Emma "Grandma" Gatewood, after climbing Katahdin at age 67 and becoming the first woman to thru-hike the Appalachian Trail

I stood on top of that rock, absorbing all the emotions coursing through my veins. I have never felt anything like that before or since. I jumped off the rock, trying to look acrobatic, but it was an ugly dismount.

Before I descended Mount Springer, I took one last look north to Maine. It was a cloudless day, and in my mind's eye I could clearly see the formidable Mount Katahdin—and she was smiling back at me.

We gazed at the view on Springer Mountain and contemplated the meaning of our little adventure. Although Lisa was the first woman to get to Georgia that season, we hardly set any records. We simply hiked our own hike and were rewarded with the most fulfilling experience of our lives.

It was October 16—a clear, chilly, and unforgettable day. We celebrated the end of our pilgrimage on the summit of Springer Mountain in Georgia. We were jubilant, euphoric, and ecstatic. However, deep inside, we were also a bit sad to be leaving the trail behind.

Epilogue:
Beyond The Hike

Two years after finishing the AT, I returned to Springer to do the infamous Approach Trail that so many Nobos had complained about all the way to Maine. I ran up the eight miles in a couple of hours and didn't see what all the fuss was about. It's really a moderate climb, an average mountain by AT standards. The trail gains only 2,000 feet over eight miles—hardly a steep climb. Compare it to the steepness of the "approach trail" Sobos have at Katahdin: 4,000 feet of elevation gain in just five miles. This explains why there are handholds on Katahdin and not on Springer.

Indeed, I was surprised by how many portions of Springer's Approach Trail were either flat or descending; all the Nobos had claimed that "it went straight up." I sat again on the wise rock at the summit of Springer and figured out why the Approach Trail is such a bad memory for so many Nobos. There are two basic problems. First, their packs are too heavy, so it makes for a miserable climb. Second, they haven't figured out how long it takes to walk eight miles. When most of us think of covering eight miles, we figure about 10 to 20 minutes in a car. "So if I'm walking, that should take an hour or two, definitely not more than three hours,"

The "approach trail" for Sobos is clearly more difficult than what the Nobos have to deal with. Here I was climbing up Mt. Katahdin thinking that the folks in Maine have stretched the definition of a "trail" a bit.

some quickly conclude. However, if your pack is heavy, and you're going uphill, and you're a bit out of shape, you'll walk at roughly one mile per hour (assuming occasional breaks). Most prospective thru-hikers don't think this through (because they didn't learn from trail lore). Therefore, after walking three hours they are depressed because they are not even halfway up the trail!

What's worse is that this eight mile trail isn't even part of the AT. It's the *approach* to the AT. When they finally get to the summit eight hours later, they're completely exhausted, and yet they're just at the starting line. They rapidly begin to doubt their ability to complete the whole trek. I confirmed this when I started flipping through the trail journal at the summit of Springer.

Thought about going to Maine, but we are tired already. I think we are headed back to Amicalola State Park.
— Tom & Joe, trail entry at the summit of Springer

I wrote this book for many reasons, but there's one reason I certainly did *not* write it for, and that's to encourage people to thru-hike the AT! Sadly, some will slam this book down and declare, "Alright! That's it darlin'! We're gonna hike that damn AT and git ourselves some wisdom!"

I can only imagine all the angry emails telling me how thru-hiking sucks. People would wonder, "How did you manage to think any deep thoughts when you're working your ass off all day long?"

It's not easy. Take it from the first woman who thru-hiked it:

I read about this [Appalachian] trail three years ago in a magazine, and the article told about the beautiful trail, how well marked it was, that it was cleared out, and that there were shelters at the end of a good day's hike. I thought it would be a nice lark. It wasn't. There were terrible blow-downs, burnt-over areas that were never remarked, gravel and sand washouts, weeds and brush

to your neck, and most of the shelters were blown down, burned down, or so filthy I chose to sleep out of doors. This is no trail. This is a nightmare. For some fool reason, they always lead you right up over the biggest rock to the top of the biggest mountain they can find. I've seen every fire station between here and Georgia. Why, an Indian would die laughing his head off if he saw [that] trail. I would never have started this trip if I had known how tough it was, but I couldn't, and I wouldn't quit.
— Emma "Grandma" Gatewood in the October 10, 1955 issue of Sports Illustrated *(she was 67 when she did the hike)*

Although the AT certainly is much better maintained than it was 50 years ago, it's still not easy. I returned to reading the trail entries in the journal on Springer Mountain:

WHAT THE HELL WAS I THINKING? 2,168 miles to go.
— "Gunner" from Biulder, Colorado, in trail entry on Springer Mountain

Clearly, there are better ways of getting wisdom. I hope this book is one of them.

May 26, 2003: Late starts mean good luck, happiness, and bird shit. Don't know how I let him talk me into this, but so far it sucks. The mood so far is fuck him, fuck this, fuck that, and we haven't even gotten to the trail. What do I have to do to get him to quit? FUCK THIS SHIT!
— Hoo-Haw, trail entry at the summit of Springer

See what I mean? That poor guy only hiked eight miles. Backpacking 2,168 miles isn't a pleasure cruise.

All these quotations reminded me of a conversation I had back in Caratunk, Maine. I met a wonderful man who had hiked both the PCT and AT, and was now giving trail magic back to the hiking community by running a bed and breakfast for hikers. Stay in a bunk for $12. And enjoy an all you can eat breakfast for $4. After watching me eat three scones, fruit, and 12 French toasts, he marveled, "Why is it always that the little scrawny guys eat more than anyone else?"

After chuckling with my mouth full, I asked him to compare the 2,650-mile Pacific Crest Trail with the 2,168-mile AT. He said, "You know, most people call the PCT the Scenic Trail and the AT the Social Trail. Even though the AT is the People Trail because so many people hike it, it's not easy. It's hard!"

The point is: don't walk away from this book concluding that you should hike the AT. It's a long hard trail that most people find insurmountable. On the other hand, the magnificent moments are phenomenal.

I do know that this has been the most amazing thing that I have ever done, and I have learned more than all my years of schooling in the past 143 days.
— Windex, a solo female AT Nobo 2001

In many ways, the AT is a microcosm of life. Its ups and downs are a metaphor for the emotional highs and lows of a lifetime. Therefore, it's not surprising that the wisdom that one can accumulate over a lifetime is condensed into this intense multi-month odyssey. The advantage the AT has over a lifetime is that you're not dead at the end of the journey (unless you had a heart attack along the way), so you can apply the wisdom you acquired on the AT in your future journeys.

Age doesn't always bring wisdom. Sometimes age comes alone. — Anonymous

Standing on the summit of Springer Mountain two years after my odyssey inundated me with memories. I vividly remembered when two wonderful women took our pictures and offered to take us back to their lodge, complete with plenty of food and a hot tub.

However, since Doug and Evelyn had already invited us, we had to decline their trail magic. Nevertheless, the ladies blessed us with some wonderful trail magic anyway by driving us down Springer, saving us the eight mile walk down to the Amicalola State Park ranger station. Later, Doug and Evelyn picked us up there. They took us to their beautiful home and Evelyn made the most perfect salmon dinner you can imagine. It was marinated in teriyaki sauce and the side dishes were equally extravagant. The dessert was delicious—ice cream with raspberries, toasted almonds, caramel and chocolate. We showered, did laundry, and slept in a luxurious bed.

I remembered how the next day we began to reintegrate into society. We flew to New Mexico for a 10 day vacation that would help us relax and transition back to the real world. We eventually returned to San Francisco on October 27, 2001 and discovered the post-911 world. The economy was in the toilet, and we were homeless and jobless. Nevertheless, our friends and family helped us readjust. After two months of job searching, we both found jobs.

Whoa! Immediately after the AT we didn't feel like walking or hanging out in humid weather, so we flew to New Mexico to enjoy the dry climate on horseback. We were so lazy and it felt so good.

One problem is we all feel as if a thru-hike should lead us to enlightenment. It's a bit of a letdown at the end of each thru-hike to realize that it hasn't exactly occurred yet. What's more, the further one hikes, the less fit one seems to be to re-enter society, at least the world of commerce. Some folks are exceptions, but I've heard it said that, 'No one who ever completed a thru hike is ever worth a shit again.' Overstated perhaps, but there's maybe a little grain of truth there. (I suppose it means that all we want to do after that is thru-hike again.) — Spur, three time AT thru-hiker (in a personal email to me). He owns a business and is semi-retired.

Spur makes a good point. Part of me was expecting that at the end of my pilgrimage there would be a big neon sign telling me everything I needed to know. However, Springer itself did not offer any insights. Instead, all my lessons were scattered throughout my trek. Although I deliberately searched for the Principles on getting the most out of life, I discovered them in unexpected ways. Many pilgrims, on the other hand, had no specific quest or objective in mind. Yet they always learned something. The AT is exceedingly generous: no pilgrim leaves empty handed.

As far as your question goes, 'What major things have I learned from the trail,' the list is long. But allow me to indulge you with a few thoughts.
1. *There is always a way around any problem.*
2. *You can't always replace a broken object (relationship, etc) so you'd better learn to fix it or learn to live without it.*
3. *I am stronger than I will ever really understand.*
4. *The world is filled with good natured people. If you live your life with integrity and continually follow your bliss, they will find you.*
5. *You don't know when you're lost unless you really understand where you're going. — Featherweight, AT Nobo 2001, in a personal email to me*

Striking a balance

I was amazed how quickly two years went by. I stood on Springer Mountain relishing it like I relished that final mile. I didn't want to leave it, even though the sun was setting and I hadn't brought a flashlight.

Nevertheless, I couldn't help but think about the Seven Principles that I had learned during my pilgrimage. It was especially clear how important it is to follow the Seven Principles if one wants to squeeze the most out of life. However, at the same time one must be careful about going overboard. Few of us will have this problem, but it's good to be aware of it. Let's see how one can take following any of these Principles to an extreme:

- **Balancing 1st and 2nd Principle:** At the end of the second chapter, we saw how you must strike a balance between following your Fun Compass and not living beyond your means. A few save so much money and never spend it, even though they would like to. Most live beyond our means and are saddled with so much debt that we can't pursue our passion.

- **Hiking with passion to a fault:** Although most of us fall short of pursuing our passion, some do it to the detriment of following the other Principles. For example, you may be so obsessed about building a business that you ignore the Fifth Principle and you never take care of your health. Or you might pursue your passion so rigorously that you forget to give to others (the Sixth Principle), even your own family. With a neglected spouse, the marriage falls apart because you're overly obsessed about your passion.

- **Overanalyzing trail lore:** As we saw in chapter 4, you can suffer from *analysis paralysis* if you spend all your time learning from history and no time making history.

- **Obsessing about your health:** Most Americans do not have this problem. However, a few of us are either hypochondriacs or so obsessed about fitness that it consumes our lives. Some may over-train, which frequently leads to injury. Others may obsess about their food choices so much that they don't reward themselves with a treat that they might enjoy, or they offend a host by not eating their food. Being overly fussy about food and spending too much time at the gym are rare problems, but you can overdo following the Fifth Principle.

- **Being overly generous:** This problem is not as rare as one might think. There are some people who spend their whole lives performing trail magic to everyone, and yet are miserable or resentful. Sometimes it might be a mother who has given her whole life to support her family, to enable everyone else to be successful, but she harbors resentment that she has not "accomplished anything." Of course, supporting a family is an incredible and fulfilling accomplishment, but perhaps she sacrificed her desire to have a part time job, pursue a hobby, or take care of her body. Also, overly generous parents may end up spoiling their kids.

- **Seeing life as one big joke:** It's easy to understand how someone can go overboard on not taking life too seriously. Consistently missing appointments, cracking jokes at funerals, and shrugging off when your son gets caught carrying a gun to school are all examples of when you might want to take life a bit more seriously. Of course, one can argue that in the grand scheme of things none of these events really matter; however, it's still bad form to treat these types of events so nonchalantly.

Therefore, you can follow each Principle to an extreme and reach a point where it becomes detrimental. Nevertheless, do not use that as an excuse to not follow them, because few overdo adhering to these Principles, whereas the majority of us fall way short of following them. Most of us:

1. Do not fully enjoy life.

2. Live beyond our means.

3. Work jobs we're not passionate about.

4. Repeat the mistakes of those who have gone before us.

5. Are unhealthy.

6. Are overly selfish.

7. Take life way too seriously.

Therefore, for most of us being overly zealous about the Seven Principles will never be problem. Most of us are ignoring some or all of them. I confess I'm no saint either. Part of the reason I wrote this book was to remind myself of the lessons I learned and to kick myself whenever I'm straying. Everyday I must work at obeying these Principles. At times it's tough, but following them is always rewarding.

> *I want to be thoroughly used up when I die. Life is no brief candle to me; it is a sort of splendid torch which I get a hold of for the moment and I want to make it burn as brightly as possible before handing it on to future generations.* — George Bernard Shaw

Final criticisms

As I walked the AT I would frequently talk to myself, constantly playing devil's advocate to sharpen my thinking. Also, my babbling would reinforce the stereotype that most thru-hikers have a few loose screws upstairs.

You may have come across one or more chapters that had you saying, "But that's obvious! Why don't you tell me something I don't know?" However, this book isn't about inventing wacky new "principles." It's about reminding us of the fundamental Principles that already exist and stuffing them all in one book. As I wrote in the beginning, the Principles are not new, they have been with us over the ages.

*All truths are easy to understand once they are
discovered; the point is to discover them.*
— Galileo Galilei (1564 - 1642)

Moreover, if these Principles are so obvious, then why are there
so many unhappy and unfulfilled people in the world? Knowing
the Principles is one thing, figuring out practical ways of following them is another. Although the AT inspired me to come up with
many concrete steps on how to do that, there are certainly more
ways. I hope to learn them and so that's why I'm still hiking.

Also, abiding by these Principles is clearly not easy; otherwise, we
would all be doing it. Part of the problem is that sometimes we
get caught up with our day-to-day obligations and we forget to
get perspective in life. This book is meant to reawaken us, to recalibrate our perspective. It's that swift kick in the pants that sometimes we need to remind ourselves what we stand for.

Lastly, I expect some people to disagree with one or more of these
Principles. Others will resist the whole book because they feel it's
too "prescriptive" or "packaged." Nearly everyone will find something to quibble about somewhere in these pages. That's why I
stress to *hike your own hike, including when it comes to using this book!*
Hiking your own hike doesn't mean that you shouldn't listen to
other people's advice. On the AT countless hikers advised me on
what shoes I should wear, how often I should take a break, why it's
no fun hiking more than 25 miles a day, and where I should go to
take a shower ASAP. I listened with an open mind, considered their
advice deeply, incorporated some of their ideas, and then hiked
my own hike. I encourage you to do the same. Therefore, if you'd
rather just grab the ideas you like and toss the rest of this book into
the campfire, then that's your way of hiking your own hike and I
respect that. However, instead of burning this book, consider doing
something more constructive with it: use it as a handy doorstop.

*From the moment I picked your book up until I laid
it down, I convulsed with laughter. Someday I intend
reading it. — Groucho Marx*

This bridge is in the White Mountains of New Hampshire. Thru-hikes are like bridges over the river of your life. They give you a perspective that you would normally never have. Such sabbaticals rejuvenate you and remind you of what really matters.

Taking time off

A multi-month odyssey is an amazing experience, and should be carefully placed in the river of your life. These journeys are like high bridges along the river. They are parts where we get off the rapids, and observe the river of our life from above. You'll gain a unique perspective that is almost impossible to see in your everyday life.

I believe that all humans can use something like a thru-hike every five to 10 years. It doesn't have to be a thru-hike. It could be a six month sabbatical in Asia, or a three month break in the Caribbean, or backpacking through Europe for two months. It doesn't really matter what you do, except that you get away to experience something you've never experienced before, and do it for at least one month. Go wander and learn.

 All action begins in rest. — Lao Tzu, Chinese philosopher and founder of Taoism

It's not healthy to do the same thing all the time for 40 years. We all could use a break; and not just a two week vacation, but a two month vacation. The more time off, the better. Many say they can't afford it, but can you afford not to? It costs less than you think. Our four month trek cost less than $5,000. That's less than most couples spend on a two week vacation in Greece or a cruise. Granted, we weren't exactly staying at the Ritz, but there are inexpensive lodging options throughout the world. It's understandable why most of us don't realize this since 80 percent of Americans still don't have a passport. Get one and go.

> *The tragedy of life is not that it ends so soon, but that we wait so long to begin it.* — W. M. Lewis

Obligations do not have to hold you back

Most adults have major responsibilities that impede them from taking time off. You probably have a job, a mortgage, a spouse, kids, and a mother-in-law. There are a few solutions.

First, solve the housing issue. Selling your property is an easy way to take care of your mortgage. Perhaps you've been looking for an excuse to sell your property and move to another neighborhood or even another country. Perhaps you've discovered that your passion is theatre or financial services, so you need to move to New York City. Or you're fond of scuba diving or rainforest preservation, so you move to Borneo and live like royalty. However, most of us don't want to leave our home permanently, so that's when renting it for a few months can solve the mortgage issue. Although your rental income may not cover your entire mortgage, it probably can help so that your adventure is not so costly. There are housing exchange programs, where you can swap houses for the summer with a family in Europe, for example. For those who rent, sublet your place. If you can't, then consider moving out and putting your stuff in storage. When you return, you can try a new neighborhood. Change is good.

A common reason for not taking two or more months off is that kids make it impossible. Yet, kids show us every year that it is possible! They take about three months off from their studies every year. Minutes after reaching the summit of Mount Katahdin, a father and son team (named Crash and Lemongrease) told me that they would be hiking the AT together, with the support of the mom of the family. They were taking advantage of the son's college graduation to hike the AT. Maybe you can section hike the AT over two summers. For example, one summer you could start in Georgia in June and finish three months later in New Jersey. The next summer you could pick up in New Jersey in June and finish in Maine at the end of August, right before school starts.

I never knew a man go for an honest day's walk for whatever distance, great or small, and not have his reward in the repossession of his soul. — George Macaulay Trevelyan, British historian, 1876—1962

Of course, the AT is only one adventure. You might want to kayak the Missouri River and relive the journey of Lewis and Clark. Some would rather bike around Europe. Perhaps sailing around the world appeals to you; or staying in a cheap bungalow in the South Pacific; or simply moving somewhere remote for the winter like that psycho in the *Shining*.

Twenty years from now you will be more disappointed by the things that you didn't do than by the ones you did do. So throw off the bowlines. Sail away from the safe harbor. Catch the trade winds in the sails. Explore. Dream. Discover. — Mark Twain

You can always come up with excuses as to why you can't do what you've always dreamed. People do this all their lives, and then, near the end of their lives, they are filled with regret. I don't want to suffer this fate, and I hope my walk has inspired you to take action now. *Create an Inflection Point in your life today.*

God bless all who inspired me. To those that followed this trip, please find a journey for yourself and start immediately to follow your dream. — Tumbleweed, AT Nobo 2001 Thru-hiker's final journal entry

If you follow the Seven Principles, you will immediately begin getting the most out of life. You won't have to wait long to feel the benefits—you'll feel them today. I've seen friends go through therapy, and one of my frustrations is to see how long it takes. I feel like the shrink is telling them the Samuel Goldwyn line: "Give me a couple of years and I'll make you an overnight success."

We can't afford to wait a couple of years. You must start squeezing the most out of life today. Squeeze it as hard as you can so you can drink every drop.

We had learned the AT parallels life.
It has peaks and valleys
joys and sorrows,
exhilarating times and ordinary times,
sunshine and rain,
laughter and tears,
healing and pain,
and, as in life,
the trail has a beginning and an end.
Likewise, the end is a new beginning.
— Madeleine Cornelius from Katahdin With Love: An Inspiration Journey, *1991*

I had been ignoring the setting sun on top of Springer Mountain. My nostalgia was too intoxicating. Now I was alone and had no flashlight. I had less than an hour of daylight to cover eight miles. I sprinted down the mountain. The last mile marker I saw said that I had three miles to go. A few minutes later, standing in the darkness, I could no longer see my hand in front of my face.

Now I felt like Bill Irwin, the blind guy who thru-hiked the AT, except for one important difference: I didn't have a Seeing Eye dog. I felt every nocturnal animal looking at me and I couldn't see anything. I could hear them though. They were probably saying, "Look at that stupid human. The idiot didn't even bring a flashlight. Talk about not learning from trail lore."

I stumbled in the moonless night. It was easy to miss the switchbacks and get off the trail. I let my feet feel the trail. If there were too many leaves on the trail, I knew I was off the path. I inched my way down as my remaining senses kicked into overdrive. After several hours I passed the spectacular Amicalola waterfall that roared in the darkness. At one point I was sure the trail was leading me straight into the river. I got down on my hands and knees and crawled closer and closer to the thundering water. I felt I was on the brink of falling into the deafening river when the trail turned sharply to the left. I breathed a sigh of relief, got up, and resumed walking slowly into the void. I'm sure that somewhere an owl was just looking at the ground, shaking his head in dismay at my stupidity.

It was nearly midnight when I finally got back to my car. It took me over four hours to inch down two and half miles of trail in the darkness. It was an adventure, but not my last one.

The wandering continues

As this book goes to press, I am already starting to write my next one. It's about my five month trek across every country in Eastern Europe. I wandered through 20 countries to learn what Eastern Europeans can teach us. Although it was a different adventure than the AT, it was also rich in wisdom and excitement. For example, I learned many lessons when I illegally entered the radioactive Chernobyl Exclusion Zone in Belarus. One side benefit from that experience is that I no longer worry about forgetting a flashlight since I now glow in the dark.

Now I am preparing to hike the Pacific Crest Trail; later I hope to hike the Continental Divide Trail. The PCT is about 2,650 miles long, roughly 500 miles (or 25 percent) longer than the AT and has dramatic changes in elevation. The CDT is approximately 3,100 miles long, about 1,000 miles longer than the AT; the CDT's greatest challenge is that it is only 70 percent complete. Therefore, 30 percent of the time I will be searching for the trail! For every book sold, I am donating half my royalty to these three trails. It's my little way to send a bit of trail magic back to the community that has given me so much.

I'm not sure what lessons I will learn from my future adventures, but this anonymous email gave me some ideas:

What I have learned as I grew older
I've learned that no matter how much I care, some people are just jerks.
I've learned that it takes years to build up trust, and it only takes suspicion, not proof, to destroy it.
I've learned that you shouldn't compare yourself to others — they are more screwed up than you think.
I've learned that you cannot make someone love you. All you can do is stalk them and hope they panic and give in.
I've learned that the people you care most about in life are taken from you too soon and all the less important ones just never go away.
I've learned that we are responsible for what we do, unless we are celebrities.
I've learned that regardless of how hot and steamy a relationship is at first, the passion fades, and there had better be a lot of money to take its place.

Now that would make an entertaining book.

Eventually I will explore Africa, Asia, and the Middle East. With nearly 200 countries in the world, my wandering is hardly over. Happy trails.

Those are my principles. If you don't like them, I have others. — Groucho Marx

Appendix 1: Why Southbound?

Why do so few people thru-hike southbound? The quick answer is simply: *it's harder than thru-hiking northbound.*

After all, if hiking southbound were the same as hiking northbound, then one would expect roughly half the thru-hikers to go south. However, only ten percent of the AT thru-hikers are Sobos. Southbound is harder than the northbound journey for four reasons:

1. **The hardest section is in the north.** Anyone who has researched a bit of trail lore will know that Maine and New Hampshire are the most challenging sections on the AT. Most people aren't physically (or mentally) prepared for a brutal beginning.

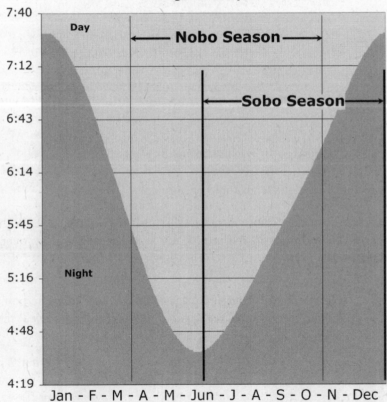

The hour the sunrises in Pennsylvania throughout the year

2. **You have a shorter hiking season than the Nobos.** Whereas Nobos can hike from March to October (seven months), Sobos wait until June, but should finish in November (five months). Therefore, the pressure to hike more miles everyday is greater for the Sobos than the Nobos. Of course, Nobos can (and do) start earlier than March, and Sobos can (and do) end later than November. Ideally Nobos should start in April, not March, because Georgia still has snow in March. Similarly, Sobos should start in early July, not June. Because of the snowmelt, Maine's rivers run high in June and the bogs of Maine are teeming with mosquitoes and other insects. The bottom line is that Sobos have less time to complete the AT than Nobos.

3. **Sobos have less daylight to hike in than Nobos.** Since night-time hiking is slow (hard to see the trail and easy to get lost), it's best to hike during the daylight. It's easier to walk 25 miles when you have 16 hours of daylight versus 10 hours of daylight. When you have lots of daylight you can take plenty of breaks and avoid overstressing your body, which can lead to injury. The longest day of the year (for those in the northern hemisphere) is June 21, the summer solstice. A Nobo starts hiking two to three months before the summer solstice and ends two to three months later. Therefore, a Nobo times the hike well because he hikes during the longest days of the year (by being halfway done by the summer solstice). The Sobo, on the other hand, starts around the summer solstice and imme-diately starts losing daylight everyday. This forces the Sobo to step on the gas. (see graph on previous page.)

4. **Greater psychological pressure.** For many Nobos it's com-forting to know that thousands have completed a northbound thru-hike. Sobos have a fraction of those role models. In fact, according to the Appalachian Trail Conservancy, in 2004 Nobos had a higher success rate than Sobos. At some point during the journey, it's easy to doubt your ability to beat the odds.

On the other hand, it's the same trail at the end of the day. It's not *that* much harder going southbound. In fact, as I like to joke, since Mount Katahdin is about 2,000 feet taller than Mount Springer, Sobos have it all downhill. It also helps if you pin the map to a wall, then it really looks like southbound is an easy descent the whole way down.

It's interesting that the other two major thru-hikes in the US (the Pacific Crest Trail and the Continental Divide Trail) have an even greater percentage of Nobos over Sobos. Ten percent go southbound on the AT, but *only two percent* go southbound on the PCT and the CDT. Why? For the same four reasons I listed above. However, PCT and CDT hikers face three additional reasons to favor going north.

1. **The desert sections are especially dry in the fall.** Both trails feature desert sections in the southern portions (Mojave Desert for the PCT and New Mexico's desert for the CDT). When the Nobos go through those sections in the early spring, the few water sources are at their best levels (which aren't that great). When the Sobos arrive in the late fall, most of those water sources have dried up. In addition, Trail Angels altruistically leave several liters of water for the Nobos at key road crossings during the springtime to help them on their journey. Since just a handful of Sobos make it to the desert portions, the Trail Angels don't leave water for them. Therefore, Sobos face the additional challenge of carrying far more water than Nobos through the desert sections of these two trails.

2. **Sobos face tougher mountain climbs and descents on the snowy mountains.** Both Sobos and Nobos run into snow in the early part of their thru-hike when they get into the mountains. However, since the Nobos are walking north, they have a slightly easier time with the snow. Why? Think about it: if you had to pick between hiking up snow and down dry trail or hiking up dry trail and walking down snow, what would you prefer? Most would prefer the latter. Why? Because hiking up dry trail is easier than hiking up snow (where you frequently sink deep in the snow, making every step harder than normal); likewise, it's easy to hike down snow, because it's low impact and if it's steep enough, you can either "ski" down in your boots or just have a blast flying down on your butt. Nobos get the easier of the two options because snow melts on the south side of the mountains first (the sun hits it all day), but lingers the longest on the north side. Therefore, since the Nobos are generally going up the south side of

mountains and descending the north side of mountains, their snow section is less arduous than the Sobo's.

3. **It's a lonely trail for Sobos.** About a dozen Sobos attempt the PCT and the CDT each year versus a couple of hundred Nobos. Sobos leave on different days, they need to keep a steady pace, and many drop out quickly; hence, it's possible that they never run into another Sobo during their multi-month pilgrimage. Of course, there are day and weekend hikers running around, but generally it's pretty deserted out there for a Sobo. That may encourage some, because they go out to the wilderness to get away from people; on the other hand, at some point even the most introverted thru-hikers crave human interaction, if only to brag about how far they walked. Because there are dozens of Nobos spread out over a few hundred miles of trail, there is a good balance of interaction and solitude. Sobos must deal with their isolation.

Therefore, while AT thru-hikers have four good reasons to hike north, PCT and CDT thru-hikers have seven! Are their any advantages in going south? Yes, four:

1. **You get the hard part over with.** All three trails have tough starts for the Sobo; whereas the trail is relatively mild for the Nobo. The only exception is the CDT; the hardest part of that trail is in the middle, Colorado. The beginning of the AT is particularly tough compared to the rest of the trail.

2. **Greater solitude.** As I mentioned above, Sobos have the trail to themselves, which can be a good thing. AT Sobos still have plenty of social opportunities because there are just as many AT Sobos as there are PCT Nobos.

3. **A shorter mosquito season.** Like spring, mosquito season heads north. Therefore, by heading north, Nobos are effectively chasing mosquitoes and prolonging their bug season. Sobos certainly cross paths with the tiny vampires, but because they're heading south, they spend at least 25 percent less time donating blood than Nobos do.

4. **You help spread out the environmental impact.** Every thru-hiker, no matter how well they practice the Leave No Trace

trail ethics (www.LNT.org), leaves some impact. The section of trail that thru-hikers use most heavily is in the southern sections. There is a mass of thru-hikers pounding the trail in Georgia, frequently 50 a day leaving out of Springer. Georgia and the Smokies get trashed during March and April. However, the attrition is so severe, that most of these hikers never get to stomp through New England (or even the Mid-Atlantic States). Therefore, New England doesn't get the same mass of thru-hikers as the southern states on the AT. The Sobos have minimal impact, not because they're more careful, but because for every Sobo starting in Maine there are at least 10 Nobos starting in Georgia. Therefore, if 10 to 50 percent of the Nobos decided to hike southbound (or to flip flop), then the environmental impact that thru-hikers leave would be distributed more evenly, and nature would have an easier time recuperating from it.

Ultimately, as Robert Frost said, I chose to go southbound simply "to go the road less traveled."

In August 2005 I was getting in shape to hike the Pacific Crest Trail in 2006. Here I'm about to go to the summit of Mount Baker in Washington State. The next weekend I tackled Mount Rainier. Although I got to the top, the 14,410 foot (4,392 meter) mountain proved that I still need to do a bit more exercise! Rainier is a toughie!

Appendix 2: Gear List

Food may be the number one topic of conversation on the trail, but gear is a close second, especially at the beginning of the expedition. Eventually, most thru-hikers get tired of the subject and talk about more meaningful subjects, like how their feet are holding up.

To answer those who are curious, here is what we carried for our 2001 AT thru-hike. It's hard for most backpackers to believe that our average pack weight (without food and water) was only seven pounds (3.17kg), including a camcorder!

Francis's Gear		
Item	Brand	Ounces
Pack	GoLite	14.2
Umbrella	GoLite	9.5
Tarp	GoLite	13.5
Stakes stowbag	GoLite	0.3
Stakes (6)	GoLite	2.0
Ground Sheet	Space Blanket	1.9
Sleeping Pad	GoLite	6.0
Water Purifier	Pristine	2.0
Cookpot bag		0.8
Stove + windscreen	Esbit	3.6
Cookpot w/ lid	Evernew Titanium	8.4
Soap (full)	Dr. Bronners	1.5
Cord (50 ft)	REI	2.5
Spoon x2	Lexan	0.6
Fuel (6 tablets)	Esbit	3.0
Shell Jacket	GoLite	7.7
Water Bag: 2L Platypus	Cascade Designs	1.5
Flashlight	Photon III	0.2
Swiss Army Knife	Victorinox Classic	0.7
Ditty bag #1	GoLite	0.3

Item	Brand	Ounces
First aid		2.0
Toothbrush		0.2
Dental floss		0.1
Vitamins		0.5
Matches		0.3
Valuables		0.5
Pad, maps, pencil		1.0
Plastic Bag		0.1
Deodorant		0.5
Head Net	Cabella	0.6
Repellent		2.0
Sunscreen		2.0
Ditty bag #2	GoLite	0.4
Camcorder w/ film & battery	Canon - Elura MC	16.2
Trowel	REI	2.0
PACK WEIGHT (oz)		**108.6**
PACK WEIGHT (lbs)		**6.78**
Lisa's Gear		
Item	**Brand**	**Ounces**
Pack	GoLite	12.5
Umbrella	GoLite	9.0
Stow sack	GoLite	1.4
Sleeping Bag	GoLite	34.2
Sleeping Pad	GoLite	6.0
No-See-Um Net		2.6
Clothes Stow Sack	GoLite	1.5
Hat: fleece (FT)	GoLite	1.5
Shirt: White (FT)	REI	5.6
Mittens: fleece (FT)	REI	1.8
Boxers (FT)	REI	3.0

Socks (FT)	REI	1.5
Hat: Fleece (LG)	GoLite	1.5
Shirt: Wicking (LG)	REI	5.0
Boxers (LG)	REI	0.8
Mittens: fleece (LG)	REI	2.4
Socks (LG)	REI	1.5
Towel	Cascade Designs	1.5
Shell pants (LG)	GoLite	5.8
Shell pants (FT)	GoLite	5.8
Shell jacket	GoLite	7.7
Head Net	Cabella	0.6
Ditty Bag: Plastic		0.2
Toilet paper		0.6
Lip balm		0.3
Sunglasses bag		0.2
Sunglasses		0.6
Flashlight	Photon II	0.2
Water Bag: 1L Platypus	Cascade Designs	0.9
PACK WEIGHT (oz)		**116.2**
PACK WEIGHT (lbs)		**7.26**
Team Pack Weight (oz)		**224.8**
Team Pack Weight (lbs)		**14.0**
Avg. Team Weight (lbs)		**7.0**
Francis Clothing Worn	**Brand**	**Ounces**
Shirt: Black	REI	9.0
Eyeglasses	Transition	0.6
Watch	Suunto Vector	1.5
Shorts: Coolmax Lycra	Dry-Fit	4.2
Socks	REI	1.5

Shoes		27.8
WORN WEIGHT (oz)		**44.6**
WORN WEIGHT (lbs)		**2.8**
Lisa Clothing Worn	**Brand**	**Ounces**
Shirt: White w/ Zipper	REI	5.3
Shorts: Coolmax Lycra	Dry-Fit	3.9
Sports Bra		3.7
Sun hat	GoLite	2.8
Knee Brace		1.0
Socks	REI	2.4
Shoes		22.8
WORN WEIGHT (oz)		**41.9**
WORN WEIGHT (lbs)		**2.6**

What about food and water? This list does not include food and water, because they are not constants. Generally each thru-hiker carries about two pounds of food and water per day. Usually we would carry no more than four days of food, or 8 extra pounds per person; with two of us, that's 16 pounds of food. I usually carried all the food and water, because I was always hungry! So when you include food and water, my total pack weight ranged from 6.8 (3kg) when empty to 30 pounds (13.6kg) when full. On average, I had about 2-3 days of food, which meant that on average I carried about 15 pounds (6.8kg), including food, water, and gear. Meanwhile, Lisa would always glide along with her 7.3 pound (3.3kg) pack!

What about cold weather clothes? One advantage of thru-hiking the AT in less than four months is that you avoid cold weather and can enjoy light backpacks. Nevertheless, Lisa carried a one pound GoLite parka at the end of the AT because it was getting chilly.

What shoes did you wear? We never wore hiking boots because they were too heavy for our ultra-light loads. If you can get your backpack to weigh less than 30 pounds, trail running shoes may be your best bet. They're comfortable, light, and quick to dry. More importantly, learn from trail lore and then hike your own hike.

Our light backpacks helped us truly enjoy going over all the mountains on the AT. Here I'm pointing to the tallest mountain on the East Coast, Mt. Mitchell. It's hard to see in the horizon and the AT doesn't go over it. Clingman's Dome in the Smoky Mountain National Park is the tallest peak on the trail. It's so accessible that you can practically drive to the top!

Jackass

As you can see from my gear list, I prefer going extremely light. But that's the way I like to hike. It's not the only way as this journal entry shows. I found it at the summit of Springer Mountain, two years after I completed my pilgrimage:

May 12, 2003

Leaving one month later than planned but that's OK. Only hiking to the Smokies. Plan on three to five miles a day. Everyone leaving in the next three weeks will be passing me, so say hello to "Rabbit."

Will be carrying a blue pack with a 77 pound load.

Yes I know. My name should be Jack-Ass-Rabbit.

Oh well. I do plan to be comfortable when I'm camping. First time here and looking for a wonderful trip.

May God keep you safe and Jesus lead the way. See ya when you pass me.

— Rabbit

Glossary

AT: Appalachian Trail. It's a 2,168-mile footpath that goes from Springer Mountain in Georgia to Mount Katahdin in Maine. More information at: www.appalachiantrail.org

ATC: Appalachian Trail Conservancy. It was formally called the "Appalachian Trail Conference." These hard workers and an army of volunteers make the AT the great trail that it is.

CDT: Continental Divide Trail. It's a 3,100 mile trail which (I'm sure you'd never guess) follows the continental divide. Its northern terminus is Glacier National Park (northern border of Montana, next to Canada) and its southern terminus is Antelope Wells (southern border of New Mexico, next to Mexico). It is only 70% complete. More at: www.cdtrail.org

DEET: is the most effective lotion to keep insects and ticks from eating you; however, prolonged use of DEET may cause neurological damage. Unless you're in an area where you could get an insect borne disease, avoid using DEET on a multi-month trip. The West Nile Virus wasn't a big deal in 2001 when we hiked the AT, so we used head-nets and thin ripstop nylon clothing to protect our skin. We also carried DEET for when the heat made clothing unbearable. But that's usually when we were sweating so much that it quickly washed away the repellent, leaving us exposed to the monsters. Now there are repellents containing picaridin or lemon eucalyptus oil that are just as effective as DEET and a bit safer.

Flip-flop: Hike the AT up to a certain point, then "flip" to another point and "flop" back to where you left it. A flip-flopper is someone who thru-hikes the AT, but not in a continuous fashion; they hike every mile, but not in the same direction. Example: hike from Georgia to Pennsylvania, and then Maine to Pennsylvania.

Inflection Point: When an old trend gets replaced with a new trend. For example, winning the lottery is an Inflection Point in your life. Quitting smoking is another. However, Inflection Points can also be negative. September 11, 2001 was an Inflection Point for many. Remember, we can create Inflection Points through our sheer will.

Nobo: Short for "Northbounder," which is a thru-hiker who hikes north. Nearly all Nobos start in Georgia and head to Maine. About 90 percent who attempt to thru-hike the AT are Nobos, although only 10 percent are successful. See *Sobo*.

PCT: Pacific Crest Trail. It's a 2,650 mile trail that goes from Manning Park, British Columbia to Campo, Mexico. It cuts through the mountains of California, Oregon, and Washington. More info: www.pcta.org

PUD: Pointless Up and Down. A PUD is when you climb up a mountain and there's nothing to see at the top—no monument, no view (because trees obscure it), and no ice cream stand. There are many PUDs on the AT, which can drive thru-hikers crazy because they wish the trail would take the low road if there's nothing to see on top.

Sobo: Short for "Southbounder," which is a thru-hiker who hikes south. Nearly all Sobos start in Maine and head to Georgia. About 10 percent who attempt to thru-hike the AT are Sobos, and about 20 percent are successful. See *Nobo*.

Trail name: A pseudonym that a thru-hiker invents or is invented for him to describe him in some way. Most people don't know the hiker's real name, they just know the trail name.

Triple Crown: All three major thru-hiking trails (AT, CDT, and PCT). You must backpack about 8,000 miles to complete the Triple Crown.

Acknowledgements

My pilgrimage was a pleasure thanks to the trail magic from my ten sponsors: Aquavie; Canon; Cascade Designs; Esbit; GoLite; Oakwood Worldwide; Pristine; REI; Sunridge Farms; and X-Terra Energy Bar. GoLite and Canon get particular recognition because they really went the extra mile for us. Some may dislike that I've plugged my sponsors' products. First, I truly recommend their products (I was using them before I asked for their sponsorship). Second, mentioning them is just my little way of thanking them for their trail magic. I hope you would do the same if someone lends you a hand.

Thank you Ben and Jerry's. No, they weren't a sponsor, I don't have a financial stake in them, I don't know anyone who works there, and I derive zero benefit from mentioning them. I just like their ice cream. That's all.

I appreciate the Fun Book Club of San Francisco for critiquing my messy first draft of this book.

Thank you Xavier Tsouo for your excellent work on the book's interior design. This was a tricky book to layout and Xav did an awesome job. Thanks to everyone at Lightbourne for designing an inspiring cover.

Thank you, Philippe, my brother. He's published two books, his writing advice was fantastic. It's great when to have a brother who can give you valuable trail lore. By the way, if you're into books off the beaten path, check out his book *A Parisian from Kansas*. It's really cool.

I must thank my parents for never taking me camping so that I could get it all out of my system later in my life. Seriously, mom and dad, thank you.

Lastly, thank you Lisa Garrett for walking 2,168 miles with me. You're not just an incredible hiker, you are an incredible woman. I will love you forever.

For more information

Thank you for reading my book or at least skipping to this section. I'd love to hear your feedback. I'm looking for ways to improve the next edition. Please visit my website to learn more, join my discussion group, or send me hate email. I'm at www.FrancisTapon.com.

I am also available for individual coaching, conducting workshops, and giving speeches to an angry mob, although I prefer friendlier crowds. See www.FrancisTapon.com for details.

If you need someone to stand on a podium and speak to your group, I love doing that. And if you want someone who can balance on a rock with one foot and look like an idiot, then I'm definitely your man.

Order more copies of Hike Your Own Hike

There are many ways to order:

- **Internet:** Visit www.FrancisTapon.com or www.SonicTrek.com for secure online ordering.
- **Email:** Info@SonicTrek.com and make sure to include the information in the Order Form below.
- **Fax:** (650) 344-9284. Send this form.
- **Postal:** SonicTrek Press, Suite 100, 315 Pepper Ave., Burlingame, CA 94010-6433 USA

Order Form

Name: _____

Address: _____

City: _____ State: _____ Zip: _____

Telephone: _____ Email: _____

Price: $24.95 per book – visit www.SonicTrek.com for quantity discounts.

Sales Tax: Please add 8.25% if you're in California.

Shipping: USA: $4.00 for the first book and $1.00 for each additional one. **International (including Canada and Mexico):** $9.00 for the first book and $2.00 for each additional one.

Payment: Check ☐ (Please mail check to the address above and make payable to *SonicTrek*.)

Credit card: Mastercard ☐ Visa ☐

Card Number: _____

Name on card: _____

Expiration Date: _____

Signature: _____

Index

Endnotes

[1] AT Statistics from http://www.appalachiantrail.org/hike/thru_hike/facts.html. Everest statistics from Raymond B. Huey and Richard Salisbury, "Success and Death on Mount Everest: How the main routes and seasons compare," *The American Alpine Journal*, 2003, p. 5. http://www.americanalpineclub.org/docs/HueyEverestAAJ_03.pdf. Obviously, Everest and the AT are completely different challenges. Everest takes about six weeks; the AT takes six months. Everest is 29,035 feet high; the tallest mountain on the AT is only 6,684 feet (Clingman's Dome in the Smoky Mountains National Park). Everest is really cold; the AT can be extremely cold but also really hot and humid. Everest has a third of the oxygen as the AT. Everest Base Camp to the summit is a bit over 22 miles; going from Maine to Georgia is nearly 2,200 miles. About 1.8 percent of climbers die on Everest, which makes it far more deadly than the AT. You have to climb about 11,400 feet to go from Everest Base Camp to the summit; AT thru-hikers climb 471,151 feet between Maine and Georgia. Despite all these differences, one thing everyone will agree with is that both of these adventures are tough. Therefore, it's interesting to compare their success rates.

[2] Bramble and Bushwack's trail journal: http://www.trailjournals.com/rudolf/

[3] Aloha! Ann's trail journal: http://www.trailjournals.com/AlohaAnn/

[4] F. Heylighen (1999): "Happiness", in: F. Heylighen, C. Joslyn and V. Turchin (editors): *Principia Cybernetica Web* (Principia Cybernetica, Brussels), URL: http://pespmc1.vub.ac.be/HAPPINES.html

[5] Stuart McCready, "In Pursuit of Happiness," *The Discovery of Happiness*, Sourcebooks, Inc., 2001, p. 16.

[6] Second hand quotation from Wang Keping, "Dao, Confucianism, and Buddhism," *The Discovery of Happiness*, Sourcebooks, Inc., 2001, p. 50. Original source is unknown.

[7] Of course, that assumes that the cost of coffee and your wage rises equally with inflation thereby canceling each other out, but these are details we don't worry about in the nominal calculation

[8] Bureau of Economic Analysis, http://www.bea.doc.gov

[9] Thomas J. Stanley and William D. Danko, *The Millionaire Next Door*, Marrena, GA, Long St. Press, 1996.

[10] Linda Formichelli, "Dream jobs? Not so much." *USA Weekend*, Feb 25-27, 2005, p. 12.

[11] Dr. David Weeks, *Eccentrics: The Scientific Investigation*, Stirling University Press, 1988, L27-50. Dr Siegried Munser, Professor of Psychiatry, University of Vienna, has carried out a similar study.

[12] Kelly Greene, "Travel Tales," *The Wall Street Journal*, June 24, 2002, p. R4.

[13] Appalachian Trail Conservancy statistic (revised 1/29/05). Prior to 2004, the ATC estimated a 20% drop-out rate.

[14] Joint Survey National Center for Health Statistics and the CDC, *San Francisco Chronicle*, March 17, 2003, P. A7.

[15] Nanci Hellmich, "A nation of obesity," *USA Today*, October 14, 2003, p. 7D and Nanci Hellmich, "How to Downsize the Student Body," *USA Today*, November 16, 2004, p. 10D.

[16] For more fun thru-hiking facts buy Roland Mueser's book, *Long-Distance Hiking: Lessons from the Appalachian Trail*, published by International Marine/Ragged Mountain Press. Sadly, "Roly" died March 9, 2004 at the age of 80.

[17] USDA's Center for Nutrition Policy and Promotion; USDA's Economic Research Service. Judy Putnam, Jane Allshouse, and Linda Scott Kantor, "U.S. Per Capita Food Supply Trends: More Calories, Refined Carbohydrates, and Fats," *FoodReview*, Vol. 25, Issue 3, p. 3.

[18] David Wessel, "We're Too Fat, and It's Technology's Fault," *The Wall Street Journal*, February 13, 2003, p. A2.

[19] National Center for Injury Prevention and Control, WISQARS Leading Causes of Deaths Reports, 1999-2002. http://webapp.cdc.gov/sasweb/ncipc/leadcaus10.html

[20] Elizabeth Frazão, "The American Diet: A Costly Health Problem," Economic Research Service, USDA, p. 1. http://www.ers.usda.gov/catalog/OneProductAtATime.asp?PDT=2&PID=1076 and http://www.ers.usda.gov/publications/foodreview/jan1996/frjan96a.pdf

[21] Tara Parker-Pope, "How to Find Out Exactly What You Can Eat and Still Lose Weight," *The Wall Street Journal*, September 16, 2003, p. D1.

[22] Margaret Talbot, "The Placebo Prescription," *New York Times Magazine*, January 9, 2000. Reprint at: http://www.nytimes.com/library/magazine/home/20000109mag-talbot7.html

[23] http://content.nejm.org/cgi/content/short/347/2/81 ; J. Bruce Moseley, M.D., and others, "A Controlled Trial of Arthroscopic Surgery for Osteoarthritis of the Knee," *The New England Journal of Medicine*, Volume 347:81-88 July 11, 2002 Number 2.

[24] Robert H. Fletcher, MD, MSc, and Kathleen M. Fairfield, MD, DrPH, *Journal of the American Medical Association*, June 19, 2002.

[25] *USA Weekend*, January 10-12, 2003, p. 8.

[26] Kevin Helliker, "Being Heavy and Healthy," *The Wall Street Journal*, July 23, 2002, p. B1.

[27] More info and statistics at http://www.tvturnoff.org

[28] John Hoeber, "Lowering carbohydrate intake with the South Beach Diet," *Marina Times*, July 2003, p. 22.

[29] David Bjerklie, "Are They Selling Us Baloney?" *Time Magazine*, May 3, 2004.

[30] Steven Pinker, *How the Mind Works*, W.W. Norton & Company, New York, 1997, p. 154.

[31] Corliss Lamont, *The Philosophy of Humanism*, Humanist Press, January 1, 1997, p. 48-49.

[32] *Oprah Magazine*, Aug 2001, p.174.

[33] Hank Herman, "Aging Gracefully, Inside and Out," *Men's Health Handbook*, Rodale Press, 1994, p. 37.

[34] John Volmer, "The Balanced Life," *Men's Health Handbook*, Rodale Press, 1994, p. 70.

[35] http://www.trailjournals.com/budderballandzokwakii/

[36] Karen Berger and Daniel Smith, *Along the Pacific Crest Trail*, Westcliffe Publishers, 1998, p.87.

[37] *Oprah Magazine*, August 2001, p.174.

[38] Dr. David Weeks, *Eccentrics: The Scientific Investigation*, Stirling University Press, 1988, L27-50.

[39] http://my.webmd.com/hw/emotional_wellness/ta4209.asp?lastselectedguid={5FE84E90-BC77-4056-A91C-9531713CA348}

[40] Ron Fisher, *Mountain Adventure: Exploring the Appalachian Trail*, National Geographic Society, 1988, p. 16.

[41] Stuart McCready, "In Pursuit of Happiness," *The Discovery of Happiness*, Sourcebooks, Inc., 2001, p. 16.

[42] For more on this concept consider reading Martin Seligman's book, *Learned Optimism: How to Change Your Mind and Your Life*, published by Free Press.